Introductory Foods

A Laboratory Manual of Food Preparation and Evaluation

Sixth Edition

Mary L. Morr
Associate Professor, Emeritus
Michigan State University

Theodore F. Irmiter
Professor, Emeritus
Kent State University

Merrill,
an imprint of Prentice Hall
Upper Saddle River, New Jersey   Columbus, Ohio

Library of Congress Cataloging-in-Publication Data

Morr, Mary L.
    Introductory foods : a laboratory manual of food preparation and evaluation/prepared
by Mary L. Morr, Theodore F. Irmiter.—6th ed.
        p.   cm.
    Includes index.
    ISBN 0-02-384142-7
    1. Food—Laboratory manuals. 2. Cookery—Laboratory manuals.
I. Irmiter, Theodore F.   II. Title
TX354.M65   1995   94-23805
641.3'0028—dc20   CIP

Editor: Kevin M. Davis
Production Editor: Christine M. Harrington
Production Buyer: Patricia A. Tonneman
Illustrations: Steve Botts

©1995 by Prentice-Hall, Inc.
Upper Saddle River, New Jersey 07458

Earlier editions © 1970, 1975, 1980, 1985, 1990 by Macmillan Publishing Company.

Printed in the United States of America

10 9 8

ISBN: 0-02-384142-7

Prentice-Hall International (UK) Limited, *London*
Prentice-Hall of Australia Pty. Limited, *Sydney*
Prentice-Hall Canada Inc., *Toronto*
Prentice-Hall Hispanoamericana, S.A., *Mexico*
Prentice-Hall of India Private Limited, *New Delhi*
Prentice-Hall of Japan, Inc., *Tokyo*
Pearson Education Asia Pte. Ltd., *Singapore*
Editora Prentice-Hall do Brasil, Ltda., *Rio de Janeiro*

Dedication

This sixth edition of *Introductory Foods: A Laboratory Manual of Food Preparation and Evaluation* is dedicated to Mary L. Morr, who passed away on 7 July 1994. She will be greatly missed.

At the time of her death we had completed the author's manuscript, so Miss Morr had made her full contribution to the work. She was responsible for the new chapter on soups and also the reworking of the chapter "Starch-Egg Combinations." I was responsible for the work on fats, including the chemistry. As in all of our editions, nothing was ever printed unless we were in complete accord. She was easy to work with and it was not difficult to smooth out the few differences we had.

Miss Morr conceived the idea of writing a manual in the mid-1960s when no satisfactory lab manual on food preparation existed. This work consisted of about 75 pages which were typed, mimeographed, and sold at the university book store. A copy was picked up by a Macmillan salesperson who approached us about putting our manuscript in a suitable form for publication by Macmillan. Obviously we agreed to do this but it was not without much discussion and soul searching. Never in our wildest imaginations did we ever think we would go into a sixth edition.

Foremost in our minds was the goal to devise a manual with a primary concern for the students who would be using it. For example, Miss Morr was most adamant that a recipe had to be totally on one page and that we spell out in full the terms appearing in the list of ingredients, i.e., "tablespoon" instead of "Tbs."

Miss Morr was an excellent classroom teacher. She tried very hard to get the best out of each student and was always available to help any student who requested help. In addition, she was an excellent academic advisor, very patient and always helping each student to have a program best suited to his or her needs.

It will now fall to my wife, a trained home economist, to assist me with the proofreading necessary to get the manual to press. Proofreading will not be new to her—everything I have written for the manual, she has already proofread, and believe me, she is tough; she has the eye of an eagle. We will do our very best so Miss Morr would be pleased with our efforts. We owe this to her.

Written at Kent, Ohio, 30 July 1994

Theodore F. Irmiter, Author

Doris L. Irmiter, Home Economist

Preface

The units included in this sixth edition of *Introductory Foods* have been selected because they illustrate the chemical and physical principles governing the preparation of food products in the home, in a restaurant, or in a factory. The teaching of skills has been subordinated to the development of an understanding of these principles. Emphasis has also been placed on the recognition and evaluation of the quality of the food products that have been prepared.

The organization and format of each unit continues the same as for all previous editions: Objectives, Product(s) to be prepared to illustrate principles, Principles, Recipes, Evaluation of Products, Summary Outlines (not in all units), and Review Questions.

The unit "Improving the Nutrient Content of Prepared Foods," has been revised, updated, and expanded to include the most recent information in the literature. Special attention has been given to the composition of fats, especially saturated fats, and new information on fat replacement and new fat substitutes has been added. Appendix C is an updated table showing the fatty acid content of selected food fats.

Three new planning units have been added: Labeling; Soups; and Meal Planning. The Labeling unit has been added to help students better understand the new Nutrition, Education and Labeling Act of 1990. The act became fully in force in May 1994.

The Soups unit is a new unit in this edition. Soups can be used in different ways, as an appetizer (served hot or cold) or as a main course. Soups are a good way to include meats, vegetables, or fruits into the diet. They are easy to make and many can be frozen for future use (cream soups are an exception to freezing). And, soups can be economical depending on the recipe.

The Meal Planning unit has been added to help clarify the relationship between good nutrition and the preparation of high-quality foods. A dietary plan will be only as good as the food prepared to meet the dietary goals.

Some recipes have been altered to give some choice in the type of fat used in the recipe. Also, any recipe that required raw eggs has been removed or revised. Raw eggs have not been used in any recipe. The use of egg substitutes has been included in some recipes; of course, a high-quality product must result.

The legal requirements for all cheese products have been updated using the most recent information in Title 21 of The Code of Federal Regulations.

A prior knowledge of chemistry for the student is helpful but not essential. The objectives of the course being taught, the choice of the accompanying textbook, and the instructor's background in chemistry will determine how much chemistry is to be included when using the manual. Some chemistry is included in the manual. The basic chemistry involved in food preparation will be found in the Principles section, which falls at the beginning of each chapter.

In this sixth edition, page 35 contains Basic Terms and Concepts, where terms essential to the understanding of food preparation are listed. A textbook or other outside reference will be required for definitions. Chemical terms and concepts also appear in the Review Questions section.

This sixth edition is designed to be used with any of the different textbooks of food preparation.

Contents

Introductory Foods

A Laboratory Manual of Food Preparation and Evaluation

Sixth Edition

Improving the Nutrient Content of Prepared Foods

The quality of a food product is the concern of everyone. Following are five of the most important objectives to be covered in this manual to improve the nutrient content of prepared foods.

1. *To increase the complex carbohydrate content of selected foods while maintaining a high-quality product.*

    In his 1988 Report, the Surgeon General of the United States recommended an increase in *"complex carbohydrates and dietary fiber "* to improve the nutrient intake of the American public. Foods containing complex carbohydrates (polysaccharides) have long been a staple in the diet of humans. The Bible tells of how the complex carbohydrate, "manna," miraculously sustained the children of Israel during their progress through the wilderness (Blumenthal, 1989).

    The terminology "complex carbohydrates" is not a precise term but generally is considered to mean a carbohydrate molecule made up of more than ten simple carbohydrate molecules. The complex carbohydrates of importance in foods are the following: dextrins, starches, the pectic substances, and dietary fiber consisting of cellulose, hemicellulose, and various vegetable gums.

    Ideally, complex carbohydrates should supply 55% of the calories in the daily diet, with fats supplying 30% or less and the remainder coming from protein (complex carbohydrates do have a sparing effect on protein, making it more available for body building functions). The following table shows the best food sources of complete carbohydrates.

Good Sources of Starch

- Breads, both whole-grain and white
- Breakfast cereals, cooked and ready-to-eat
- Flours, whole-grain and white
- Pastas, such as macaroni and spaghetti
- Barley and rice
- Legumes, such as dried peas, beans, and lentils
- Starchy vegetables, such as potatoes, butter beans, corn, sweet peas, lima beans, and navy beans

Good Sources of Fiber

- Whole-grain breads, other grain bakery products
- Whole-grain cereals, cooked and ready-to-eat
- Legumes, kidney beans, lima beans, navy beans, and split peas
- Fruits, especially the skins and edible seeds
- Nuts and seeds

(Blumenthal, 1989)

The water insoluble dietary fiber serves to increase fecal bulk, resulting in faster intestinal transit time and promotion of regularity. Some types of water soluble dietary fiber (such as oat gum) have significantly reduced serum cholesterol levels, including the Low Density Lipoprotein (LDL) portion, while actually raising the amount of High Density Lipoprotein (HDL) present (Kirby et al. 1981). Similar reductions in blood triglyceride levels have been found with soluble fiber diets (Anderson, 1986).

Fruits, vegetables, and certain breads and cereals are the usual sources of fiber in the diet. The average estimated dietary fiber intake of Westerners ranges between 20–25 grams per day. Though no Recommended Daily Allowance (RDA) or other officially sanctioned estimate for a desirable intake of dietary fiber is available, experts recommend intakes in the 35–40 grams per day range. Thus, an approximate doubling of dietary fiber intake is being advocated (Hughes, 1989).

Hughes (1989) also gives a brief summary of some commonly consumed foods and their relative insoluble and soluble dietary fiber contents.

Low in both insoluble and soluble dietary fiber:
   enriched wheat flour products, most breakfast cereals, white rice

High in insoluble and low in soluble dietary fiber:
   wheat bran, corn bran, most bran breakfast cereals, whole wheat flour products

Low in insoluble and high in soluble dietary fiber:
   psyllium seeds, guar gum, locust bean gum, gum arabic, carrageenan

High in both insoluble and soluble dietary fiber:
   oat bran, oatmeal, most legumes, including beans and lentils

Most fresh vegetables are also good sources of both insoluble and soluble dietary fiber, but comparisons are difficult because of their high water content.

It is easy to add dietary fiber to foods such as muffins, yeast rolls, pancakes, waffles, and as toppings on selected *au gratin* dishes without decreasing the quality of the finished product. In this sixth edition, all recipes for these products meet this objective.

2. *To reduce the caloric content of selected foods and especially to reduce the calories derived from fat.*

This objective can be achieved in selected products by making certain changes without reducing the quality of the finished product.

Following is a list of recommended changes:
a. Use skim, 1%, or 2% milk in place of whole milk. In all recipes in this sixth edition, these four types of milk may be used interchangeably.
b. Use non-nutritive sweeteners in selected products.
c. Limit portion size: when the portion served is larger than that recommended, an excess of calories will be ingested. Following the requirements of the Food Pyramid for portion size will supply the optimum caloric intake.
d. Reduce the amount of fat used both in the recipe and that used to prevent sticking; you can also use non-stick sprays to prevent sticking.
e. Use less fatty cuts of meats.
f. Trim fat from the outside of meat.
g. Emphasize proper methods of deep-fat frying to reduce the absorption of fat.
h. Broil meat and fish and poach fish in place of the various frying methods.
i. Where a range is given for the amount of fat in products such as baked goods, hold the amount of fat in the recipe at the lower end of the range.
j. In certain baked products, substitute egg whites for mixed whole egg or use egg substitutes.

3. *To reduce the sodium content of the recipe.*

We accomplished this objective to some extent in the earlier editions of this manual. We have made further reductions where possible without decreasing the quality of the product. Remember that in certain products such as yeast breads the amount of salt required cannot be altered.

4. *To reduce the quantity of cholesterol in the recipe.*

We addressed this objective both in Objective 1 where the increase of soluble dietary fiber will help to lower the cholesterol level and in Objective 2 where the total amount of fat has been reduced. Also, we recommend, where possible, vegetable oils or fats in preference to animal fats.

5. *To select the proper fat to use in a recipe.*

Current practice recommends not more than 30% of the calories in the diet should come from fats. The most recent research indicates the amount of fat is not the only factor but, in addition, the nature and the chemical composition of the fat is probably more important for good nutrition. Fats containing higher amounts of saturated fatty acids (largely animal fats) are less desirable than vegetable fats and oils, which have a higher content of unsaturated fatty acids and are more desirable; further, polyunsaturated fats are more desirable than monounsaturated fats. Appendixes C and D show the composition of many of the fats that are available in retail grocery stores.

The Nutrition and Labeling Act of 1990 gave the Food and Drug Administration the authority to require nutritional labeling on most foods (Dairy Council Digest *64:* No. 3, May/June 1993). The law took effect in the spring of 1994. We discuss this new labeling law in the next unit of this manual.

THE RELATIONSHIP OF THE CHEMICAL COMPOSITION OF FATS TO THEIR PHYSICAL PROPERTIES AND TO THEIR NUTRITIONAL ACTIVITY

A good place to start is to examine some simplified formulas of the structure of fat molecules. The most common food fats are called triglycerides and are composed of one molecule of glycerol to which are attached three molecules of fatty acids.

$$
\begin{array}{l}
\text{H} \\
\text{H--C--OH} \\
\text{H--C--OH} \\
\text{H--C--OH} \\
\text{H}
\end{array}
$$

A glycerol molecule.

A fatty acid molecule where R is a short or long chain of carbon and hydrogen atoms as shown:

$$CH_3\text{-}CH_2\text{-}CH_2\text{-}COOH$$

Butyric acid (found in butter).

$$
\begin{array}{l}
\text{H} \\
\text{H--C--OOR}_1 \\
\text{H--C--OOR}_2 \\
\text{H--C--OOR}_3 \\
\text{H}
\end{array}
$$

A fat molecule where R_1, R_2, R_3 are fatty acids.

If there is one bond between two atoms as C-H or C-OH, it is called a single bond. However, some of the fatty acid molecules have less than a full complement of hydrogen atoms and are designated as unsaturated fatty acids. If only 2 hydrogen atoms are missing, the fatty acid is classified as monounsaturated; and if 4 or more of the hydrogen atoms are missing, it is classified as polyunsaturated. Some of the polyunsaturated fatty acids are *essential* fatty acids, i.e., they must be supplied in the diet. The linkage between 2 carbon atoms changes when hydrogen atoms are missing, illustrated as follows:

$$-HC = CH-$$ The linkage between the 2
C atoms is called a double bond.

Following are the structures of 4 fatty acids:

Name	Number of Carbon Atoms	Number of Double Bonds	Structure
Oleic	18	1	$CH_3(CH_2)_7CH=CH(CH_2)_7COOH$
Linoleic	18	2	$CH_3(CH_2)_3(CH_2CH=CH)_2(CH_2)_7COOH$
Linolinic	18	3	$CH_3(CH_2CH=CH)_3(CH_2)_7COOH$
Arachidonic	20	4	$CH_3(CH_2)_3(CH_2CH=CH)_4(CH_2)_3COOH$

The following is an unsaturated fatty acid (oleic acid) showing the double bond more clearly:

$$CH_3 - (CH_2)_7 - CH = CH - (CH_2)_7 - COOH$$

These relatively small changes in chemical structure cause physical changes in the fat. For example, the following table shows the changes in the melting points of the different fatty acids as affected by the length of the carbon chain and the number of double bonds.

FATTY ACIDS FOUND IN FOODS

Saturated		
Carbon Atoms	Name	Melting Pt. °C*
4	Butyric	−7.9
6	Caproic	−3.4
8	Caprylic	16.7
10	Capric	31.6
12	Lauric	44.2
14	Myristic	54.1
16	Palmitic	62.7
18	Stearic	69.6

Unsaturated			
Carbon Atoms	Double Bonds	Name	Melting Pt. °C*
18	1	Oleic	10.5
18	2	Linoleic	−5.0
18	3	Linolenic	−11.0
18	4	Arachadonic	−49.5

* Coultate, T.P. (1989) *FOOD: The Chemistry of Its Components*, 2nd ed. Royal Society of Chemistry.

One further point, three different fatty acids may be attached to the glycerol molecule, but in some fats two of the fatty acids may be the same and the third one different. In natural foods there is not likely to be three of the same fatty acids attached to a single glycerol molecule.

Up to this point, only fats containing three fatty acids, triglycerides, have been discussed. There are two other types of fats that are important in foods. Some fats may have only two fatty acids and are referred to as *diglycerides,* while other fats may have only one fatty acid in their structure and are called *monoglycerides.*

Diglyceride

$$
\begin{array}{c}
H \\
| \\
H\text{–}C\text{-}OOCR_1 \\
| \\
H\text{–}C\text{-}OOCR_2 \\
| \\
H\text{–}C\text{-}OH \\
| \\
H
\end{array}
$$

Monoglyceride

$$
\begin{array}{c}
H \\
| \\
H\text{–}C\text{–}OOCR_1 \\
| \\
H\text{–}C\text{–}OH \\
| \\
H\text{–}C\text{–}OH \\
| \\
H
\end{array}
$$

Monoglycerides and diglycerides are not available in retail stores but are sold to various food manufacturers to be incorporated into a variety of food products such as salad dressings, margarines, margarine-type spreads, and cake mixes (this is only a partial list). Their primary function is to serve as an emulsifying agent.

BASIC TERMS

(See also page 35.)

Single bond	Monoglyceride	Saturated fat
Double bond	Diglyceride	Unsaturated fat
Glycerol	Triglyceride	Fat/Oil
Fatty acid	Emulsions	Emulsifying agent

The preceding discussion of the chemical composition of fats should help you understand the labeling information on food packages. These important food ingredients will be discussed in the unit Fats and Oils starting on page 91.

NEW TECHNOLOGY/NEW INGREDIENTS FOR FOOD PRODUCTS

The effort to reduce the amount of fat consumed by the American public has given rise to a group of new products referred to as all-natural fat substitutes that may be used in many different types of food products. The use of fat substitutes may reduce the fat content of foods by 50% to 95%, with a calorie reduction of 50% to 80%. There will also be a reduction in the cholesterol content of the food. Three different types of fat substitutes will be described as examples of these new products.

One company makes a patented product utilizing naturally occurring food proteins such as egg white, whey, and milk protein. The resulting product is small, round, hydrated particles of uniform size. The particles roll easily over one another, and the product is perceived as a creamy fluid giving the same mouth feel as fats. The product may be used in dairy-based products, that is, sour cream, dips, ice cream, yogurt, butter (spread), natural and processed cheese, cream cheese, cheese spreads, frostings, refrigerated desserts, and baked cheese cake. It may also be used in oil-based products, such as salad dressings, mayonnaise, and margarine (spread).

Dried plum juice concentrate, paste, powder, or purée may be used to replace fat and can be used to replace multiple ingredients without affecting taste and texture. For example, the plum product helps to replace the dough strengthening and softening effects of artificial emulsifiers. These products have the added advantage of being high in fiber, half of which is pectin, which helps entrap air particles to make stable foams. The product may be used in baked products such as muffins, cookies, and brownies.

There are two fat replacers available that are made from oats utilizing the properties of the hydrocolloids in the oats. This product has been used in bakery goods, dairy products, and processed meats. The fat can be taken out of the products without altering the taste or the texture.

All of these products are supplied to food manufacturers only and there is no indication they will be sold in grocery stores in the near future.

DISCLAIMER. The products just described have been given as examples only. Mention of these products does not imply endorsement by the authors, their universities, or the publisher.

REFERENCES

1. Anderson, J. S. et al. (1986). Dietary Fiber: Hyperlipidemia, Hypertension and Coronary Heart Disease. Am. J. of Gastroenterology 81:907.

2. Blumenthal, D. (1989). A Simple Guide to Complex Carbohydrates. FDA Consumer 23: No. 3, 18.

3. Hughes, J. S. (1989). Keeping Current on Dietary Fiber. Audits International/Monthly, February 1989.

4. Kirby, R. W. et al. (1981). Oat Bran Intake Selectively Lowers Serum Low-Density Lipoprotein Cholesterol Concentration. Am. J. Clin. Nutrit. 34:824.

5. Dairy Council Digest *64*: No. 3, May/June 1993.

The Nutrition Labeling and Education Act of 1990 (NLEA)

CAVEAT

There has been a tremendous amount of information written about this subject; the new FDA and USDA nutrition-labeling proposals take up 961 pages in the *Federal Register* of January 6, 1993. In addition, a large number of papers explaining the proposals have appeared in technical journals and in publications of various government agencies and food manufacturers.

It is beyond the scope of this manual to delve deeply into this literature. Only enough will be presented to help you understand the basic concepts and to use the information to plan menus for preparing foods that are both nutritionally accurate and highly palatable. A reference list is presented that will help you explore the new regulations in more depth.

INTRODUCTION—A BRIEF HISTORY

The first steps to devise some plan for helping consumers be better shoppers came about during World War II when many foods were in limited supply or not available at all; many basic foods were rationed. In 1946, at the end of the war, the USDA published a brochure entitled "The Basic 7." This scheme was difficult for the consumer to use and so was of limited value.

In 1955 the Department of Nutrition at Harvard University published the first "Basic 4." This was much simpler than the Basic 7 to use but needed further refinement; in 1980 the USDA published a modified version of the "Basic 4." This was a great improvement but still did not do much to help the shopper in the store for a variety of reasons (Freeland-Graves and Peckham, 1987).

These problems led to the passage of the Nutrition, Labeling and Education Act of 1990. The reaction of several scientific organizations to the new regulations may be found in the Journal Food Tech *46* : No. 7, pages 64–67.

PURPOSE OF FOOD LABELS

1. Food labels describe the product and identify its producer.
2. They point to significant material information about the attributes of the food itself.
3. They provide nutrient content information on the basis of scientifically accepted relationships between nutrients and health or disease.
4. They point to known health or safety risks for selected individuals.

(Brooks, 1993)

WHAT HAS BEEN MANDATED

1. Nutrition labeling is mandatory for almost all packaged foods and voluntary for raw fruit, vegetables, and fish as long as a sufficient number of retailers participate. The voluntary labeling will appear in the stores and is the responsibility of the store management (Kurtzweil, Jan.–Feb., 1993).

     The law permits voluntary nutrition labeling on single-ingredient, raw meat and poultry products and requires nutrition labeling on most other meat and poultry products (Mermelstein, 1993).
     Note: Many stores had this nutrition information posted in-store in late 1993 even though it was not required by law until May 1994.
2. Nutrients for which information must be provided has been revised.
3. A new standard for dietary intake will be used (percent of Daily Value instead of percent of U.S. RDA).
4. Serving sizes have been established for more than 130 food categories and the values will be presented in household measures.
5. Ten product descriptors have been defined.
6. Acceptable health claims have been stated (Mermelstein, 1992).

SOME SPECIFIC CHANGES

1. The revised Nutrition Panel is titled Nutrition Facts.
2. A revised list of mandatory and optional dietary components listed in a specified order has been given. No other components may be listed.
3. Data must be given to support any nutritional claims.
4. A format has been given for giving grams per serving and Daily Value for micronutrients.
5. The data will be based on both a 2,000 and a 2,500 calorie daily diet. A footnote must state, "Your daily value may be higher or lower depending on your calorie needs."
     A sample of a package panel is in Appendix E.

DIETARY GUIDELINES

Apart from and different than the NLEA, the Department of Health and Human Services and the U.S. Department of Agriculture have developed 7 dietary guidelines that represent the best and most current nutrition advice for healthy Americans 2 years and older:

1. Eat a variety of foods.
2. Maintain a healthy weight.
3. Choose a diet low in fat, saturated fat, and cholesterol.
4. Choose a diet with plenty of vegetables, fruits, and grain products.
5. Use sugars only in moderation.
6. Use salt and other forms of sodium only in moderation.
7. If you drink alcoholic beverages, do so in moderation.

(Saltos, 1993)

APPLICATION OF THE DIETARY GUIDELINES: THE FOOD GUIDE PYRAMID

For many years dietitians and homemakers have used the "Basic 4" or the "Old Basic 4 Circle" to translate nutritional requirements into food choices. With the advent of NLEA and a more up-to-date set of Dietary Guidelines, a new method of putting these guidelines into action was essential. To accomplish this the U.S. Department of Agriculture, supported by the Department of Health and Human Services, developed "**The Food Guide Pyramid: A Guide to Daily Food Choices**" (Saltos, 1993).

The Food Guide Pyramid emphasizes food from the five major food groups shown in the three lower sections of the pyramid. Each of these food groups provides some, but not all, of the nutrients you need. Foods in one group cannot replace those in another. No one food group is more important than another—for good health, *you need them all.*

Note: Each student should have a personal copy of this document; if this is not possible, the instructor should have several copies for classroom use.

FOOD GUIDE PYRAMID: A GUIDE TO DAILY FOOD CHOICES

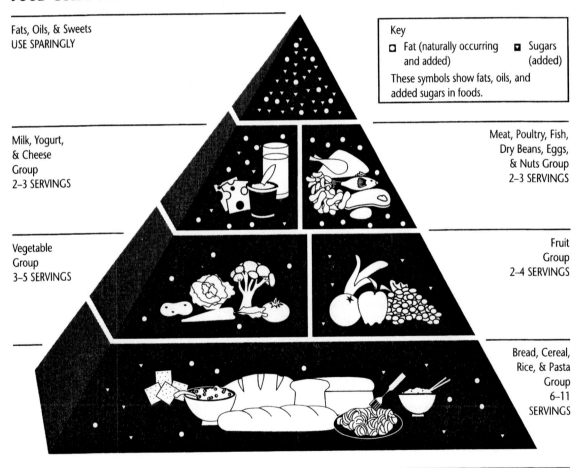

The Food Guide Pyramid is available from a County Extension Home Economist or from the following address: U.S. Department of Agriculture, Human Nutrition Information Service, 6505 Belcrest Road, Hyattsville, MD 20782.

WHAT IS A SERVING?

Food Groups
  Bread, Cereal, and Pasta
    1 slice of bread
    1 ounce of ready-to-eat cereal
    1/2 cup of cooked cereal, rice, or pasta
  Vegetable
    1 cup of raw leafy vegetables
    1/2 cup of other vegetables, cooked or chopped raw
    3/4 cup of vegetable juice
  Fruit
    1 medium apple, banana, orange
    1/2 cup of chopped, cooked, or canned fruit
    3/4 cup of fruit juice
  Milk, Yogurt, and Cheese
    1 cup of milk or yogurt
    1 1/2 ounces of natural cheese
    2 ounces of process cheese
  Meat, Poultry, Fish, Dry Beans, Eggs, and Nuts
    2 to 3 ounces of cooked lean meat, poultry, or fish
    1/2 cup of cooked dry beans, 1 egg, or 2 tablespoons of peanut butter count as 1
      ounce of lean meat

If you eat a larger portion, count it as more than 1 serving; if you eat a smaller portion, count it as a fraction of a serving.

OTHER CONSIDERATIONS

1. Fat—depends on calorie needs; limit to 30% of calories; limit amount of saturated fat.
2. Limit the amount of cholesterol-containing foods.
3. Avoid getting too many calories from sugars; calorie intake will determine the amount of added sugars.
4. Salt and sodium should be limited to 3,000 mg of total salt per day.

Home and Garden Bulletin Number 252 contains more detailed information on the items mentioned above and in addition gives information on how to obtain the necessary foods. The information given here will be sufficient for the Meal Planning Lesson to come later.

REFERENCES

Anon. (1992). Food Guide Pyramid Replaces Old Basic 4 Circle. Food Tech *46*: No. 7, 64–67.

Anon. (1993). New Food Labeling Regulations. Dairy Council Digest *64*: No. 3.

Anon. (1993). Dietary Supplements and NLEA. FDA Consumer *27*: No. 1, Jan.–Feb., 3.

Anon. (1993). New Rules for Protein Labeling. Prot. Tech. Int., Checkerboard Square, St. Louis, MO.

Anon. (1993). Nutrition Labeling Update: Determination of the Protein Quality of Food Products; New Rules for Protein Labeling; New Rules for Labeling Dietary Fiber; Protein Technologies International, Checkerboard Square, St. Louis, MO.

Anon. (1993). The Food Guide Pyramid. USDA, Home and Garden Bulletin Number 252.

Anon. (1993). New Food Labeling Regulations. Dairy Council Digest *64*: No. 3.

Barcenas, Camdelaria (1993). A System for Tracking Food Components for Labeling and Other Purposes. Food Tech *47*: No. 5, 99–102.

Brooks, Ellen (1993). Politics of Biotechnology Dictate Food Label's Fate. Food Tech *47*: No. 8, 22.

Dean, Bob (1993). Sorting Out the New Nutrition Labeling Regulations. Food Processing *54*: No. 8, 20–23.

Freeland-Graves, J. and Peckham, G. (1987). Foundations of Food Preparation, Fifth Edition. Macmillan Publishing Company, New York.

Kurtzweil, Paula (1993). Honey Bears, Snowmen, and Other Exceptions to Food Label Rules. FDA Consumer *27*: No. 10, December, 5–9.

Kurtzweil, Paula (1993). Nutrition Information Available for Raw Fruits, Vegetables, and Fish. FDA Consumer *27*: No. 1, Jan.–Feb., 7–9.

Kurtzweil, Paula (1994). Food Label Close-Up. FDA Consumer *28*: No. 3, April, 15–19.

Kushner, Gary J. (1993). The Last Word on the NLEA. Food Processing *54*: No. 8, 51–52.

Mermelstein, Neil H. (1992). A Guide to the New Nutrition Labeling Proposals. Food Tech *46*: No. 1, 56–62.

Mermelstein, Neil H. (1993). A New Era in Food Labeling. Food Tech *47*: No. 2, 81–96.

Pszcaola, Donald E. (1993). "Friendly" Labels; Responding to Consumer Desires. Food Tech *47*: No. 5, 124.

Saltos, Etta (1993). The Food Pyramid–Food Label Connection. FDA Consumer *27*: No. 5, June, 17–21.

Segal, Marian (1993). What's in a Food? FDA Consumer *27*: No. 3, April, 14–18.

Stare, F. J. (1993). The Facts About Food Scares. Priorities *5*: No. 3, 3.

Stehlin, Dori (1993). A Little "LITE" Reading. FDA Consumer *27*: No. 5, June, 12–16.

Troiano, Joan (1993–94). Have You Looked at Our Data Base Lately? FOOD NEWS—for Consumers *10*: No. 4, 13.

Woodburn, Margy and Rabb, C. (1993). Product Care Directions on Food Labels; Status and Needs. Food Tech *47*: No. 2, 97–99.

Special References

The following references are found in a single journal: FDA Consumer *27*: No. 4, May 1993.

Paula Kurtzweil, "Good Reading for Good Eating," pp. 7–13.

Dixie Farley, "Look for LEGIT Health Claims on Foods," pp. 14–21.

Paula Kurtzweil, NUTRITION FACTS to Help Consumers Eat Smart," pp. 22–27.

Paula Kurtzweil, DAILY VALUES Encourage Healthy Diet," pp. 28–32.

Judith E. Foulke, "Cooking Up the New Food Label," pp. 33–38.

The following references are found in a single journal: FOOD NEWS—for Consumers *10*: No. 1–2, Spring–Summer 1993.

Barbara O'Brien, "Answering Your Questions on Nutrition and Nutrition Labeling," pp. 4–5.

Mary Ann Parmely, "Minnie's Story—Using the Nutrition Panel," pp. 6–7.

Marianne H. Gravely, "Understanding the New Meat and Poultry Labels," pp. 8–9.

Pat Moriarty, "Food Labeling and the Law," p. 10.

Mary Ann Parmely, "Who Needs Help Interpreting the New Nutrition Labels and Why," pp. 11–12.

Joan Troiano, "The Latest Pubs and Videos," p. 13.

Herb Bantz, "Label . . . . What Label?" p. 14.

Objectives of the Laboratory Experience

*1. To illustrate the principles discussed in lecture and demonstrate the application of these principles in the actual preparation of food.

2. To acquaint students with acceptable method(s) for the preparation of selected food products including microwave cooking.

3. To acquaint students with established standards for food products.

**4. To acquaint students with one method for evaluating the quality of food products for compliance with established standards.

5. To give students the opportunity to observe the effect of certain manipulative procedures on the quality of selected food products.

6. To acquaint students with acceptable sanitary standards and procedures for handling food products and to impress upon the student the absolute necessity for adherence to these standards.

7. To foster a professional attitude in students toward their work.

8. To introduce the most recent advances in nutrition, especially the role of fiber and fats.

*The same principles apply to small portions (2–4 servings) as well as to large quantities (100–400 servings). In the preparation of large quantities, additional principles may be involved; these principles would not be applicable to the smaller portions.

**Other techniques for recording observations will be used occasionally.

Laboratory Conduct and Responsibilities

PERSONAL CONDUCT

1. Do not chew gum, eat candy, or drink beverages other than water during the laboratory period.
2. Do not read magazines or newspapers during the laboratory period.
3. Do not use work units, supply tables, or window ledges as seats.
4. Be responsible for washing your own equipment. Keep work surfaces and sinks clean.
5. Assist in general housekeeping of the laboratory.

PERSONAL HYGIENE

1. Wash your hands with soap before working with food. Do not dry your hands on dish towels.
2. Wash your hands after using a tissue or handkerchief, before handling foods again.
3. Avoid touching your hair or face while working with food; wash your hands after each contact.
4. Do *not* comb your hair in the laboratory at any time. You should do this before you enter the laboratory.

FOOD HANDLING

1. Do *not* lick spoons and/or rubber spatulas used for blending or stirring food ingredients.
2. Use a special spoon or fork for sampling any food product to test for degree of doneness or for amount of seasoning.
3. Wash any spoon or fork placed in the mouth before you use it for further food sampling.
4. Observe the special instructions for preparation of fresh foods where indicated in a lesson.

DISHWASHING

Preparation for Washing

1. Rinse and/or soak soiled utensils immediately after use.
   a. Greasy pans

        (1)   Wipe pans with paper toweling to absorb grease.

        (2)   Put detergent in the pan with hot water for soaking.

   b. Sugar syrups or similar
       Soak in hot water.

   c. Protein foods

        (1)   Soak in cold water.

        (2)   Rinse egg beaters in cold tap water immediately after use.

   d. Starchy foods
       Soak in cold water.

2. If a food scorches or burns in a cooking pan, remove pan immediately from heat.
   a. Transfer food quickly into another container.
   b. If a cooking utensil is glass or enamel, allow it to cool before adding hot water. Place the utensil over low heat for 10–15 minutes after hot water has been added. *Caution:* Oven glassware cannot be put over direct heat.
3. Place any large pieces of food material which have soaked free from the cooking pan in the garbage. Do *not* scrape flour into any sink.
4. Use a rubber or plastic spatula or paper toweling to remove loosened food material from utensils.
5. Rinse dishes with hot water. Stack for washing with detergent.

Washing Procedure

1. Run several inches of hot (120°F or 49°C) water into a sink or dishpan.
2. Add enough detergent to form a suds which remains sudsy during the dishwashing.
3. Place several of the rinsed dishes in the hot, soapy water. Wash with a clean brush or dishcloth.
4. Rinse the washed dishes in ample hot water (150°F or 66°C) in order to remove the soapy film.
5. Place the rinsed dishes in dish drainers. Dry all utensils with a clean, dry dish towel. Do *not* carry dish towels about on your shoulder or use for drying your hands.
6. All pieces of equipment must be thoroughly dry before they are stored.
7. Dry dish pans, dish drainers, and drainer mats before you return them to their storage area.

Care of Sinks

1. Each student is expected to assume responsibility for the use and care of sinks.
2. Do *not* discard food material in sinks that have no disposal units. Place refuse either in disposal sinks or pans for garbage.
3. Aluminum pans leave gray streaks on porcelain sinks. Use care in handling pans in the sink. At the end of dishwashing use cleanser to scour aluminum stains off the porcelain.
4. Each person is responsible for washing out his or her sink with hot, sudsy water at the end of the dishwashing. Rinse suds away with ample hot water.
5. Leave water taps clean and dry.

Use and Care of Dishcloths and Dish Towels

1. Use dish towels for drying dishes *only*.
2. Wring dishcloths dry at the end of the dishwashing period.
3. Handle used towels and dishcloths as directed by the instructor.

CHECKOUT OF UNITS

1. Each student is responsible for returning all equipment to its proper location in the unit. Each piece of equipment should be cleaned and dried before it is returned to its storage area.
2. Instructors may inspect units before students leave the laboratory at the end of the day's work.

Evaluation of Food Products

INTRODUCTION

To accomplish the objectives of studying the principles of food preparation and their application to the actual preparation of food, you will carefully prepare food products and then carefully evaluate them in a systematic manner to determine if the characteristics of the product meet the established standards of quality. Every food product will be "right" for the treatment it has received; for example, a burned cake has obviously been baked at too high an oven temperature for the recommended baking time, or it has been in the oven for too long a time at the proper baking temperature. Evaluation of the characteristics which influence the quality of the prepared product is seldom as simple as the observations for the burned cake.

It is true, "the proof of the pudding is in the eating." Difficulties begin in attempting to determine the quality of the pudding because the evaluation of any food product is complex. One might take a bite of the pudding and decide, "I like it" or "I dislike it," but even this simple decision is quite complex. Furthermore, such a decision tells very little about the quality of the product.

The simple decision "I like it" is based on a combination of ethnic, cultural, religious, psychological, and physiological factors. Most of these factors probably were not consciously considered in making the decision, but they nevertheless influenced the decision. Once you recognize the existence of all these factors, you can exert a conscious effort to base your evaluation on only the pertinent factors.

Great progress has been made in the last few years in the procedures and techniques used for evaluation of food products. Tests based on sensory evaluations are subjective in nature and may represent personal bias; tests run on machines, however, are objective and reflect a minimum of personal bias, although taking data from machines may be influenced by human accuracy. The choice of the type of test to be used is largely dependent on the information desired. One type of test will be used by the food manufacturer who wishes to know how the public will accept a new product he plans to market; an entirely different test would be used by the research worker who is studying the effects of different methods of cooking on muscles of the beef round.

It is beyond the scope of this manual to discuss all of the methods for the evaluation of food products. For the purposes of this manual, we will present and develop one sensory method of evaluation of foods. This method is based on a systematic evaluation of the physiological factors of sight, feel, aroma, and taste. It takes considerable skill, developed only through diligent practice, to become proficient in evaluating foods. Other methods of sensory evaluation, such as the triangle test, the duo-trio test, paired comparison, ranking, and other more sophisticated tests belong in a more advanced foods course.

QUALITY OF PRODUCTS

A worker carefully following a balanced recipe, accurately measuring ingredients, and diligently carrying out the manipulative procedure will obtain a product that has certain desirable quality characteristics.

Quality characteristics are dependent on the nature and type of food product. Products prepared within the scope of this laboratory outline will usually be evaluated on the characteristics of appearance, texture, tenderness, and flavor. These characteristics will be discussed in detail as they are encountered in the various products.

Appearance includes the shape, size, color, and condition of the outside surface, and in some products (certain baked products and some meats) the interior color.

Texture refers to the nature of the structure of the product. For baked products, texture refers to the size of the gas cells and to the thickness of the cell walls. In meat, texture refers to the size of the muscle fibers and/or the size of the bundles of muscle fibers. In some food products, such as tomato soup and cornstarch pudding, the textural characteristics are referred to as *body* or *consistency*.

Flavor of food is the taste and aroma of the food as it is chewed and will be typical of the product being evaluated. Deviations from the typical flavor are referred to as "off flavors" and may arise from a number of causes.

In some products it may be desirable to evaluate other characteristics such as tenderness and moistness in baked products and tenderness and juiciness in meat. *Tenderness* refers to the ease with which a product may be cut, broken, or chewed.

However, a product may not have the characteristics associated with a high-quality product and may be something less than an acceptable product. One subjective procedure for determining how closely a product achieves the characteristic of high quality is detailed in the following sections.

GENERAL DESCRIPTION OF THE SELECTED TEST

You will use a scalar scoring procedure for the most part throughout this manual; that is, a numerical value will be used to score each of the quality characteristics of the product. Descriptive terms may be used in addition to the assigned numerical score. Study the evaluation sheet which follows this discussion to see the format and how it looks when it is filled out.

This particular procedure has been selected because it aids in meeting the objectives of the course. When properly carried out, the scalar scoring procedure will tell how the product deviates from the standard, by how much it deviates, and will offer a clue as to *why* the product deviates. In this latter instance the scoring procedure shows what happens when the principles of food preparation are improperly applied or ignored.

RATING SCALES

Many different scales have been proposed for scoring food products. Some scales have as few as three points whereas others have as many as one hundred; some scales have all positive numbers whereas others have both positive and negative numbers. If there are too few points on the scale, the scorer cannot be sufficiently discriminating to accurately evaluate the sample. On the other hand, if there are too many points on the scale, the scorer becomes confused and is inclined to guess. The results, in either case, are less accurate than if an appropriate number of points are chosen for the scale.

It has been found that an odd number of points is better than an even number of points on a rating scale. In this way, the mid-point of the scale becomes a neutral point and there are an equal number of points on the good side and on the poor side of the scale. Usually, low numbers signify poor quality whereas high numbers signify good quality. You will use this concept of high numbers indicating high quality in evaluating the food products presented in this manual. Use only whole numbers. No attempt should be made to assign fractional values as most people do not have a sufficient power of discrimination to justify their use.

LABORATORY PROCEDURE FOR EVALUATION

Each person *must* do his or her own work: there must not be any talking while foods are being evaluated. Generally class discussion led by the instructor will follow the individual evaluation of the products.

The success of the entire scoring procedure depends on the degree to which you can put yourself into the position of an impartial judge. Ethnic, religious, and psychological (personal) prejudices *must* be put aside. You must consciously decide to do a careful evaluation. Diligence in the evaluation of foods is as important as care in the preparation of foods. You must also develop a "scoring attitude" (i.e., get psyched up). This requires complete concentration on the evaluation—the setting must be such that there is no interruption while the evaluations are taking place. You must have a positive attitude toward the whole evaluation process. It would be well to read the admonition—the last paragraph of this section.

Individual evaluation will enable you to determine how closely the quality characteristics of your product match the desired quality characteristics of the product. Rarely will a high-quality product be available for direct comparison with the product you are scoring. Therefore, you have the responsibility for learning the described quality characteristics for the various products. You will be guided in making the judgments necessary for evaluating your product against the described quality characteristics of a high-quality product.

An evaluation sheet can be found at the end of each lesson in the baked products unit. The left-hand column of the evaluation sheet lists the quality characteristics to be evaluated. These characteristics may be changed for certain types of products, for example, *juiciness* in addition to *texture* for meats.

In the space at the top of each column identify the product being evaluated. Score the visual characteristics (appearance, texture, and so on) first. After you read the descriptions for the quality characteristics of the high-quality product, you must decide how closely the product characteristics match the description: if it matches closely, score the product 6 or 7. If the product does not match the description, score it at some lesser value; the farther the product characteristic deviates from the description, the lower the score you assign. Record the numerical score in the small box in the upper left-hand corner. Use the remainder of the box for the descriptive terms justifying or giving validity to the particular numerical score assigned. If the score lies in the range of excellent to good products (7–5) the descriptive terms may be omitted; however, if the score lies in the medium to very poor (4–1), the proper descriptive terms *must* be used. Keep descriptive terms brief but clear. Score each quality characteristic in this manner.

For many products the characteristic of "Overall Eating Quality" will be evaluated. This represents the judge's overall estimate of the product and is *not* an average of the scores assigned to all of the other quality characteristics. (Is the product servable to friends and acquaintances? Is the product saleable in a high-quality restaurant?)

A word of caution about two sources of error in scoring of foods: First, by being careless, a scorer may miss the differences that should have been detected and, second, a scorer may be hypercritical and mark down deviations that in reality do not exist. One type of error is just as bad as the other.

EXAMPLES

The sample evaluation sheet, page 21, shows how several types of products might be scored.

The muffin did not meet the established quality standards and would be rated a poor product: the numerical values tell that much. The descriptive terms are clues indicating why this muffin was a poor product and, as will be shown later, the terms describe a muffin that has been overmixed.

Note that the characteristic of tenderness is not scored for a product like soup.

The tomato soup leaves much to be desired, but the reasons may not be obvious. The fact that the soup is too thin might indicate any of several deviations:

1. Incorrect measurements—too much milk, too much tomato juice, or too little starch
2. Undercooking—starch not gelatinized
3. Overcooking—starch hydrolyzed

However, when all of the other comments are considered, it appears the soup has been undercooked. The first clue is the oily surface, indicating an unstable emulsion due to incomplete gelatinization of the starch. The second clue is the starchy flavor, which can be due only to undercooked starch. Other possible causes of the thin consistency cannot be completely ruled out: the cook might have made more than one error!

The pork chop as prepared rated as a high-quality product; therefore, the use of descriptive terms is not essential for denoting quality, but the use of descriptive terms emphasizes the desirable characteristics of a high-quality product.

The olive green color of the green beans is an indication of the effect of acid on chlorophyll. Volatile acids normally present in the vegetable are trapped within the saucepan when the pan is covered and the nonvolatile acids react with the green pigment to produce the olive green color. The mushy surface and mushy texture indicate excessive breakdown of cell structure as a result of overcooking.

The Quick Mix Cake must be given a low rating due to the bitter flavor, although the appearance, texture, and tenderness scores seem to indicate the cake was a high-quality product.

CONCLUSION

Careful evaluation of food products can substantially increase your knowledge and understanding of food preparation. The information obtained by scoring will be in direct proportion to the care and diligence used in carrying out the evaluation.

EVALUATION OF PRODUCTS

Name: _____

Date: _____

Score System

Points	Quality
7	Excellent
6	Very good
5	Good
4	Medium
3	Fair
2	Poor
1	Very Poor

Directions:
1. Place the numerical score in the box in the upper left-hand corner.
2. Comments should justify the numerical score. Comments must be brief.
3. Evaluation of the food products must be on an *individual* basis.

Products

Quality Characteristic	Muffin		Tomato Soup		Pork Chop		Green Beans		Quick Mix Cake	
Appearance	3	Smooth, shiny, peaked, pale	4	Oily surface	5	Evenly browned	3	Olive green color, surface mushy	6	Even top crust, golden color
Consistency or Texture	2	Tunnels	2	Thin	5	Fine grained	3	Disintegrates in mouth, mushy	6	Fine, even cell structure
Tenderness	3	Tough	1		6	Tender	2	Very soft, little resistance to bite	6	Very little resistance to bite
Flavor	5	Bland, slightly sweet	4	Starchy	6		4	Lacks fresh bean flavor	3	Bitter
Overall Eating Quality	3		3		6		2	Poor	3	Poor Flavor
	(Overmixed)		(Starch undercooked)		(Standard)		(Overcooked in closed pan)		(Too much vanilla)	

Metric Conversion

INTRODUCTION

The process of conversion from our customary* system of measurements to the metric system is on a voluntary basis and this has led to different approaches for making the conversion. For a complete discussion of the conversion process, refer to the publication, *Think Metric: Handbook for Metric Usage*, published by the American Home Economics Association in 1977. A "soft" conversion is one of vocabulary only; one quart equals 0.946 liter, so one cup would contain 236.6 milliliters; fractional measures would derive from this. "Hard" conversion involves a real quantitative measurement change to even metric units such as one liter (1 L); thus a "metric cup" would contain 250 milliliters. "Hard" conversion has required resizing of measuring equipment to standard metric modules. The figures in Table 1 compare these quantitative differences and the resizing is evident in the column marked "Hard" Conversion. The standards on which resizing has been based were established by a committee of the American National Standards Institute. One may purchase measuring devices based on both "soft" and "hard" conversions for metric measurement of foods in the home.

TABLE 1

Customary U.S.A.	"Soft" Conversion	"Hard" Conversion
1 cup	236.6 ml	250 ml
1/2 cup	118.3 ml	125 ml
1/3 cup**	78.8 ml	**
1/4 cup	59.1 ml	60 ml

**A measure equivalent to this size is not available in "sets" of measuring devices.

*Customary measurements are referred to in this manual as U.S.A. measurements.

PROCEDURE AND DISCUSSION

The "hard" conversion procedure has been used in this manual although it does not yield precise, quantitative, equivalent measures; conversion factors which have been used appear in Part I, Table I and Part III in the Tables of Equivalents (see page 24). We have accepted the recommendation on page 11 of *Think Metric: Handbook for Metric Usage*, ". . . metric devices should not be called *cups* or *spoons*"; metric measuring utensils should be referred to as *measures* or *measuring devices*. The system of "hard" conversion does *not* yield a precise mathematical conversion but rather a new system of measurements that embodies the inherent simplicity of the metric system. The two systems, however, do share a common ground in that the 250 milliliter measure has the same 4 to 1 ratio to a liter that one cup has to a quart; this may help to put the two systems of measurements into proper perspective.

In selecting metric measurements, we have taken care to be sure the ratio of ingredients will yield a satisfactory product and that the measurements are practical to make; it is important in the laboratory for you to be able to measure ingredients quickly and with a minimum of error. In those instances where quantitative differences in the amount of an ingredient indicated that the quality of the product would be affected, the recipe has been carefully tested and the resulting product deemed acceptable.

In addition to the conversion of recipes to metric units, sizes of food pieces, pan sizes, and cooking or baking temperatures have also been converted to metric units. Part III in the Tables of Equivalents (page 25) contains the length measure conversions; temperature conversions appear on the thermometer diagram (page 26).

The volumetric system of measurements is more suited to use in the home; the metric system presented herein does not require basic changes in the techniques of measuring, but only a change in units employed. Gravimetric measuring of ingredients as currently practiced in quantity food preparation will be continued and will need to be converted to metric units of grams and kilograms, a matter which is beyond the scope of this manual.

Either the customary (U.S.A.) or metric measurements may be used with the expectation of obtaining a high-quality product when the recipe is followed carefully. In using metric measures one must learn to "think metric" and resist the strong temptation to make mental conversions from customary units to metric units.

Tables of Equivalents

Discussion material explains why by "hard" conversion 1/4 cup is equal to only 60 ml (see page 22).

Part I Volumetric Measurements

TABLE 1 "HARD" CONVERSION AS USED IN THIS MANUAL

1 cup	=	250 ml	1 tablespoon	=	15 ml
1/2 cup	=	125 ml	1 teaspoon	=	5 ml
1/4 cup	=	60 ml	1/2 teaspoon	=	2 ml
			1/4 teaspoon	=	1 ml
			1/8 teaspoon	=	0.5 ml

TABLE 2 "SOFT" CONVERSION NOT USED IN THIS MANUAL

1 quart	=	946.0 ml (0.946 L)	1/2 cup	=	118.3 ml
1 cup	=	236.6 ml	1/3 cup	=	78.8 ml
			1/4 cup	=	59.1 ml

TABLE 3 FRACTIONAL U.S. MEASUREMENTS

1 quart	=	4 cups	1 cup	=	8 ounces liquid measure
1 pint	=	2 cups			
1 cup	=	16 tablespoons			
1 tablespoon	=	3 teaspoons			

Part II Gravimetric (Weight) Measurements

16 ounces	=	1 pound	=	453.6 grams
		1 ounce	=	28.4 grams

Part III Length Measurements

12 inches = 1 foot = 30.8 cm
1 inch = 2.5 cm

Fractional measures as used in this manual

3/4 inch = 2.0 cm
1/2 inch = 1.3 cm
3/8 inch = 1.0 cm
1/4 inch = 0.6 cm
1/8 inch = 0.3 cm
1/16 inch = 0.2 cm

Part IV Abbreviations (to be memorized)

qt	= quart	lb	= pound	L	= liter
pt	= pint	oz	= ounce	ml	= milliliter
c	= cup	ft	= foot	g	= gram
tbsp	= tablespoon	in	= inch	cm	= centimeter
tsp	= teaspoon				

TEMPERATURES USED IN FOOD PREPARATION

(Degrees Fahrenheit) °F   °C (Degrees Celsius)

Oven Temperatures:

Extremely hot oven — — — 525 — 274
500 — 260

Very hot oven — — — — — 475 — 246
450 — 232

Hot oven — — — — — — — 425 — 218 — — (Muffins, biscuits, pie pastry)
400 — 205

Moderate oven — — — — — 375 — 190 (Angel and sponge cakes, custards and
350 — 176 souffles— set in pan of water; macaroni

Slow oven — — — — — — 325 — 163 and cheese—all 350°F)
300 — 149 (Roasting large roasts of meat, roasting
poultry—325°F)

Deep-Fat Frying:
395   201   (French-fried potatoes)
375   190   (Croquettes, onions, eggplant)
350   177   (Chicken, fish, fritters)

Sugar Cookery:
338   170   (Caramelization of sugar)
320   160   (Granulated sugar liquifies)
310   154   (Hard crack—peanut brittle)
290   143   (Soft crack—taffy, butterscotch)
266   130   (Hard ball—divinity, marshmallows)
248   120   (Firm ball—caramels)
239   115   (Soft ball—fudge, penuche)
234   112   (Very soft ball—fondant)

Steam Pressure:
250   121 — — — (15 lbs. pressure at sea level)
240   115 — — — (10 lbs. pressure at sea level)
228   109 — — — (5 lbs. pressure at sea level)

Water Temperatures:
Boiling water   212   100 — — — (0 lbs. pressure at sea level)
Simmering range — — — 210   99 (Bubbles vigorously break on surface)
185   85

Scalding   149   65
Lukewarm   104   40

Changes in Foods: 214   101 — — — (Coagulation of protein in baked
products of low sugar content)

208   98 — — — (Steep beverages: tea, coffee)
203   95 — — — (Maximum gelatinization of starch)

Temperature Effect on   170   77 — — — (End temp. in cooking pork to kill
Bacterial Growth/Survival: 165   74 trichinae; well-done beef)

165–140° F (74–60°C) Prevents   160   70 — — — (Medium beef; egg yolk and whole
growth; allows survival.   egg coagulate)

140–120° F (60–49°C) Some   149   65 — — — (Complete coagulation egg white;
growth occurs; many bacteria   starch begins to gelantinize)
survive.   140   60 — — — (Rare beef)

120–60°F (49–15°C) Danger   125   52 — — — (Coagulation of egg white begins)
Zone: 120   49

1) Bacteria grow rapidly.   115   46 — — — (Maximum for rehydration of dry yeast)
2) Toxins produced by some   104   40 — — — (Optimum activity of rennin enzyme)
bacteria.   90   33 — — — (Optimum for yeast fermentation)

60–40°F (15–4°C) Some bac-   60   15
terial growth occurs.   45   7 — — — (Maximum temp. for refrigeration)
40   5

40–32°F (4–0°C) Slow growth   35   2 — — — (Optimum temp. for refrigeration)
of bacteria causing food   32   0 — — — (Freezing temp. of water)
spoilage.   29   − 1.7 — — — (Cold storage of eggs in shell)

32–0°F (0° to–18°C) Some   0   −17.8 — (Range for freezer storage of foods)
bacteria survive freezing.   −10   −23.3
No growth at low temp.

140–40°F (60–4°C) Critical
temp. range for food poison-
ing bacteria.

Microwave Cooking

OBJECTIVES

1. To introduce and apply the basic principles of microwave cooking.
2. To illustrate principles using various techniques of microwave cooking with selected foods.

PRODUCTS TO BE PREPARED TO ILLUSTRATE PRINCIPLES

Cinnamon sugar muffins (page 40)
Chocolate pudding (page 124)
*Cheese sauce (page 123)
*Scrambled eggs (page 157)
Chocolate cake, package mix (page 71)
Yellow cake, package mix (page 71)
Clam chowder (page 206)
White sauce (page 123)

Broccoli (page 226)
Baked potatoes (page 216)
Savory spinach (page 225)
*Apple sauce (page 238)
Bacon (page 180)
Ground beef patties (page 176)
Squash in cream sauce (page 225)
Stuffed zucchini (page 221)

*Require a microwave oven with variable power capabilities.

PRINCIPLES

1. Microwaves have very short wave lengths; fewer than five inches for microwaves are used to heat foods.
2. Microwaves may behave in three ways:
   a. Be absorbed by the material causing heating; this causes the cooking of food.
   b. Pass through the material with no reaction; substances exhibiting this property may be used as containers for the food in microwave ovens.
   c. Bounce off metals, thereby limiting the use of metals in microwave cooking.
3. Microwaves penetrate the food from all directions.
4. Microwaves reverse direction 2,450,000,000 times a second, causing the food molecules to vibrate. The friction of the molecules in motion generates heat, which cooks the food very quickly.
5. Microwaves penetrate food to a depth of 3/4–1 1/2 inches (2–3.8 cm) causing heating in the area which they penetrate. Heat is transferred to the center (cold area) by conduction, the mechanism of heat transfer in conventional cooking.
6. Some foods may cook further after removal from the oven.

7. The rate of cooking is influenced by many factors:
   a. Water, fat, and sugar absorb microwave energy more readily and therefore cook faster.
   b. Well-marbled meat cooks more evenly.
   c. Small amounts of food cook faster than large amounts.
   d. Thinner parts of foods which are not evenly shaped cook faster than thicker parts.
   e. Porous foods absorb energy more easily and cook faster than denser foods.
   f. Bone conducts heat and may cause uneven heating if it is on one side of a cut of meat. Boneless cuts of meat cook more slowly but more evenly.
8. Covering the food container will speed up cooking. Microwave cooking is essentially a moist heat method of cooking.
9. Some food products brown in the microwave oven while others do not. Large items (such as a whole turkey) which have a long cooking time (60–90 minutes) will brown. Small items (such as cupcakes) which have a short cooking time (2–4 minutes) do not brown; moisture on the surface of the cupcake would also be a factor in preventing browning.
10. It may be necessary to stir the food, to rearrange it in the pan, or to rotate the pan to get more even heating.

SPECIAL NOTE

The cooking times given in these recipes are based on a microwave oven with an output of 600–700 watts. If the oven used does not have an output within this range, adjustments in cooking time will be required; for ovens with an output of less than 600 watts, a longer cooking time will be required while ovens with an output of more than 700 watts will require a shorter cooking time. The total power consumption of a microwave oven will always be greater than the actual cooking power (output). The total power consumption will be about 1500 watts.

REVIEW QUESTIONS

1. Explain how microwaves cause heating in foods.
2. Why can paper, some glass, and some plastics be used as containers to hold food while it is being cooked in a microwave oven?
3. a. Explain why scrambled eggs cannot be cooked in a stainless steel bowl.
   b. What else would happen if metal pans were used in a microwave oven?
4. Relate cooking time to quantity of food being cooked.
5. Discuss the effect of shape in cooking
   a. a chicken leg and thigh
   b. fresh broccoli spears
6. Fat comes to the surface of a whole turkey being cooked in the microwave oven. What effect will this have on browning? On juiciness?

Introduction and Demonstration

OBJECTIVES

1. To discuss expectations from a food preparation laboratory:
   a. from student's viewpoint
   b. from instructor's viewpoint
2. To acquaint students with procedural patterns for laboratory sessions.
3. To demonstrate and discuss acceptable methods for measurement of selected ingredients.
4. To acquaint students with selected equipment used in food preparation.
5. To acquaint students with temperatures used in the preparation of food products.
6. To introduce a systematic procedure for the evaluation of the quality of food products.

PRODUCT TO BE PREPARED TO ILLUSTRATE PRINCIPLES

Instructor demonstration of Methods of Measurement of Muffins

PRINCIPLES

1. Separation of particles of a dry ingredient by sifting, rolling, and/or stirring equalizes the density of the ingredient.
2. Volume measurements may be less accurate than weight measurements.
3. Use of an equivalent measurement may increase accuracy of measurement.
4. High standards of safety and sanitation must be maintained in handling and preparing food.
5. The quality characteristics of food products must be evaluated as objectively as possible.

METHODS OF MEASUREMENT—MUFFINS*

Ingredient	Measurement	Techniques Used
Flour, all-purpose	1 cup *or* 250 ml	
Baking powder	2 teaspoons *or* 10 ml	
Salt	1/2 teaspoon *or* 2 ml	
Sugar	3 tablespoons *or* 45 ml	
Milk	1/2 cup *or* 125 ml	
Egg, blended	2 tablespoons *or* 30 ml	
Vegetable oil**	2 tablespoons *or* 30 ml	

*These measurements will yield 5 or 6 muffins. Use Muffin Method on page 45 for combining ingredients.

**Demonstrate techniques of measuring solid fat at beginning of Baking Powder Biscuit lesson on page 50.

CHARACTERISTICS OF HIGH-QUALITY MUFFINS

Appearance: Top crust has a cauliflower-like appearance; is rather rough or pebbled; is golden brown.

Texture: Uniform distribution of gas cells; gas cells may be fairly large; the cell walls are of medium thickness.

Tenderness: Very little resistance when bitten and chewed.

Flavor: Usually bland or very slightly sweet.

Eating Quality: Overall satisfaction in serving and eating this product is high.

EVALUATION OF PRODUCTS

Name: _____

Date: _____

Score System

Points	Quality
7	Excellent
6	Very good
5	Good
4	Medium
3	Fair
2	Poor
1	Very poor

Directions:

1. Place the numerical score in the box in the upper left-hand corner.
2. Comments should justify the numerical score. Comments must be brief.
3. Evaluation of the food products must be on an *individual* basis.

Products

Quality Characteristic					
Appearance					
Consistency or Texture					
Tenderness					
Flavor					
Overall Eating Quality					

REVIEW QUESTIONS

Methods of Measurement

1. a. Why is flour usually sifted before it is measured?
   b. Under what circumstances is flour *not* sifted before measuring?
2. a. What types of dry ingredients are not sifted before measuring?
   b. State the reason for not sifting each ingredient listed in 2a.
3. Why must the mark on the glass measuring cup be at eye level?
4. How would you measure 1/8 teaspoon of cream of tarter?
5. How would you measure 1/8 cup of milk? Of flour?
6. How would you measure 4 tablespoons of sugar? Of flour? Why?
7. How would you measure 3 teaspoons of baking powder? Why?
8. How would you measure 1/6 cup?
9. How would you measure 1/2 cup of brown sugar?
10. How would you measure 3/8 cup of solid fat?
11. Triple all quantities in the following recipe and indicate how each ingredient would be correctly measured.

MUFFIN RECIPE

Ingredient	Amount	3X Amount	How Measured
Flour, all-purpose	1 cup		
Baking powder	2 teaspoons		
Salt	1/2 teaspoon		
Milk	1/2 cup		
Egg	2 tablespoons		
Vegetable oil	2 tablespoons		
Sugar	3 tablespoons		

12. How would you measure 25 milliliters of sugar? Of milk? Of vegetable oil?
13. How would you measure 45 milliliters of sugar? 50 milliliters of sugar? 150 milliliters of sugar?
14. How would you measure 0.5 milliliter of salt?
15. How would you measure 30 milliliters of milk?
16. How would you measure 1.5 liters of flour?

17. Reduce all quantities by one-fourth in the following recipe. Indicate how each ingredient would be correctly measured.

MUFFIN RECIPE—METRIC MEASURES

Ingredient	Amount	One-Fourth Amount	How Measured
Flour, all-purpose	1 L		
Baking powder	40 ml		
Salt	8 ml		
Milk	500 ml		
Vegetable oil	120 ml		
Sugar	180 ml		

Safety and Sanitation

1. a. Why are uniforms required for each student in the laboratory?
   b. Why are hairnets or caps required?
2. a. Why are pans and utensils used for preparing protein foods and starchy foods rinsed in cold water? (*Note*: An understanding of the terms *coagulation* and *gelatinization* is required.)
   b. Why is hot water used to rinse pans which contained
      (1) fats (after most of fat has been wiped out with paper toweling)?
      (2) sugar or sugar syrups?
3. a. What is the relationship between water temperature and destruction of micro-organisms?
   b. What are the two functions of soap in washing dishes?
4. What is the proper water temperature for washing dishes? For rinsing dishes?

Evaluation of Foods

1. List some of the personal factors which may influence evaluation of a food product.
2. a. Name the two general types of tests which may be used to evaluate a food product.
   b. Which of these two tests embodies the least personal bias?
3. List the factors one considers or steps one takes if his or her evaluation of a food product is to be as objective as possible.

Basic Terms and Concepts

This is a basic vocabulary for food study. A good working knowledge of these terms and concepts is essential for an understanding of the changes taking place in food preparation. Students need to learn these terms early to be able to read and understand textbooks. Refer to a textbook and the American Home Economics Association *Handbook of Food Preparation*. Additional terms appear in most of the Review Questions at the end of each unit.

Food Constituents

Proteins
Fats
Carbohydrates
    Sugars
    Starches
    Pectins
    Cellulose
Vitamins
    Fat soluble
    Water soluble
Enzymes
Water
Minerals

Protein Terms and Processes

Peptization
Denaturation
Coagulation

Starch Terms and Processes

Gelatinization
Syneresis

Dispersion Systems

True solutions
    Solute
    Solvent
Colloids
    Dispersed phase
    Dispersion medium
    Interface
    Emulsions
    Foams
    Sol
    Gel
Suspensions

Reactions or Processes

(Starches and proteins)
Hydration
Hydration capacity
Polymers
Gelation

Fat and Oil Terms and Processes

Oxidation
Oxidative rancidity
Hydrolytic rancidity
Hydrogenation
Flash point
Smoke point

Baked Products

Browning mechanisms
    Dextrinization
    Caramelization
    Maillard reaction
Leavening system
Leavening agent
Leavening gas

Physical Properties

Density
Specific gravity
Suface tension
Viscosity
Heat of fusion
Heat of vaporization
Molal lowering of freezing point
Crystallization

Descriptive Terms Used in Judging Characteristics of Baked Products

Volume: The amount of a baked product produced from a specific amount of batter. Volume will be small (poor), average (good), large (excellent).

Appearance: The shape, condition of the top crust, and the color of the exterior surface (may at times include the color of interior crumb).
Shape: Symmetrical, asymmetrical.
Condition of top crust : Level, sunken, rounded, erupted (volcano-like), pebbled, sticky, greasy, dry.
Exterior color: Pale, practically no browning, golden brown, light brown, dark brown, black (burned).
Interior color: May be affected by ingredients used, especially where egg is an ingredient.

*Texture**: The size of the air cell and thickness of the cell wall constitute the "grain" of the baked product. A product is heavy, compact, or light by characteristics of cell wall and air cell.
Air cell: Small, medium, large.
Cell wall: Thin, medium, thick.
Flakiness: The layering or development of "flakes" in the crumb of certain pastries.
Mealiness: Lack of flakiness: pastry is crumbly.

Velvetiness: Smoothness of crumb as it comes between palate and the back of the tongue. Lacking velvetiness, the crumb may be harsh and rough.

Moistness: The degree of moisture within the crumb. The crumb may be wet, soggy, gummy, pleasingly moist, dry.

Tenderness: The ease with which a product may be cut, broken, or chewed. Products may vary from very tough to extremely tender. Pastries may be designated as *brittle* and *hard*.

Flavor: Should be characteristic of product. Aroma becomes part of flavor as product is eaten. A partial list of terms to describe flavor may include: sweet, bitter, soapy, nutlike, floury, flat, rancid fat, wheat-like, eggy, yeasty, bland, sour.

Note: Many authors describe texture attributes of baked products in terms of "grain"; for example, a pound cake has a close grain.

Muffins

OBJECTIVES

*1. To give students the experience of applying principles of measurement of ingredients.
2. To acquaint students with the Muffin Method for combining ingredients for baked products.
3. To observe changes that occur in muffin batter with extended stirring of ingredients.
*4. To acquaint students with one method for evaluating quality characteristics of a food product.

PRODUCTS TO BE PREPARED TO ILLUSTRATE PRINCIPLES

Plain muffins
Whole wheat muffins
Corn meal muffins
Oatmeal muffins

Cinnamon sugar muffins (Microwave)
High-fiber muffins (Wheat fiber)
High-fiber muffins (Oat bran or oatmeal)

PRINCIPLES

*1. Flour proteins (glutenin and gliadin) plus milk (water) plus work result in the formation of gluten.
*2. Role of liquids
   a. Water only
      1. Solvent
      2. Hydration of protein
      3. Imbibition
      4. Gelatinization
   b. Fruit juices and milk in addition to furnishing water contribute to
      1. Flavor
      2. Tenderness
      3. Browning
*3. The quality of the gluten structure formed determines the quality of the baked product.

*4. Coagulation of certain proteins retains structure.
  a. Gluten
  b. Egg (if present); mixed whole egg is usually used, although egg whites may be used in some instances.
*5. Sugar
  a. Contributes to flavor
  b. Affects gluten structure
  c. Affects tenderness
*6. Sugar substitutes contribute only to flavor.
*7. Fats and oils
  a. Affects gluten structure
  b. Incorporation of air
  c. Affect leavening gas
  d. Affect crumb and mouth feel
*8. Leavening agents affects elastic protein
  a. Production of gas
  b. Expansion of gas
  c. Effect of baking powder residue on gluten
*9. Leavening action of baking powder is affected by
  a. Addition of liquid (water)
  b. Temperature of baking
10. Leavening action of yeast is affected by
  a. Sugar
  b. Salt
  c. Temperature
*11. Salt contributes to flavor
  a. Saltiness
  b. Sweetness
*12. Mechanisms of browning
  a. Caramelization of sugar
  b. Dextrinization of starch
  c. Protein-carbohydrate interaction (Maillard Reaction)
13. Dietary fiber
  a. Affects gluten
  b. Improves nutritional quality of product
  c. Many cereals are an excellent source of dietary fiber. (See Appendix A.)
14. See Appendices B, C, and D for the composition of various fats and oils.

*Objectives and principles indicated by an asterisk are inherent in all baked products.

Muffins

Flour, all-purpose	1 cup	250 ml
Baking powder	2 teaspoons	10 ml
Salt	1/2 teaspoon	2 ml
Sugar	3 tablespoons	45 ml
Milk	1/2 cup	125 ml
Egg, blended	2 tablespoons	30 ml
Vegetable oil	2 tablespoons	30 ml

1. Preheat oven to 425°F (220°C).
2. Lightly grease the *bottoms* (not the sides) of a set of 6 muffin cups. Use additional oil.
3. Always stir flour in storage container to aerate before measuring.
4. Sift together flour, baking powder, salt, and sugar in a 2-quart (2-L) bowl.
5. Blend together the milk, egg, and liquid shortening with the egg beater in a 1-quart (1-L) bowl. Do *not* beat until foamy, but oil should be broken up into fairly small globules.
6. Make a depression or "well" in the dry ingredients with a tablespoon. Add the liquid ingredients immediately.
7. Stir 5 or 6 strokes with a metal tablespoon. Some of the dry ingredients will not be wetted at this stage of blending. Remove enough batter for one muffin. (Muffin cups should be approximately 2/3 full.)
8. Stir remaining batter an additional 5 or 10 strokes or just enough until all dry ingredients are wetted. The batter should appear lumpy at this stage. Remove enough batter for four muffins. (These muffins should be typical high-quality muffins when baked.)
9. Stir the remaining batter an additional 50 strokes. At this stage the batter should be extremely smooth. (Be sure to note changes in the consistency of the batter during the stirring periods.) Remove enough batter for one muffin.
10. Bake in 425°F (220°C) oven for 15–20 minutes. The typical or standard muffins should be a golden brown at the end of the baking period.
11. Record total working time: _____minutes.

Variations

Whole Wheat Muffins
1. Follow Steps 1 and 2 as given for Muffins.
2. Substitute 1 cup (250 ml) finely ground whole wheat flour for the all-purpose flour.
3. In a 2-quart (2-L) bowl stir together all dry ingredients until thoroughly blended.
4. Follow Steps 5 and 6 as given for Muffins.
5. Stir liquid and dry ingredients 10–15 strokes until just blended. Fill cups approximately 2/3 full.
6. Bake as given in Step 10 for Muffins.

Oatmeal Muffins
1. Substitute 1/2 cup (125 ml) quick cooking oatmeal for 1/2 cup (125 ml) of the all-purpose flour.
2. Follow directions (other than Step 2) as given for Whole Wheat Muffins.

Corn Meal Muffins
Use only 1/2 cup of all-purpose flour. Add 1/2 cup yellow or white corn meal. Mix as directed for Whole Wheat Muffins.

Cinnamon Sugar Muffins (Microwave)

Flour, all-purpose	1 cup	250 ml
Baking powder	2 teaspoons	10 ml
Salt	1/2 teaspoon	2 ml
Sugar	3 tablespoons	45 ml
Milk	1/2 cup	125 ml
Egg, blended	2 tablespoons	30 ml
Vegetable oil	2 tablespoons	30 ml

Topping

Sugar	2 tablespoons	30 ml
Cinnamon	1/8 teaspoon	0.5 ml

1. Sift together flour, baking powder, salt, and 3 tablespoons (45 ml) sugar.
2. Use a rotary egg beater to thoroughly blend milk, egg, and vegetable oil so the oil is in fine globules when liquid ingredients are added to dry ingredients.
3. Add liquid to dry ingredients. Stir 15–20 strokes. All dry ingredients should be wetted, but the batter should still be lumpy.
*4. Carefully spoon batter into custard cups; do not fill more than half-full.
5. Spoon some of the topping over each muffin.
6. Do not microwave more than 6 muffins at one time. Place custard cups in a circle in the oven. Microwave at *high* power for 1 minute; turn 1/2 turn. Microwave 1 more minute at *high* power; turn 1/4 turn. Microwave 30 seconds at *high* power or until muffins appear to be baked. Tops may be slightly moist but will dry with standing. *Avoid overbaking.*
7. Remove muffins immediately from custard cups; place muffins on cooling rack.
8. Record total working time: _____minutes.

*Only custard cups made of materials safe for microwave cooking should be used. Bottoms of glass custard cups can be greased and batter put directly into the custard cups or cupcake paper cups can be used in the custard cups; two paper liners are used in each cup. Paper liners are to be filled no more than half-full.

CHARACTERISTICS OF HIGH-QUALITY MUFFINS

Appearance: Top crust has a cauliflower-like appearance; is rather rough or pebbled; is golden brown.
Texture: Uniform distribution of gas cells; gas holes may be fairly large; the cell walls are of medium thickness.
Tenderness: Very little resistance when bitten and chewed.
Flavor: Usually bland or very slightly sweet.
Eating Quality: Overall satisfaction in serving and eating this product is high.

High-Fiber Muffins
(Except oat bran and oatmeal)

Flour, all-purpose	3/8	cup	100 ml
Baking powder	2	teaspoons	10 ml
Salt	1/2	teaspoon	2 ml
Sugar	1/4	cup	60 ml
Milk	3/8	cup	100 ml
Egg, blended	2	tablespoons	30 ml
Vegetable oil	2	tablespoons	30 ml
High-fiber cereal*	1/2–1	cup	125–250 ml

1. Preheat oven to 425°F (220°C).
2. Lightly grease the *bottoms* (not the sides) of a set of 6 muffin cups. Use additional oil.
3. Sift together flour, baking powder, salt, and sugar in a 2-quart (2-L) bowl.
4. Blend together the milk and high-fiber cereal in a 1-quart (1-L) bowl and let stand 5 minutes. Add the egg and vegetable oil and mix with a whip or egg beater. Do not beat until foamy, but oil should be broken up into fairly small globules.
5. Make a depression or "well" in the dry ingredients with a tablespoon. Add liquid ingredients immediately.
6. Stir 10 to 15 strokes or just until all dry ingredients are wetted. The batter should appear lumpy at this stage.
7. Carefully spoon the batter into the muffin cups; use about 1 tablespoon full and push into the cup with the back of a teaspoon (muffin cups should be about 2/3 full).
8. Bake in a 425°F oven for 15–18 minutes or until the muffins are an even light brown color.
9. Record total working time: _____ minutes.

*The cereal used must contain 10–15 g dietary fiber per serving in order to supply a significant quantity of dietary fiber in each muffin. The amount used will depend on the density of the product; see the package for proper amount to use.

From the preceding directions, each muffin will contain from 2.0 to 4.7 grams of dietary fiber, depending on the amount of dietary fiber in the cereal or flour used, as shown in the following table.

Dietary Fiber per serving**	Dietary Fiber per muffin
04 g	2.0 g
10 g	3.3 g
13 g	4.3 g
14 g	4.7 g

Good nutritional practice indicates dietary fiber should come from a number of different foods in the diet and not from one source only. A well-balanced diet will achieve this.

**See Appendix A or nutritional content on side label of package.

High-Fiber Muffins with Oat Bran

Oat bran cereal, finely ground	1 cup	250 ml
Brown sugar, firmly packed	1/4 cup	60 ml
Baking powder	1 teaspoon	4 ml
Salt (optional)	1/4 teaspoon	1 ml
Milk	1/2 cup	125 ml
Egg white	1	1
Honey or molasses	2 tablespoons	30 ml
Vegetable oil	1 tablespoon	15 ml

1. Preheat oven to 425°F (220°C).
2. Lightly grease the *bottoms* (not the sides) of a set of 6 muffin cups. Use extra vegetable oil.
3. Combine all of the dry ingredients in a 2-quart (2-L) bowl.
4. In a 1-quart (1-L) bowl blend together the milk, egg white, honey, and vegetable oil with a whip or egg beater.
5. Make a depression or a "well" in the dry ingredients with a tablespoon. Add the liquid ingredients immediately.
6. Stir 10–15 strokes or until the dry ingredients are just wetted. The batter should be lumpy at this stage.
7. Fill each muffin cup about 3/4 full.
8. In a 425°F oven, bake for 15–17 minutes or until golden brown.
9. Record total preparation time: _____minutes.

Each muffin will contain approximately 2.0 grams dietary fiber.

EVALUATION OF PRODUCTS

Name: _____

Date: _____

Score System

Points	Quality
7	Excellent
6	Very good
5	Good
4	Medium
3	Fair
2	Poor
1	Very poor

Directions:

1. Place the numerical score in the box in the upper left-hand corner.
2. Comments should justify the numerical score. Comments must be brief.
3. Evaluation of the food products must be on an *individual* basis.

Products

Quality Characteristic					
Appearance					
Consistency or Texture					
Tenderness					
Flavor					
Overall Eating Quality					

SUMMARY OUTLINE: _____MUFFINS_____ Name: _____
(Product)

Date: _____

Summary Outlines emphasize application of principles to basic steps in preparation of a food product. Principles may have been discussed in lecture or in laboratory, or may have been assigned in readings. Include cooking or baking temperature and know _why_ a low, medium, or high temperature is used. Summaries are excellent means for review.

List of Ingredients

Flour, all-purpose	1 cup	250 ml
Baking powder	2 teaspoons	10 ml
Salt	1/2 teaspoon	2 ml
Sugar	3 tablespoons	45 ml
Milk	1/2 cup	125 ml
Egg, blended	2 tablespoons	30 ml
Vegetable oil	2 tablespoons	30 ml

Steps in Preparation	Principles Applied
1. Preheat oven to 425°F (220°C).	1. Have oven ready for immediate heating of batter.
2. Lightly grease bottoms of muffin pans.	2. So batter can be transferred rapidly with least loss of carbon dioxide.
3. Sift together all dry ingredients.	3. For more even distribution, especially of baking powder (leavening agent).
4. With rotary beater blend together milk, egg, and vegetable oil.	4. a. For more even distribution of liquid ingredients; egg must be thoroughly blended with milk; oil must be broken into small globules. b. For easier blending of liquid and dry ingredients.
5. Add liquid ingredients to dry ingredients. Stir approximately 15–20 strokes. Stir only until mixture appears lumpy and dry ingredients are wetted.	5. a. To hydrate flour b. To dissolve sugar and salt. c. To initiate leavening reaction. d. To regulate gluten development.
6. Carefully spoon batter into pans.	6. a. To prevent stretching of gluten. b. To prevent loss of leavening gas. c. To avoid trapping air, which forms pockets and gives poor texture.

7. Bake at 425°F (220°C) for 15–20 minutes.	7. a. High temperature necessary for rapid production of carbon dioxide.
	b. Coagulate proteins for structure.
	c. Gelatinize starch for structure.
	d. Browning reactions include
	  (1) Caramelization of sucrose and lactose (sugars)
	  (2) Dextrinization of starch
	  (3) Maillard reaction

Note: A Summary Outline sheet is placed at the end of each lesson in the baked products unit.

REVIEW QUESTIONS

1. What leavening system is used in muffins?
2. What is the effect of dropping the batter from a distance into the muffin pan?
3. What is the effect of overmanipulation of the batter on the quality of the finished muffin?
4. a. Why is there less danger of overmixing muffins if they are made with a higher proportion of sugar to flour?
   b. Why is there less danger of overmixing muffins if cornmeal or whole wheat flour is substituted for a part of the all-purpose flour?
5. List the characteristics of a high-quality muffin.
6. List several possible defects which might be found in muffins and indicate the cause(s) of each defect.
7. Describe how the addition of whole wheat flour to the muffin recipe affects each of the following Quality Characteristics:
   a. color and appearance
   b. texture
   c. tenderness
   d. flavor
8. Describe how the addition of high-fiber cereal to the muffin recipe affects each of the following Quality Characteristics:
   a. color and appearance
   b. texture
   c. tenderness
   d. flavor
9. a. Name two fruits which could be added to muffins to increase the level of complex carbohydrates.
   b. Which type(s) of complex carbohydrate would be increased?
10. Compare the following Quality Characteristics of muffins baked in a microwave oven with those baked in a regular oven:
    a. texture
    b. tenderness

GENERAL REVIEW QUESTIONS ON BAKED PRODUCTS

Note: Students may be unable to answer some of these questions at this early stage in their study of the principles of food preparation. However, these questions should serve as a guide to some of the important principles that are to be covered. Specific review questions on each of the baked products follow the lesson on that product.

1. Give the essential steps in each of the following methods of combining ingredients:
   a. Muffin method
   b. Biscuit method
   c. Pastry method
   d. Cake, Conventional method
   e. Cake, Quick Mix method
   f. Foam-Type Cake method
   g. Cream Puff method
2. a. How are the proteins of wheat (glutenin and gliadin) transformed to gluten?
   b. What effect does heat have on the gluten structure?
3. List the function(s) of each of the following ingredients in baked products:
   a. Flour
   b. Sugar
   c. Baking powder
   d. Salt
   e. Egg
   f. Water
   g. Milk
4. a. What are the three gases which produce leavening action?
   b. Briefly describe how each gas can be produced.
5. Tell how each of the following will affect the formation and/or the resulting characteristics of the gluten structure:
   a. Type of flour
   b. Amount of flour
   c. Sugar
   d. Baking powder residue
   e. Salt
   f. Egg
   g. An increase or decrease of milk or water
   h. Fat
   i. Whole wheat flour
   j. Corn meal
   k. Oat flour
6. What advantage is gained by adding complex carbohydrates to baked products?
7. What problem(s) might arise with this addition?
8. Explain what two functions the added dietary fiber plays in the body.
9. Name at least five food products which are high in both *insoluble* and *soluble* dietary fiber.
10. a. In preparing certain baked products the oven must be preheated and the pan prepared before measuring the ingredients. Why?
    b. List the products where this is required.

11. Summarize the reactions that take place as any baked product is heated in the oven. Give some indication as to when in the baking process each reaction takes place (this could be done as a timeline). Be sure to account for each of the following constituents or reactions: leavening agents, fats, sugars, salts, protein, starch, water, and browning reactions (Maillard Reaction, caramelization, and dextrinization).

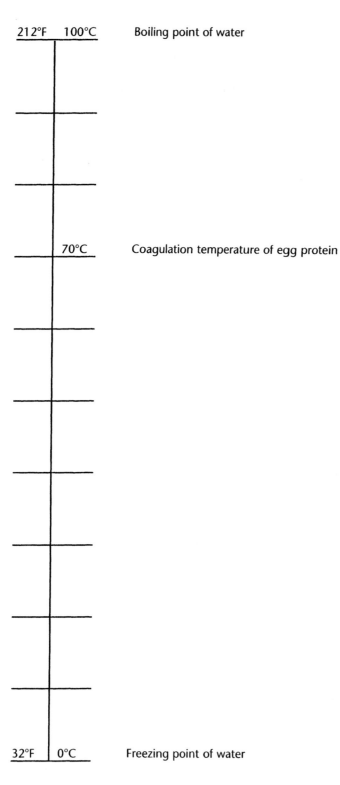

212°F 100°C — Boiling point of water

70°C — Coagulation temperature of egg protein

32°F 0°C — Freezing point of water

12. Each baked product has an optimum oven temperature for obtaining the highest quality finished product. For each of the products listed below, state the optimum oven temperature and tell briefly why it is the optimum temperature for that product.

Muffins
    Temperature: _____
    Reason(s)

Cream puffs
    Temperature: _____
    Reason(s)

Baking powder biscuits
    Temperature: _____
    Reason(s)

Yeast-leavened products
    Temperature: _____
    Reason(s)

Butter-type cakes
    Temperature: _____
    Reason(s)

Pie pastry
    Temperature: _____
    Reason(s)

Foam-type cakes
    Temperature: _____
    Reason(s)

Baking Powder Biscuits

OBJECTIVES

1. To acquaint students with the Biscuit Method for combining ingredients for baked products.
2. To observe the effect of kneading on the biscuit dough.
3. Toobserve changes that occur in a baking powder biscuit as a result of kneading.
4. To demonstrate the effect of buttermilk (acid)-soda leavening system on selected quality characteristics.
5. To explain the format for applying principles of preparation to the product.

PRODUCT TO BE PREPARED TO ILLUSTRATE PRINCIPLES

Baking powder biscuits
Buttermilk biscuits
Whole wheat biscuits

Note: When a cereal high in dietary fiber was added to the recipe for biscuits, an unsatisfactory product resulted. The biscuits tended to be dry and crumbly and the texture was more like a muffin than a biscuit. We do not recommend the addition of cereals high in dietary fiber to the biscuit recipe.

PRINCIPLES

1. Flakiness depends on
   a. Type of fat used
   b. The kneading process
2. After carbon dioxide has been released in the leavening reaction, residues from the system remain in the baked product and may affect flavor and/or tenderness.
3. Principles 1, 2, 3, 4, 7, 8, 9, 11, and 12 given in the lesson on muffins also apply to baking powder biscuits. See pages 37–38.

Baking Powder Biscuits (Kneaded)

Flour, all purpose	1 1/2 cups	375 ml
Baking powder	2 teaspoons	10 ml
Salt	1/2 teaspoon	2 ml
*Shortening	1/4 cup	60 ml
Milk	1/2 cup + 1 tablespoon	140 ml

1. Preheat oven to 425°F (220°C).
2. Lightly grease a 2-inch (5-cm) diameter portion of the baking sheet for the Drop Biscuit (Step 6).
3. Sift together all dry ingredients.
4. Cut shortening into dry ingredients until it has been cut into pieces the size of small grains of rice. (Use pastry blender.)
5. Add the milk all in one portion. Stir with a metal tablespoon for approximately 10 strokes.
6. Cut out enough dough for one "drop" biscuit. Place the dough on greased portion of baking sheet. See the note following Characteristics of High-Quality Drop Biscuits.
7. Use approximately 1 tablespoon (15 ml) more flour to lightly flour the breadboard.
8. Turn remaining dough out onto the lightly floured board. Dip fingertips into small amount of flour and pat out dough to 1 inch (2.5 cm) thickness. Fold half of the dough onto the other half. If necessary, lightly flour portion of board from which dough has been removed.
9. Again pat dough 1 inch (2.5 cm) thick. Repeat manipulation processes in Step 8 until the dough has been patted out and folded at least 5 or 6 times (total).
10. After the last folding of the dough, roll the dough 3/4 inch (2 cm) thick with a lightly floured rolling pin.
11. Dip biscuit cutter into flour before cutting each biscuit. Use even pressure in cutting down on the dough to get more evenly shaped biscuits.
12. Place the cut biscuits on an ungreased baking sheet. Have sides of biscuits touching if soft biscuits are desired. Set biscuits apart for crisp crusted biscuits. These should be typical, control, or standard-kneaded biscuits.
13. Knead the scraps of dough together until the dough becomes very elastic (about 50 kneading strokes). Roll dough 3/4 inch (cm) thick. Cut several biscuits of these "re-rolls." Place on ungreased baking sheet with biscuits cut at Step 12.
14. Place in an oven preheated to 425°F (220°C). Bake for approximately 15 minutes. Typical biscuits will be golden brown.
15. Record total working time: _____ minutes.

*Measuring solid (plastic) fat
1. Select appropriate measuring device, for example, 1 tablespoon measure or 1/2 cup measure.
2. Using a straight-edged spatula, press the fat into the measure until it is slightly more than full.
3. Draw the straight edge of the spatula evenly over the top of the cup to level the surface of the fat.
4. Remove the fat cleanly from the cup with a rubber spatula.

Variations

Whole Wheat Biscuits

Replace the all-purpose flour totally with whole wheat flour. Follow the directions for the kneaded baking powder biscuits.

Buttermilk Biscuits (Kneaded)

Flour, all-purpose	1 1/2 cups	375 ml
Baking powder	1 teaspoon	5 ml
Soda	1/2 teaspoon	2 ml
Salt	1/2 teaspoon	2 ml
*Shortening	1/4 cup	60 ml
Buttermilk	2/3 cup	150 ml

Follow directions as given for Baking Powder Biscuits (Kneaded). *Note:* If the dough is stiff at the end of Step 5, add 1 tablespoon buttermilk.

*See note on preceding page.

CHARACTERISTICS OF HIGH-QUALITY BAKING POWDER BISCUITS

Appearance: Top crust is a pale, golden brown; top crust is slightly rough; sides are straight.
Texture: Uniform small gas cells; relatively thin cell walls; crumb will peel off in "sheets" or layers.
Tenderness: Outer crust is crisp, yet tender; little resistance to bite. Interior is tender with little resistance to bite.
Flavor: Very bland, mild; flavor of table fat or jelly will predominate.

CHARACTERISTICS OF HIGH-QUALITY DROP BISCUITS

Appearance
  Exterior: Top crust is pale, golden brown; top crust is slightly rough.
  Interior: Crumb color will be white.
Texture: Gas cells larger and less uniform than in kneaded biscuits; cell walls slightly thicker.
Tenderness: Outer crust should be very crisp, yet tender; interior very tender, little resistance to bite.
Flavor: Very bland, mild; flavor of table fat or jelly will predominate.

Note: In order to make drop biscuits of optimum quality the dough must be more moist than for kneaded biscuits. The recipe for kneaded biscuits may be used for drop biscuits by increasing the milk to 1 cup (250 ml).

CHARACTERISTICS OF HIGH-QUALITY BUTTERMILK BISCUITS

Appearance:
  Exterior: Top crust is golden brown; may be slightly rough; sides are straight.
  Interior: Crumb color will be creamy white.
Texture: Gas cells vary in size from small to medium large. Cell walls may vary from slightly thick to relatively thin. Crumb will "peel off" in small sheets or layers.
Tenderness: Outer crust is crisp, yet tender; very little resistance to bite. Interior is extremely tender; practically no resistance to bite.
Flavor: Bland, mild flavor with a slightly acid aftertaste.

EVALUATION OF PRODUCTS

Name: _____

Date: _____

Score System

Points	Quality
7	Excellent
6	Very good
5	Good
4	Medium
3	Fair
2	Poor
1	Very poor

Directions:

1. Place the numerical score in the box in the upper left-hand corner.
2. Comments should justify the numerical score. Comments must be brief.
3. Evaluation of the food products must be on an *individual* basis.

Products

Quality Characteristic					
Appearance					
Consistency or Texture					
Tenderness					
Flavor					
Overall Eating Quality					

SUMMARY OUTLINE: _____ Name: _____

(Product)

Date: _____

Summary Outlines emphasize application of principles to basic steps in preparation of a food product. Principles may have been discussed in lecture or in laboratory, or may have been assigned in readings. Include cooking or baking temperature and know _why_ a low, medium, or high temperature is used. Summaries are excellent means for review.

List of Ingredients:

Steps in Preparation	Principles Applied
1.	1.

REVIEW QUESTIONS

1. *Flakiness* in biscuits:
   a. What is the role of fat? Of flour?
   b. What type of fat must be used?
   c. At what steps in the procedure is flakiness developed?
2. Describe how each of the following treatments would affect the quality of the finished biscuit. Why is this effect produced?
   a. Overkneading the dough
   b. Too much liquid
   c. Biscuit cut over the edge of the dough
   d. Tops brushed with milk
3. Why is an oven temperature of 425°F (220°C) used for baking biscuits?
4. Distinguish between *flakiness* and *tenderness*. What different factors influence each of these quality characteristics?
5. List the characteristics of a high-quality kneaded biscuit.
6. List the characteristics of a high-quality buttermilk biscuit.
7. a. How is carbon dioxide produced in the buttermilk-soda system?
   b. How does this differ from the leavening system in a baking powder biscuit?
8. Why is a buttermilk biscuit more tender than a baking powder biscuit?
9. Describe how the addition of whole wheat flour to the recipe for baking powder biscuits affects each of the Quality Characteristics:
   a. Color and appearance
   b. Texture
   c. Tenderness
   d. Flavor
10. Explain why it is not feasible to add oat flour to the recipe for baking powder biscuits.

Yeast Breads

OBJECTIVES

1. To give students the opportunity to prepare a product leavened by yeast.
2. To acquaint students with three selected factors that will affect quality characteristics of yeast dough:
   a. Temperature for yeast activity
   b. Effect of salt on yeast activity
   c. Effect of kneading
3. To give students the opportunity to use dried milk solids in a baked product.
4. To develop an extremely elastic gluten structure in the dough.

PRODUCTS TO BE PREPARED TO ILLUSTRATE PRINCIPLES

Yeast rolls, all-purpose flour
Yeast rolls, whole wheat flour
Yeast rolls, all-purpose flour, oat flour or quick cooking oatmeal added

PRINCIPLES

1. Dry yeast is blended with warm (105°–115°F)(41°–46°C) water and sugar. This yeast mixture is then held at a warm temperature. This procedure will
   a. Hydrate dry yeast cells.
   b. Provide sugar for growth of yeast cells, thereby producing carbon dioxide for leavening.
   c. Provide a warm temperature for more rapid growth of yeast cells. Cold temperature delays yeast growth; too high a temperature kills yeast cells.
   d. Avoid depressing effect of salt on rate of yeast growth.
2. Kneading of dough develops extremely elastic gluten structure essential for proper fermentation.
3. Kneading of dough more evenly distributes yeast cells throughout the dough structure for more even leavening action.
4. Kneading dough after first fermentation period further increases dispersion of yeast and gas cells.
5. Oven heat causes rapid increase in yeast activity with increase in loaf volume during the first part of the baking period.
6. Factors which contribute to the browning of the crust
   a. Dextrinization of starch
   b. Caramelization of sugars (glucose, lactose, and sucrose)
   c. Maillard Reaction—interaction of carbohydrate and protein

58

Yeast Rolls

Water, warm	1/2 cup	125 ml
Sugar	1 tablespoon	15 ml
†Dried milk solids	2 tablespoons	30 ml
*Yeast, dried	1 package	1 package
**Flour, all-purpose	2 cups	500 ml
Salt	1/2 teaspoon	2 ml
Shortening (at room temp.)	2 tablespoons	30 ml
Egg	1	1

1. Preheat oven to 400°F (200°C).
2. Measure the sugar and the dried milk solids.
*** 3. Measure the water and place in a 2-quart (2-L) bowl. Add the dried yeast. Stir until blended. Add the sugar and the dried milk solids. Stir until blended. Allow this yeast mixture to stand while measuring the remaining ingredients. The yeast activity is initiated.
4. Measure remaining ingredients.
*** 5. Add the egg and 1 cup (250 ml) of the flour to the yeast mixture. Beat until the batter is smooth (about 100 strokes).
*** 6. Add the salt, shortening, and half of the remaining flour. Stir until the mixture is smooth and well blended. If the dough is sticky at this stage, add about half of the remaining flour. Stir until well blended.
7. If the dough is still too sticky to turn out on a lightly floured board, add the remaining portion of flour and stir into dough. If the dough is not sticky at the end of Step 6, use the flour that was not put into the dough to lightly flour the breadboard.
8. Put the dough onto the lightly floured board. Knead the dough until it is lightly blistered under the surface. The dough has a satiny sheen and has become resilient. When punched lightly with a finger, the dough springs back.
9. Place the dough in a lightly greased bowl. Lightly grease the surface of the dough. Allow dough to rise at least 10 minutes; to double in bulk is preferable if time permits. Use a plate or a clean, damp cloth to cover the bowl during fermentation.
10. *Lightly* knead the dough to evenly distribute gas cells.
***11. Shape dough into rolls. Place rolls in a well-greased baking pan. Dough will make 12 pan rolls. Cut dough into 12 equal portions. Round surface of the dough against the palm of the hand, or on the breadboard (not floured for this). A thin film of shortening on the surface of the rolls will keep them from drying during the proofing period.
12. Allow the shaped rolls to rise until double in bulk. This may take 20 minutes or longer. Do not have rolls in too warm a place for this second rising period.
13. Bake rolls in an oven preheated to 400°F (200°C) for 20–25 minutes. (Rolls baked individually as in muffin pans will bake more quickly than rolls placed touching each other in a layer cake pan.)
14. Record total working time: _____ minutes.

†, *, **, *** Special information is given on page 60.

Variations

Yeast Rolls, Whole Wheat

Replace 1 cup of all-purpose flour with 1 cup of whole wheat flour.

Special Notes: Ingredients and Method of Combining Yeast Rolls

†*Milk* :
a. The processing procedure to make dry milk solids requires heating the milk to a temperature at which enzymes in milk are inactivated and bacteria are destroyed. Consequently the reconstituted dried milk solids do not need to be heated and cooled in preparing yeast leavened products.
b. One-half cup (125 ml) fresh, fluid milk can be substituted for the water plus dried milk solids. Heat milk to lukewarm. Add yeast and sugar. Stir to thoroughly blend. Continue at Step 4, page 59.

*Yeast:
Two times the normal amount of yeast has been used because of the limited amount of time for fermentation of the dough. Use the rapid or quick rising type of yeast.

**Flour:
All-purpose flour is used so the rolls can be completed within a 2-hour laboratory period. Other types of flour (alone or in combinations) usually require a longer rising time and the rolls may not be completed within the limited time period.

***Combining ingredients—Shaping of dough:
a. The straight dough method of combining ingredients has been modified to provide more rapid yeast growth by delaying the addition of those ingredients (fat and salt) that inhibit the growth of yeast.
b. The dough is shaped and baked as pan rolls because less time is needed; however, the dough may be formed into a loaf, which may require a longer rising and baking period.

CHARACTERISTICS OF HIGH-QUALITY YEAST ROLLS

Appearance: Surface of each roll is smooth; top crust is golden brown.
Texture: Gas cells are evenly distributed; gas cells should be fairly small and uniform in size; cell walls are fairly thin.
Tenderness: Some, but very little resistance when bitten and chewed.
Flavor: Fairly bland (may be slightly yeasty if roll is warm when tasted).

Yeast Rolls with Oat Flour

Water, warm	1/2 cup	125 ml
Honey	1 tablespoon	15 ml
†Dried milk solids	2 tablespoons	30 ml
*Yeast, dried, rapid acting	1 package	1 package
**Flour, all-purpose	1 1/8 cup	280 ml
Flour, oat	1 cup	250 ml
Salt	1/2 teaspoon	2 ml
Shortening (room temperature)	2 tablespoons	30 ml
Egg, extra large	1	1

Variation

Use 1 cup of quick cooking oatmeal in place of the oat flour. Increase the all-purpose flour to 1 1/2 cups.

1. Preheat oven to 400°F (220°C).
2. Measure the dried milk solids.
***3. Measure the water and place in a 2–quart (2-L) bowl. Add the honey, the dried yeast, and the dried milk solids. Stir until blended. Allow this mixture to stand while measuring the remaining ingredients. The yeast activity is initiated.
4. Measure the remaining ingredients.
***5. Add the egg, shortening, and 7/8 cup (215 ml) of all-purpose flour to the mixture. Beat until the batter is smooth (about 100 strokes).
***6. Add salt, half of the remaining all-purpose flour, and the oat flour or the oatmeal. Stir until the mixture is smooth and well blended. If the dough is sticky at this stage, add about half of the remaining flour. Stir until well blended.
7. If the dough is still too sticky to turn out on a lightly floured board, add the remaining portion of the flour and stir into the dough. If the dough is not sticky at the end of Step 6, use the flour that was not put into the dough to lightly flour the breadboard.
8. Put the dough onto the lightly floured board. Knead the dough intil it is lightly blistered under the surface. The dough has a satiny sheen and has become resilient. When punched lightly with a finger, the dough springs back.
9. Place the dough in a lightly greased bowl. Lightly grease the surface of the dough. Allow the dough to rise at least 10 minutes; to double in bulk is perferable if time permits. Use a clean, damp cloth to cover the bowl during fermentation.
10. *Lightly* knead the dough to evenly distribute gas cells.
***11. Shape dough into rolls; place rolls in a well-greased baking pan. Dough will make 8 pan rolls. Cut dough into 8 equal portions; round surface of the dough against the palm of the hand, or on the breadboard (not floured for this). A thin film of shortening on the surface of the rolls will keep them from drying during the proofing period.
12. Allow the shaped rolls to rise until double in bulk. This may take 20 minutes or longer. Do not have the rolls in too warm a place for this second rising period.
13. Bake rolls in an oven preheated to 400°F (200°C) for 20-25 minutes. (Rolls baked individually as in muffin pans will bake more quickly than rolls placed touching each other in a layer cake pan.)
14. Record total working time: _____ minutes.

†, *, **, *** See Special Notes on page 60.

EVALUATION OF PRODUCTS

Name: _____

Date: _____

Score System

Points	Quality
7	Excellent
6	Very good
5	Good
4	Medium
3	Fair
2	Poor
1	Very poor

Directions:
1. Place the numerical score in the box in the upper left-hand corner.
2. Comments should justify the numerical score. Comments must be brief.
3. Evaluation of the food products must be on an *individual* basis.

Products

Quality Characteristic					
Appearance					
Consistency or Texture					
Tenderness					
Flavor					
Overall Eating Quality					

SUMMARY OUTLINE: _____   Name: _____

(Product)

Date: _____

Summary Outlines emphasize application of principles to basic steps in preparation of a food product. Principles may have been discussed in lecture or in laboratory, or may have been assigned in readings. Include cooking or baking temperature and know _why_ a low, medium, or high temperature is used. Summaries are excellent means for review.

List of Ingredients:

Steps in Preparation	Principles Applied
1.	1.

REVIEW QUESTIONS

1. a. Why are the yeast, water, sugar, and milk powder mixed together?
    b. Why is warm water used?
    c. Why is the mixture allowed to stand for 15–20 minutes?
    d. Does the flour furnish any food for the growth of the yeast? How?
    e. Why are salt and fat added so late in the mixing procedure?
2. a. Why is an extremely elastic gluten structure desirable in bread and rolls?
    b. What steps are taken to achieve this elastic structure?
3. What is the primary purpose of the second kneading operation?
4. a. Why is the surface of the rolls covered with fat during the proofing period?
    b. What other technique is also used that accomplishes the same purpose?
5. What is meant by each of the following terms?
    a. Oven spring
    b. Dextrinization
    c. Caramelization
6. Describe the characteristics of a high-quality yeast roll.
7. Describe how the addition of whole wheat flour to the recipe for yeast breads affects each of the Quality Characteristics:
    a. Color and appearance
    b. Texture
    c. Tenderness
    d. Flavor
8. Describe how the addition of oat flour or oatmeal to the recipe for yeast breads affects each of the Quality Characteristics:
    a. Color and appearance
    b. Texture
    c. Tenderness
    d. Flavor
9. Compare the Quality Characteristics of texture, tenderness, and flavor of rolls made with all-purpose flour, whole wheat flour, and oat flour.

Butter-Type Cakes

OBJECTIVES

1. To acquaint students with two frequently used methods for combining cake ingredients:
   a. Conventional Method
   b. Quick Mix Method
2. To provide an opportunity to compare quality characteristics of cakes baked by these two methods.
3. To have students recognize the importance of the relationship between proportion of ingredients and the type and amount of manipulation required to produce a typical cake by either method for combining cake ingredients.
4. To prepare a cake utilizing a food acid-baking soda leavening system.
5. To compare specially formulated microwave cakes with cakes prepared by standard methods.

PRODUCTS TO BE PREPARED TO ILLUSTRATE PRINCIPLES

Conventional Method cake
Quick Mix Method cake
Devil's Food cake

Microwave cakes
  Chocolate
  Yellow

PRINCIPLES

1. Cake flour contains the smallest amount of protein of any of the wheat flours.
2. Cake flour protein produces a weak gluten structure.
3. Plastic fat can entrap air incorporated with addition of sugar to the fat during the creaming process. The amount of air incorporated depends on two factors:
   a. Rate at which sugar is added to the fat
   b. Amount of work done in "creaming" the fat and sugar after each addition of sugar
4. Gluten formation is delayed or inhibited by
   a. Sugar
   b. Fat
   c. High ratio of liquid to flour
   d. Baking powder residues
5. Gluten formation is fostered by
   a. Low ratio of liquid to flour
   b. Stirring or beating
6. Gluten structure is augmented by egg protein.
7. Sulphate-phosphate baking powder requires heat for full carbon dioxide production.
8. Emulsifiers in shortening give greater dispersion of the fat in the batter and the baked cake.

9. Most flavors used in cakes are fat soluble.
10. Standardization of manipulation by "strokes" and not time alone makes for more standardized quality in the baked cakes.
11. Common flavors (sugar, vanilla, lemon, spice, chocolate, and so on) may mask flavor of baking powder residues.
12. Certain foods are decidedly acid and when used in conjunction with baking soda (a base) form a leavening system.
13. Low-fat margarine, whipped margarines, or whipped butter will not yield satisfactory products in these cake recipes.
14. The sugar crystals are necessary to incorporate air during creaming; therefore, non-crystalline sweeteners cannot be substituted.
15. Dutch-type cocoa is produced by treating the raw cocoa with an alkali. This treatment produces a deep, rich color and a mellow chocolate flavor.

Butter-Type Cake—Conventional Method

Margarine or butter	1/4 cup	60 ml
Sugar	2/3 cup	150 ml
Vanilla	1/2 teaspoon	2 ml
Egg	1	1
Flour, cake	1 cup	250 ml
Baking powder	1 teaspoon	5 ml
Salt	1/4 teaspoon	1 ml
Milk	1/3 cup	75 ml

1. Preheat oven to 350°F (175°C).
2. Cut waxed paper to fit bottom of 8- or 9-inch (20–22 cm) diameter layer cake pan.
3. Grease *only* bottom of the cake pan. Insert the waxed paper and grease it also.
4. Sift together the flour, salt, and baking powder.

By Electric Mixer:
5. Place the shortening and vanilla in the bowl. Set the mixer at medium speed. Add sugar *very* gradually. Cream until the mass is light and fluffy. The mass should be soft enough to remain on the bottom of the bowl; the mass should *not* remain balled up around the mixer blades. Total creaming time may be as long as 5–7 minutes. This creaming step is critical.
6. Add the beaten egg in two portions. Beat for 1 minute after each addition.
7. Add approximately half the flour mixture and half the milk. Beat at medium speed for 1 minute.
8. Add the last portion of flour and liquid. Blend for 30 seconds at medium speed; beat for 3 more minutes at high speed.
9. Push all of the batter at one time into the pan. Bake at 350°F (175°C) for approximately 25 minutes.
10. Cool in upright position at least 5 minutes before removing from cake pan.
11. Record total working time: _____ minutes.

By Hand Mixing:
5. Place the shortening and the vanilla in a bowl. Add about 1 teaspoon of sugar. Stir the sugar thoroughly into the shortening.
6. Repeat Step 5 until all the sugar has been added. Be sure the fat-sugar mixture is beaten until light and fluffy after each addition of the sugar. (The degree of creaming at this stage determines the texture and eating quality of the baked cake.) At this stage the fat-sugar mass should be light, fluffy, and soft enough to stay on the bottom and the sides of the mixing bowl. The mixture should be stirred or beaten beyond the stage where the mass tends to cling to the mixing spoon.
7. Add approximately half the beaten egg. Blend thoroughly with the fat-sugar mixture.
8. Repeat Step 7.
9. Add about one-third of the flour mixture to the fat-sugar mixture. Stir about 75 strokes.
10. Add about half of the milk. Stir about 15 strokes.
11. Add about half of the remaining flour. Stir 75 strokes.
12. Add the last portion of milk. Stir about 15 strokes.
13. Add the last portion of flour. Stir about 150 strokes.
14. Push all of the batter at one time into the pan. Bake at 350°F (175°C) for approximately 25 minutes.
15. Cool in upright position at least 5 minutes before removing from cake pan.
16. Record total working time: _____ minutes.

Butter-Type Cake—Quick Mix Method

Flour, cake	1 cup	250 ml
Sugar	2/3 cup	150 ml
Salt	1/4 teaspoon	1 ml
Baking powder	1 1/2 teaspoons	7 ml
*Shortening	1/4 cup	60 ml
Milk	1/2 cup	125 ml
Vanilla	1/2 teaspoon	2 ml
Egg	1	1

1. Preheat oven to 350°F (175°C).
2. Cut waxed paper to fit bottom of an 8- or 9-inch (20–22 cm) diameter layer cake pan.
3. Grease *only* the bottom of the cake pan. Insert the waxed paper and grease it also.
4. Sift together into a large mixing bowl the flour, sugar, salt, and baking powder.
5. Add the shortening, approximately half of the milk, and the vanilla. Beat vigorously for 2 minutes. If beaten by hand, use 150 strokes per minute. Scrape batter from the sides and bottom of bowl while mixing in order to blend uniformly. Use medium speed if using an electric mixer.
6. Add unbeaten egg and the remaining portion of milk. Beat two minutes longer at 150 strokes per minute. Use medium speed if using an electric mixer.
7. Push all of the batter at one time into cake pan. Bake at 350°F (175°C) for approximately 25 minutes.
8. Cool in an upright position at least 5 minutes before removing from cake pan.
9. Record total working time:_____ minutes.

*We recommend a shortening which contains mono- and/or diglyceride-type emulsifiers for all cakes combined by the Quick Mix Method.

CHARACTERISTICS OF HIGH-QUALITY BUTTER-TYPE CAKES

Appearance: Top crust should be slightly rounded toward the center of the layer; top crust should be pale, golden brown.

Texture: Uniform distribution of small gas cells; cell walls should be quite thin.

Tenderness: Crumb should be so tender as to "melt in the mouth" when bitten. There should be practically no resistance to bite.

Mouth Feel: Crumb should feel "velvety" or extremely smooth as it comes into contact with the palate and the back of the mouth; crumb should be slightly moist.

Flavor: Mild sweet flavor will predominate. If butter is used, butter flavor may be apparent.

Variations of Quick Mix Cake—Microwave Cakes

Chocolate
Yellow

Purchase Microwave Cake Mix with Microwave Pan. (Some brands also contain a pouch of frosting.) Carefully follow the package directions. Always use the special pan which comes with the mix; do not use the pan with any other brand of cake mix.

Devil's Food Cake

Flour, cake	1	cup	250	ml
Sugar	3/4	cup	175	ml
Soda	3/4	teaspoon	3	ml
Salt	1/2	teaspoon	2	ml
Cocoa	1/4	cup	60	ml
*Shortening	1/4	cup	60	ml
Buttermilk	1/2	cup	125	ml
Vanilla	1/2	teaspoon	2	ml
Egg	1		1	

Fat and flour for baking pan (see Step 2)

1. Preheat oven to 350°F (175°C).
2. Lightly grease bottom of 9-inch (22-cm) diameter layer cake pan. Insert waxed paper and lightly grease it. Evenly shake 1/2 teaspoon (2 ml) flour over bottom of pan. Invert the pan to remove excess flour.
3. Sift together cake flour, sugar, soda, salt, and cocoa.
4. Add vanilla to buttermilk. Add approximately 2/3 of buttermilk mixture and shortening to the dry ingredients.
5. Beat for 1 minute at medium speed with an electric mixer or for 150 strokes if mixed by hand. Use a rubber spatula to scrape batter from sides of bowl. Beat for 1 more minute, medium speed of mixer, or stir an additional 150 strokes by hand. Scrape batter from sides of bowl.
6. Add remaining buttermilk and the unbeaten egg. Beat for 3 more minutes, medium speed of the mixer, or stir an additional 450 strokes.
7. Use a rubber spatula to push all the batter to side of bowl; then push batter into baking pan in as large masses as possible. *Note:* Texture of baked cake can be impaired by the way in which batter is transferred to baking pan.
8. Bake in 350°F (175°C) oven for 30–35 minutes.
9. Cool in an upright position at least 10 minutes before removing from cake pan. This is an extremely tender cake so use special care to remove cake from pan.
10. Record total working time: _____ minutes.

*We recommend a shortening which contains mono- and/or diglyceride-type emulsifiers for all cakes combined by the Quick Mix Method. This type of shortening is derived from vegetable oil with no cholesterol and only a limited amount of saturated fat. The quantity used in this recipe adds about 1 1/2 teaspoons of fat (36–45 calories per serving).

CHARACTERISTICS OF HIGH-QUALITY DEVIL'S FOOD CAKE

Appearance
Exterior: Top crust should be slightly rounded toward the center of the layer; top crust is lightly browned, but mahogany red color predominates.
Interior: Crumb color is mahogany red.
Texture: Uniform distribution of very small gas cells; cell walls should be very thin.
Tenderness: Crumb is extremely tender with practically no resistance to bite.
Mouth Feel: Crumb is dry and may be slightly harsh as it comes into contact with the tongue and the roof of the mouth.
Flavor: Aroma and flavor of chocolate; slightly sweet.

REVIEW QUESTIONS

1. a. What are the differences between all-purpose flour and cake flour?
    b. How would the substitution of all-purpose flour for cake flour affect the texture and tenderness of a cake?
2. a. What type of fat must be used in a quick mix cake?
    b. What fats can be used successfully in conventional cakes?
3. What are the differences in proportion of ingredients between a conventional mix cake and a quick mix cake?
4. a. Describe briefly the creaming process.
    b. How can the maximum volume of air be incorporated during the creaming process?
    c. Is there a "creaming process" in the Quick Mix Method?
5. List the quality characteristics of high-quality butter-type cakes.
6. List the quality characteristics of a high-quality devil's food cake.
7. a. Explain the leavening system used in this devil's food cake recipe.
    b. How does this leavening system influence the rate of manipulation?
8. List the factors that affect the color of a devil's food cake.
9. Why would you expect the devil's food cake to be more tender than the plain butter-type cake?

EVALUATION OF PRODUCTS

Name: _____

Date: _____

Score System

Points	Quality
7	Excellent
6	Very good
5	Good
4	Medium
3	Fair
2	Poor
1	Very poor

Directions:
1. Place the numerical score in the box in the upper left-hand corner.
2. Comments should justify the numerical score. Comments must be brief.
3. Evaluation of the food products must be on an *individual* basis.

Products

Quality Characteristic					
Appearance					
Consistency or Texture					
Tenderness					
Flavor					
Overall Eating Quality					

SUMMARY OUTLINE: _____   Name: _____
(Product)
Date: _____

Summary Outlines emphasize application of principles to basic steps in preparation of a food product. Principles may have been discussed in lecture or in laboratory, or may have been assigned in readings. Include cooking or baking temperature and know *why* a low, medium, or high temperature is used. Summaries are excellent means for review.

List of Ingredients:

Steps in Preparation	Principles Applied
1.	1.

SUMMARY OUTLINE: _____   Name: _____
(Product)
Date: _____

Summary Outlines emphasize application of principles to basic steps in preparation of a food product. Principles may have been discussed in lecture or in laboratory, or may have been assigned in readings. Include cooking or baking temperature and know _why_ a low, medium, or high temperature is used. Summaries are excellent means for review.

List of Ingredients:

Steps in Preparation	Principles Applied
1.	1.

Cream Puffs and Popovers

OBJECTIVES

1. To illustrate leavening action as water is converted to steam in a baked product.
2. To illustrate emulsifying properties of egg protein.
3. To illustrate the extensibility of egg protein.
4. To acquaint students with unique method for combining ingredients for cream puffs.

PRODUCTS TO BE PREPARED TO ILLUSTRATE PRINCIPLES

Cream puffs
Popovers

PRINCIPLES

1. Starch plus water plus heat in correct ratios produce a gelatinized starch gel.
2. Melted fat separates the starch granules in flour.
3. Separated starch granules have the ability to absorb liquid equally when flour is added to boiling water-fat mixture.
4. Boiling temperature of water is essential for maximum gelatinization of starch.
5. Cool starch paste (140°F or 60°C) to prevent premature coagulation of egg protein.
6. Presence of fat inhibits or delays gluten formation.
7. Popovers contain no fat; therefore development of gluten structure is critical.
8. Steam formation for leavening action is dependent on initial oven temperature.

Cream Puff Shells

Water	1/4 cup	60 ml
Margarine or butter	2 tablespoons	30 ml
Salt	few grains	few grains
Flour, all-purpose	1/4 cup	60 ml
Egg, well-blended (not foamy)	1	1

1. Preheat oven to 425°F (220°C).
2. Lightly grease three areas of baking sheet, each area approximately 2 inches in diameter. Allow approximately 3 inches between greased areas.
3. Place water, butter, and salt in smallest size saucepan. Heat until the butter is melted and the water boils *vigorously.*
4. Add the flour all in one portion to the vigorously boiling water-fat mixture. Stir quickly with a wooden spoon to get flour well blended with the water-fat mixture. Remove saucepan from the heat for the last part of the stirring process. As the flour becomes well blended, it tends to form a ball around the spoon. The partially cooked starch should hold the imprint of a metal spoon if the flour has been properly blended and heated sufficiently.
5. Partially cool the cooked starch paste.
6. Add half of the well-beaten egg to the starch paste. Stir vigorously to blend.
7. Add the remaining half of the egg. Stir vigorously to blend.
8. Clean sides of pan and mixing spoon with rubber spatula. If necessary, blend so final paste mixture is smooth throughout.
9. Divide paste mixture into approximately three equal portions. Place one portion on each of the greased areas of the baking sheet.
10. Bake in a 425°F (220°C) oven until lightly golden brown (15–20 minutes). Reduce oven setting to 350°F (175°C). Bake for 20 more minutes. Reduce heat still further and bake until centers are fairly dry. Puffs can be pricked with a fork about 10 minutes before removing from oven in order to speed the drying.
11. Puff shells should be cold before they are filled.
12. Record total working time: _____ minutes.

CHARACTERISTICS OF HIGH-QUALITY CREAM PUFF SHELLS

Appearance: Top surface is irregular; top crust is golden brown.
Texture: At least one large gas cell formed in the interior of the puff.
Tenderness: Outer crust is tender.
Moistness: Outer crust is crisp; interior membranes may be slightly moist.
Flavor: Outer crust should be bland; if butter is used, its flavor may be apparent.

Popovers

Flour, all-purpose	1/2 cup	125 ml
Salt	1/4 teaspoon	1 ml
Milk	1/2 cup	125 ml
Egg	1	1

Vegetable oil to grease custard cups

1. Preheat oven to 425°F (220°C).
2. Thoroughly grease bottom and sides of 3 or 4 deep custard cups, cast-iron popover pans, or deep aluminum muffin tins.
3. Sift salt and flour together into a 1-quart (1-L) mixing bowl.
4. Add egg to milk. Blend.
5. Add egg-milk mixture to flour mixture. Use a rotary beater to blend liquid and dry ingredients. Beat until mixture is just smooth. (Overbeating will reduce volume.)
6. Fill custard cups or popover pans 1/3 to 1/2 full. Fill muffin tins 1/2 full.
7. Set custard cups in a shallow cake pan. This is for convenience in handling cups during baking. Place pan in oven.
8. Bake in a 425°F (220°C) oven until medium golden brown (40–45 minutes). Oven temperature may be reduced to 350°F (175°C) for last 10 minutes of baking to prevent overbrowning.
9. Popovers customarily are served hot from the oven.
10. Record total working time: _____ minutes

CHARACTERISTICS OF HIGH-QUALITY POPOVERS

Appearance: Irregular contour; surface smooth. Top crust is golden brown.
Texture: At least 1 large gas hole formed in the interior of the popover. With formation of several medium-size gas cells, several medium thick cell walls will have formed as "sheets" between gas cells.
Tenderness: Outer crust is crisp. Interior portions have slight resistance to bite.
Moistness: Outer crust is relatively dry; interior membranes may be moist.
Flavor: Bland; possible slight egg flavor.

REVIEW QUESTIONS

1. a. Into what type of colloid system is the fat dispersed in cream puffs?
   b. List some other food products that are also examples of this system.
2. a. Why must the fat-water mixture be boiling vigorously before the flour is added when making cream puffs?
   b. What functions do eggs serve in cream puffs? In popovers?
   c. What happens if the starch paste is too hot when the egg is added?
   d. Why are cream puffs and popovers started in a 425°F (220°C) oven?
   e. Why is the temperature reduced to 350°F (175°C)?
   f. Why are cream puffs pricked during baking?
   g. Why is the baking sheet greased only in spots?
3. Describe briefly the leavening of cream puffs and popovers.
4. List the quality characteristics of a high-quality cream puff.
5. List the quality characteristics of a high-quality popover.
6. How might overbeating cause reduced volume in a popover?

EVALUATION OF PRODUCTS

Name: _____

Date: _____

Score System

Points	Quality
7	Excellent
6	Very good
5	Good
4	Medium
3	Fair
2	Poor
1	Very poor

Directions:
1. Place the numerical score in the box in the upper left-hand corner.
2. Comments should justify the numerical score. Comments must be brief.
3. Evaluation of the food products must be on an *individual* basis.

Products

Quality Characteristic					
Appearance					
Consistency or Texture					
Tenderness					
Flavor					
Overall Eating Quality					

SUMMARY OUTLINE: _____ Name: _____
                          (Product)

                                        Date: _____

Summary Outlines emphasize application of principles to basic steps in preparation of a food product. Principles may have been discussed in lecture or in laboratory, or may have been assigned in readings. Include cooking or baking temperature and know _why_ a low, medium, or high temperature is used. Summaries are excellent means for review.

List of Ingredients:

Steps in Preparation	Principles Applied
1.	1.

SUMMARY OUTLINE: _____ Name: _____
(Product)

Date: _____

Summary Outlines emphasize application of principles to basic steps in preparation of a food product. Principles may have been discussed in lecture or in laboratory or may have been assigned in readings. Include cooking or baking temperature and know _why_ a low, medium, or high temperature is used. Summaries are excellent means for review.

List of Ingredients:

Steps in Preparation	Principles Applied
1.	1.

Fats and Oils

OBJECTIVES

1. To make students aware of the variety of fats and oils and how the properties of each are dependent on source and processing treatment.
2. To acquaint students with quality characteristics of a selected group of fats and oils.

PRODUCTS TO BE INSPECTED TO ILLUSTRATE PRINCIPLES

Butters: stick, whipped
Margarines: stick, whipped, imitation (low-fat)
Hydrogenated vegetable oils: plain, butter-flavored
Hydrogenated animal fat blended with hydrogenated vegetable oils
Lard   Canola oil   Safflower oil
Soya oil   Corn oil   Sunflower oil
Olive oil

PRINCIPLES

1. Degree of plasticity of a fat at room temperature depends on these factors:
   a. Length of carbon chains in the fatty acid
   b. Number of double bonds (degree of unsaturation) in the fatty acid
   c. Amount of air incorporated
2. Hydrogenation process reduces the number of double bonds in a fat or oil.
3. Nutrient value can be fortified by addition of vitamins.
4. Addition of emulsifiers to shortening increases the degree of dispersion of the shortening in baked products.
5. Source of fat or oil may contribute a characteristic flavor to the product.
6. Whipped products
   a. Plasticity depends on the amount of air incorporated.
   b. The incorporated air changes the density of the fat.
   c. Whipped fats cannot be used to substitute for solid fat in the recipes in this manual.
7. Oil alone will not form gluten when mixed with all-purpose flour.
8. Tenderness of baked products is related to fat content.

Note: Please refer to Appendices B, C, and D for the composition of various fats and oils.

CHARACTERISTICS OF FATS AND OILS

Type of Fat	Source	Consistency at 72°F (22°C)	Percentage Fat As Purchased	Added Ingredients	Flavor

CHARACTERISTICS OF FATS AND OILS

Type of Fat	Source	Consistency at 72°F (22°C)	Percentage Fat As Purchased	Added Ingredients	Flavor

REVIEW QUESTIONS

1. Define or describe briefly each of the following terms:
   a. Saturated fatty acid
   b. Unsaturated fatty acid
   c. Hydrogenation
   d. Smoke point
   e. Emulsion
   f. Immiscible
   g. Emulsifying agent
   h. Polar molecule
   i. Antioxidant
   j. Synergist
   k. Pro-oxidant
   l. Sequestering agent

2. List several common fats and give the source of each fat.
   a. With a high content of unsaturated fatty acids.
   b. With a high content of saturated fatty acids.

3. a. What are the two types of emulsions?
   b. In the table, list several foods which are examples of emulsions.

Food	Type of Emulsion	Dispersed Phase	Dispersing Medium	Emulsifier(s)
Cream puff	O/W	Butterfat	Water	Egg yolk Gelatinized starch
Butter	W/O	Water	Butterfat	Milk proteins
Milk				
Cheese				

   c. Why must considerable work be done in making an emulsion?
   d. How are emulsions stabilized?

4. a. Name several antioxidants which can legally be used in foods.
   b. Which of the antioxidants named in part (a) has the best "carry through" properties in baked goods?

Pie Pastry: Fruit Pies

OBJECTIVES

1. To acquaint students with the Pastry Method for combining ingredients.
2. To give students the opportunity to study the following factors which affect the quality characteristics of pie pastry:
   a. Ratio of fat to flour
   b. Type of fat used
   c. Amount of fat used
   d. Type of flour used
   e. Amount of liquid used
   f. Extent to which fat is cut into the flour
   g. Kind and extent of manipulation
3. To illustrate factors that affect quality characteristics of a baked pastry shell.
4. To discuss principles related to the preparation of fruit-filled pies.

PRODUCTS TO BE PREPARED TO ILLUSTRATE PRINCIPLES

Pie pastry
  Flaky pie dough
  Mealy pie dough

Apple pie—fresh fruit
Commercial frozen pies:
  Apple
  Cherry

PRINCIPLES

1. Pieces of plastic fat coated with flour particles are pressed into "sheets" or "layers" between strands of gluten during the rolling process.
2. There are two types of pastry dough, flaky or mealy. The type of dough obtained will depend on the amount of fat and water used and on the degree to which the fat is cut into the flour.
   a. Flaky dough contains more water and fat than mealy dough.
   b. For flaky dough the fat particles are larger in size than the particles of fat for mealy dough.
3. During baking the fat melts into the gluten framework, thus leaving "sheets" or "flakes" of gluten structure in the baked pastry. The nature of the gluten structure will depend on the type of dough being prepared.
4. Rerolling pastry dough
   a. Develops the strength of the gluten framework
   b. Entraps air between layers of gluten. Air will expand during the baking period.
5. Air is the primary leavening agent; steam is the secondary leavening agent.

6. Unbaked gluten is elastic and is easily stretched.
7. Gluten contracts as the coagulation temperature of the flour protein is reached.
8. Pared, light-colored fresh fruit may darken unless air is kept from the cut surface.
9. Fruit may be covered with one of the following to exclude air:
    a. Tap water
    b. Lemon juice
    c. Sugar
    d. Vitamin C (ascorbic acid)
    e. Mixture of vitamin C and citric acid
10. Sugar separates starch granules.
11. Separated starch granules have equal opportunity to absorb liquid as heat is applied.
12. Thickening the fruit juice by gelatinizing the starch before adding thawed fruit retains flavor in the pie.
13. Initial high temperature will cause coagulation of flour protein before fruit juice can "soak" the bottom crust.
14. Cornstarch and tapioca give more translucent pie fillings than flour.
15. Waxy maize starch contains a higher percentage of the amylopectin-type molecule; this gives the starch some special properties. These starches will thicken but will not gel nor will they form a skin on the surface. They may be used in pie fillings and puddings where the product is to be frozen; the starch paste will not thin out upon thawing. They may also be used in salad dressings. Waxy maize starch may be difficult to find in the retail market; however, it is found widely in commercial products such as frozen fruit pies and canned puddings.

Pie Pastry—Single-Crust (Flaky Type)

Flour, all-purpose	3/4 cup	175 ml
Salt	1/8 teaspoon	0.5 ml
Texturated lard or hydrogenated shortening	1/4 cup	60 ml
Milk (or water)	2 to 3 tablespoons	30–45 ml

1. Preheat oven to 425°F (220°C).
2. Sift flour and salt together into small mixing bowl. Cut the lard into the flour with a pastry blender until the fat pieces are the size of small peas.
3. Sprinkle the milk, a half teaspoon at a time, over the fat-flour mixture. Use a fork to lightly toss the moistened fat-flour mixture to the side of the bowl so all dry ingredients can come in contact with the milk as it is added. Use only enough milk to form a stiff dough. Avoid a wet, sticky dough.
4. When time permits, allow the dough to stand for 5–10 minutes for more even hydration of the flour. However, for class, there is not time for this hydration period.
5. Place the dough between two sheets of heavy waxed paper. Roll the dough to 1/8 inch (0.3 cm) thickness. Place the rolling pin at the center of the mound of dough and roll from the center toward the outer edges of the dough. Keep even pressure on the rolling pin so the pastry will be of uniform thickness. It may be necessary to loosen the waxed paper from the pastry during the rolling period to keep the paper smooth and to obtain pastry of even thickness. Roll the dough to a circle at least 1 inch (2.5 cm) larger than the pie pan. Pastry can be formed into two 6-inch (15-cm) or one 8-inch (20-cm) pie shells.
6. Loosen pastry dough from the waxed paper with a minimum stretching of the pastry.
7. Ease the dough into the pie pan but be careful not to stretch the dough. Gently press the pastry dough against the bottom and sides of the pie pan. Trim the crust even with the edge of the pie pan.
8. With a fork prick the bottom and sides of the crust to allow escape of steam.
9. Bake in a 425°F (220°C) oven for 8–10 minutes or until very pale, golden brown.
10. If air is trapped under the pastry, the crust will tend to "hump" during the baking period. Check the pastry shell after the first 4 or 5 minutes of baking to be sure the pastry is not "humping." If the pastry is bulging up from the bottom of the pan, quickly prick the pastry before it is "set" with baking.
11. If time permits, reroll the remaining dough 5–8 times. Roll 1/8 inch (0.3 cm) thick, place on baking sheet, prick, and bake. Compare with pastry shell for tenderness and flakiness.
12. Record total working time: _____ minutes.

Note: For cream pie fillings see pages 170 to 171.

Variation

Mealy Pie Crust

Reduce the fat to 3 1/2 tablespoons (43 ml) and reduce the water to 1.5–2.5 (18–38 ml) tablespoons. At Step 2, cut the lard into the flour until it is the size of coarse corn meal.

   Note: In commercial bakeries, mealy pie crust is used for the bottom crust in fruit pies. It is also used for custard and soft-type pies.

Pie Pastry—Double-Crust for 6-Inch Fruit Pie (Flaky Type)

Flour, all-purpose	1 cup	250 ml
Salt	1/4 teaspoon	1 ml
Texturated lard or shortening	1/3 cup	75 ml
Milk	3 tablespoons	45 ml

1. Preheat oven to 425°F (220°C).
2. Sift together flour and salt into a small bowl. With a pastry blender, cut the fat into the flour until the fat is the size of small peas, approximately 1/4 inch (0.6 cm) diameter.
3. Add milk gradually, stirring with a fork to evenly distribute the liquid. Add as little liquid as possible to hold the dough together.
4. Divide dough into two portions. Use approximately two-thirds of dough for the lower crust. Shape dough into rounds. Place dough between sheets of waxed paper for rolling.
5. Roll dough not more than 1/8 inch (0.3 cm) thick. (Invert pie pan over dough to be sure dough extends 1 inch (2.5 cm) beyond the rim of the pie pan. Excess dough beyond the 1-inch (2.5-cm) perimeter can be trimmed away after the waxed paper has been removed from one side.)
6. Ease dough into pie pan, being careful not to stretch the pastry. Lightly hold pastry in position at center of pie pan while arranging the pastry against the sides. Cut excess pastry away from the rim of the pie pan using a sharp knife.
7. Add pie filling.
8. Lightly moisten the edge of the pastry around the rim of the pie pan with water (use a moistened fingertip).
9. Roll pastry for top crust—also not more than 1/8 inch (0.3 cm) thick. Place on pie filling. Gently press against the moistened pastry of bottom crust. This aids in sealing the two crusts together.
10. Trim away excess pastry as in Step 6. Dip a 3- or 4-tined fork into flour. Gently press fork against the pastry and rim of pie pan to leave firm imprint of fork in pastry. Repeat around entire rim. This further aids in binding top and bottom crusts together.
11. Use a sharp knife to make four or five 1-inch (2.5-cm) slits in the upper crust. This allows steam to escape during the baking period.
12. Place pie in oven preheated to 425°F (220°C). If top crust appears to be getting too brown, reduce heat to 350°F (175°C) after 15–20 minutes at the higher temperature. Total time: 45 minutes.
13. Place a piece of aluminum foil on a rack placed just above the floor of the oven to catch juices if pie boils over. Wash foil under hot water at end of baking period.
14. Record total working time: _____ minutes.

CHARACTERISTICS OF HIGH-QUALITY PIE PASTRY (FLAKY TYPE)

Appearance: Surface of pastry may have small "blisters" apparent; top is very pale golden brown; edges may be *slightly* darker.

Texture: Pastry should show evidences of layers or "flakes." Gas cells should be medium large.

Tenderness: The pastry should "melt in the mouth." There should be *very* little resistance when bitten or when cut with a fork.

Flavor: Usually quite bland, but type of fat used may influence the flavor of the pastry.

FRUIT PIE FILLING

Apple Pie (One 6-Inch Pie)

Apples, cooking variety	1 cup	250 ml
Sugar, depending on ripeness of apples	1–2 tablespoons	15–30 ml
Cornstarch	1/2 teaspoon	2 ml
Lemon juice, if apples are very ripe	1 teaspoon	5 ml
Cinnamon or nutmeg	1/8 teaspoon or less	0.5 ml or less

1. Wash, pare, and core apples. Slice into 3/8–1/2 inch (1.0–1.3 cm) slices.
2. Add lemon juice. Lemon juice added to the apple slices reduces the tendency of the apples to brown. If the apples are quite ripe, the lemon juice improves the flavor.
3. Blend cornstarch with sugar and spice. Stir into apples (use a fork).
4. Place seasoned apples in pastry-lined pie pan.
5. Place top crust on apples.
6. Complete as indicated in the directions for Double-Crust Pie Pastry.

CHARACTERISTICS OF HIGH-QUALITY FRUIT PIES

Pastry (Flaky Type)

Appearance: Top crust is golden brown: edges may be *slightly* darker; surface may have small "blisters" apparent.

Texture: *Slightly* moist and friable (easily broken); flaky.

Tenderness: Pastry should "melt in the mouth."

Flavor: Bland, depends on fat used.

Pastry (Mealy Type)

Appearance: Golden brown, not likely to blister; however, generally not used as a top crust.

Texture: Very small granules; tends to be dry and slightly crumbly, not likely to be flaky.

Tenderness: Very tender and friable.

Flavor: Bland, depends on fat used.

Fillings

Appearance: Fruit pieces should appear intact; apple slices will appear moist; cherries should appear plump.

Body and Texture: Fruit pieces are tender and soft; juice has the consistency of a soft starch pudding.

Flavor: Typical of fruit used; spice flavor must be mild.

Variation

Purchase two brand-name commercial pies, an apple and a cherry. Evaluate these two pies at the same time as the pie made in the laboratory using the Characteristics of High-Quality Fruit Pies. Carefully examine the crust of all three pies.

REVIEW QUESTIONS

1. a. What are the similarities in the Pastry Method and Biscuit Method of combining ingredients?
    b. What are the differences?
2. How do the basic steps in the manipulative procedure affect the characteristics of the finished pastry?
3. a. Discuss flakiness and tenderness in a pie crust.
    b. What causes a pie crust to be flaky and not tender?
    c. What causes a pie crust to be tender and not flaky?
4. What happens when too much water or milk is added to a pie dough?
5. What is the advantage of milk over water in making pie pastry?
6. Describe how each of the following treatments would affect the quality of the finished pastry.
    a. An increased amount of fat
    b. Use of a very soft (low melting point) plastic fat
    c. Use of cake flour rather than all-purpose flour
7. a. Why is the bottom of a single-shell pastry pricked with a fork before baking?
    b. How can a soggy bottom crust in a cherry pie be prevented?
8. Describe the characteristics of a high-quality pie.
9. Why is it desirable to use a mealy-type pie crust in a cherry pie?
10. a. How is waxy maize starch different chemically than cornstarch?
    b. How is waxy maize starch different in performance in food products than cornstarch?

EVALUATION OF PRODUCTS

(Evaluate only the pastry here.)

Name: _____

Date: _____

Score System

Points	Quality
7	Excellent
6	Very good
5	Good
4	Medium
3	Fair
2	Poor
1	Very poor

Directions:

1. Place the numerical score in the box in the upper left-hand corner.
2. Comments should justify the numerical score. Comments must be brief.
3. Evaluation of the food products must be on an *individual* basis.

Products

Quality Characteristic					
Appearance					
Consistency or Texture					
Tenderness					
Flavor					
Overall Eating Quality					

EVALUATION OF TWO-CRUST PIES

Name: _____

Date: _____

Type of Filling: _____

Quality Characteristic	7 Excellent	6 Very Good	5 Good	4 Medium	3 Fair	2 Poor	1 Very Poor
Crust: Color and Appearance							
Crust: Texture							
Crust: Tenderness							
Filling: Appearance							
Filling: Body and Texture							
Filling: Flavor							
Overall Eating Quality							

Note: A two-crust pie is evaluated on quality characteristics of pastry, quality characteristics of the filling, and finally for its overall eating quality (pastry + filling). For example, place comments for a pastry to be rated "Good" in column 5.

SUMMARY OUTLINE: _____   Name: _____

(Product)

Date: _____

Summary Outlines emphasize application of principles to basic steps in preparation of a food product. Principles may have been discussed in lecture or in laboratory, or may have been assigned in readings. Include cooking or baking temperature and know _why_ a low, medium, or high temperature is used. Summaries are excellent means for review.

List of Ingredients:

Steps in Preparation	Principles Applied
1.	1.

Deep-Fat Frying

OBJECTIVES

1. To give students an opportunity to relate properties of fats and oils to factors to be considered in deep-fat frying.
2. To acquaint students with the relationship between composition of the food product and temperature at which food is deep-fat fried.
3. To acquaint students with the following factors and their interrelationships that affect the quality of deep-fat fried batter and dough products:
   a. Type of ingredients used
   b. Proportion of ingredients used
   c. Extent of manipulation
4. To acquaint students with factors that influence fat absorption by deep-fat fried products.

PRODUCTS TO BE PREPARED TO ILLUSTRATE PRINCIPLES

Doughnut holes
Fruit and/or vegetable fritters

PRINCIPLES

1. Fats or oils used for the frying medium should have a high smoke point.
   a. The smoke point is lowered by the presence of low molecular weight fatty acids in the fat.
   b. The smoke point is lowered by the presence of mono- and/or diglycerides in superglycerinated fats.
   c. The smoke point is lowered by the presence of free fatty acids in the fat.
      (1) Not all free fatty acids may have been removed during commercial processing of the fat.
      (2) Free fatty acids are liberated by breakdown of the fat during heating (cooking of food product).
   d. The smoke point of each fat is lowered as the surface area of the fat in the frying pan is increased.
   e. The smoke point is lowered by the presence of food particles that break away from the food being fried and remain in the fat during the frying period.
   f. The smoke point for a fat is lowered each time the fat is used for deep-fat frying.

2. The rate at which a fat breaks down depends on the following factors:
   a. Temperature to which fat is heated
   b. Length of time the fat is heated during a frying period
   c. Accumulation of food particles in the fat during the frying period
   d. Surface area of fat exposed to air during the frying period
3. The temperature at which a food product is fried is dependent on characteristics of that food.
   a. Raw meat or fish which is to be cooked during the frying period must be cooked slowly at a relatively low temperature.
   b. Foods which are quickly cooked, such as doughnuts or fritters, can be cooked at higher temperatures.
4. The amount of fat absorbed by a food product during frying depends on the following factors:
   a. Smoke point of the fat used for the frying medium
   b. Temperature-time relationship during the frying period
   c. Composition of the food product being fried
      (1) Batter and dough products are affected by
         (a) Amount of flour
         (b) Amount of liquid
         (c) Amount of sugar
         (d) Amount of fat
         (e) Amount of manipulation related to the ingredients used and their proportion
      (2) Fatty foods absorb more fat than less fatty foods.
   d. Surface area of the food product being fried.
5. Factors to consider in selecting a fat for deep-fat frying
   a. Smoke point: low smoke point indicates rapid breakdown of fat with accompanying changes in flavor.
   b. Presence of mono- and/or diglyceride emulsifiers: smoke point is lower with these emulsifiers present.
   c. Since oils remain liquid at room temperature, oil absorbed during frying will remain liquid during storage of a product such as doughnuts. The surface of the stored doughnuts feels "oily."
   d. Natural flavor of the fat. Usually a bland flavor is desired so the flavor of the food will predominate.
   e. Cost of the fat or oil.
   f. Temperature to which the fat will be heated relates to the stability of the fat during the heating period.
6. Browning of deep-fat fried products depends on the following:
   a. Time-temperature relationship during frying
   b. Amount of carbohydrate in food or coating material
   c. Type of carbohydrate in food or coating material
   d. The degree of gluten development

Note of caution: Temperatures used for deep-fat frying, 365°–375°F (185°–190°C), are much higher than the boiling point of water. *Handle hot fats with extreme caution!*

Doughnut Holes

Flour, all-purpose	2 cups	500 ml
Baking powder	1 tablespoon	15 ml
Salt	1/2 teaspoon	2 ml
Nutmeg	1/4 teaspoon	1 ml
Cinnamon	1/4 teaspoon	1 ml
Sugar	1/2 cup	125 ml
Vegetable oil	2 tablespoons	30 ml
Milk	2/3 cup	150 ml
Egg yolks	2	2
*Fat for deep-fat frying	2 pounds	1 kg

1. Place fat for frying in a pan 5–6 inches (12–15 cm) deep with a diameter 6–7 inches (15–18 cm). There should be 2–3 inches (5–8 cm) of melted fat in the pan. Do not use less than 2 inches (5 cm) or more than 3 inches (8 cm) of fat. Hold over low heat while preparing the doughnut batter.
2. Sift together all dry ingredients into a large bowl.
3. In a small bowl blend together the egg yolks, milk, and vegetable oil. Use the egg beater for blending. The oil must be thoroughly blended with the egg yolk and milk as the liquid mixture is added to the dry ingredients.
4. Add liquid ingredients to dry ingredients and stir 75 strokes. Scrape down sides of bowl and clean spoon with rubber spatula midway in the stirring period. Allow the batter to stand 5 minutes before frying.
5. Have the frying fat at 365°F (185°C) at the beginning of each frying period.
6. Use a teaspoon to cut a spoonful of batter for each doughnut. Keep the surface of the batter as smooth as possible during the cutting and spooning of the batter. The raw batter should not be larger than 1 inch in diameter for each doughnut hole.
7. Place the spoon containing the raw batter at the surface of the hot fat. Use the back of a second teaspoon to push the batter into the hot fat. (*Do not use a rubber spatula.*) Keep surfaces as smooth as possible. Do not fry more than 5 or 6 doughnut holes at one time. Remember to have fat at 365°F (185°C) for each frying.
8. Cook the doughnut holes for approximately 4 minutes. The doughnuts tend to turn over in the hot fat as the first side becomes brown. It will be necessary to turn a second time to get even browning during frying.
9. Use a slotted spoon to remove the cooked doughnut holes from the fat. Place doughnut holes on several layers of paper toweling to drain off excess fat.
10. For evaluation do not roll doughnut holes in sugar. Doughnut holes not used for evaluation may be rolled in sugar.
11. Record total working time: _____ minutes.

*Fats to be used in a deep-fat fryer must have a high smoke point (above 229°F–444°F). Vegetable oils such as peanut, cottonseed, and canola oils may be used. Many hydrogenated fats may be used only if they do not contain mono- or diglycerides because these compounds lower the smoke point.

CHARACTERISTICS OF HIGH-QUALITY DOUGHNUT HOLES

Appearance: *Outer crust* is evenly golden brown; surface is relatively smooth; doughnut hole is round. *Interior* is white to grayish white. (Fat absorption can be noted by greasy appearance just under the crust. A high-quality doughnut hole does not have or has very little greasy crumb in the fried doughnut.)

Texture: Fairly compact structure; small gas cells; cell walls of medium thickness.

Tenderness: Tender, little resistance to bite; exterior may be slightly crisp immediately after frying.

Flavor: Mild, slightly spicy.

Special Notes Relative to Evaluation

1. The spices, especially the cinnamon, may cause a slightly grayish cast to the interior of the doughnut holes.
2. With the ratio of spices used in the recipe, the spice flavor will be quite mild immediately after the batter is fried. However, the spice flavor becomes more intense as the doughnut holes may be held in storage.
3. Immediately after frying the crust is fairly crisp. With storage sugar absorbs moisture from the air and/or there is time for equalization of moisture within the doughnut hole so the crust becomes soft.

Fruit or Vegetable Fritter Batter (A Thick Batter)

Flour, all-purpose	1/2 cup	125 ml
Baking powder	1/2 teaspoon	2 ml
Salt	1/2 teaspoon	2 ml
Sugar (for fruit fritters only)	1 teaspoon	5 ml
Egg	1	1
Milk	1/4 cup	60 ml
Vegetable oil	1 teaspoon	5 ml
Pineapple, crushed	1/2 cup	125 ml
or		
Corn, whole kernel	1/2 cup	125 ml
Fat for deep-fat frying	2 pounds	1 kg

1. Drain the crushed pineapple or whole kernel corn thoroughly. Press the juice from the pineapple with a spoon. The fruit or vegetable must be dry as it is added to the batter.
2. Place fat for frying in a pan 5–6 inches (12–15 cm) deep with a diameter 6–7 inches (15–18 cm). There should be between 2–3 inches (5–8 cm) of melted fat in pan. Do not use less than 2 inches (5 cm) or more than 3 inches (8 cm) of fat. Hold over low heat while preparing the fritter batter.
3. Sift together all the dry ingredients. (Use sugar *only* in batter for *fruit* fritters.)
4. Place the egg in a small bowl. Add the milk and blend thoroughly with egg beater.
5. Add the liquid to the dry ingredients. Stir a maximum of 25 strokes to blend. Add the vegetable oil and stir a maximum of 10 strokes to blend.
6. Add either the well-drained pineapple or the corn. Blend with not more than 4 or 5 strokes.
7. Have the frying fat heated to 375°F (190°C).
*8. Carefully spoon the fritter batter into the hot fat. Have the spoon near the surface of the fat. Push the fritter batter into the fat with the back of a second spoon. (*Do not use a rubber spatula.*) Do not fry more than four fritters at one frying. Cook fritters until golden. Turn and cook until second side is golden—approximately 2 minutes for each side. (The larger the fritter, the longer the time to cook the center of the fritter.)
9. Use a slotted spoon to remove the cooked fritters from the hot fat. Allow fat to drain away from the spoon before placing the fritter on several thicknesses of paper toweling to drain off excess fat.
10. Fritters may be kept warm by placing on a baking sheet in an oven preheated to 300°F (150°C).
11. For evaluation serve fritters without powdered sugar or table syrup.
12. Record total working time: _____ minutes.

*A No. 20 ice cream scoop may be used for putting batter into the hot fat. Hold the scoop at the surface of the hot fat for putting batter into the fat.

CHARACTERISTICS OF HIGH-QUALITY FRUIT OR VEGETABLE FRITTERS

Appearance: Deep golden brown; fairly smooth, even surface.

Texture: Medium-size gas cells fairly evenly distributed; cell walls may be fairly thick; evenly dispersed fruit or vegetable pieces.

Tenderness: Slight resistance to bite; fork cuts easily through crust of fritter.

Flavor: "Batter" portion is bland in flavor; flavor of fruit or vegetable should predominate.

REVIEW QUESTIONS

1. List the characteristics of composition that would give an ideal fat to use for deep-fat frying.
2. a. List some factors which will speed up the breakdown of the fat used in a deep-fat fryer.
   b. List some practical steps which might be taken to retard the rate of breakdown of the fat and extend its frying life in deep-fat frying.
3. Why are products such as breaded pork chops, chicken, and fish fillets fried at lower temperatures than doughnuts?
4. a. Doughnut recipe A uses 1 tablespoon (15 ml) vegetable oil per cup of flour whereas doughnut recipe B uses 1 1/2 tablespoons (25 ml) vegetable oil per cup of flour. If the same quantities of other ingredients are used in both A and B, doughnuts from which recipe will absorb more fat during frying? Why?
   b. If only sugar were increased in recipe B, which recipe would now be likely to have the greater fat absorption? Why?
   c. How would the increase in sugar in (b) affect the rate of browning of the doughnuts on frying?
   d. How can the change in browning be compensated for in frying the doughnuts?
   e. What practical consideration might limit the composition for browning in (d)?
5. Explain what might have been done to the doughnuts and fritters to account for the evaluations given in the following table:

Score System

Points	Quality
7	Excellent
6	Very good
5	Good
4	Medium
3	Fair
2	Poor
1	Very poor

EVALUATION OF PRODUCTS

Name: _____

Date: _____

Directions:
1. Place the numerical score in the box in the upper left-hand corner.
2. Comments should justify the numerical score. Comments must be brief.
3. Evaluation of the food products must be on an *individual* basis.

Quality Characteristic	Doughnut A	Doughnut B	Doughnut C	Corn fritter	Pineapple fritter
Appearance	3 Color too light	2 Too dark	4 Greasy	5	6
Consistency or Texture	3 Wet in center	3 Wet in center	3 Greasy	4 Gas cells too large	5 Even, well-distributed gas cells
Tenderness	5	4 Crust too crisp	5	4 Too soft	6
Flavor	4 Raw dough	3 Sweet	4 Greasy	4 Batter tastes like corn	6 Pineapple
Overall Eating Quality	3	3	4	4	6

Starch

OBJECTIVES

1. To emphasize the necessity for separation of starch granules for even hydration and gelatinization.
2. To illustrate methods for separation of starch granules before gelatinization of the starch.
3. To illustrate the effect of source of starch on thickening properties and translucency of starch gels.
4. To illustrate the effect of commercial processing of starch on gel characteristics.
5. To study quality characteristics of selected starch-thickened food products.
6. To demonstrate that starch-thickened products increase in viscosity as the starch paste cools.
7. To illustrate acceptable methods for the preparation of white sauce.
8. To show the relative degrees of consistency of white sauces prepared with varying ratios of flour to milk and to discuss the use of these sauces in food preparation.

PRODUCTS TO BE PREPARED TO ILLUSTRATE PRINCIPLES

Chocolate pudding
Selected commercial starch puddings
White sauce—thin, medium, thick, very thick
Selected starch gels

PRINCIPLES

1. Starch granules in the dry form tend to pack together.
2. Starch granules can be separated by
   a. Melted fat
   b. Other dry ingredients such as sugar
   c. Cold liquid
3. Separated starch granules have more equal opportunity for absorbing liquid during the cooking period.
4. Starch granules will settle to the bottom of the pan during cooking unless the starch mixture is stirred enough to keep the starch granules evenly dispersed throughout the mixture.
5. Gelatinization depends on the following:
   a. Ratio of liquid to starch (concentration of starch)
   b. Temperature to which the starch mixture is cooked
   c. Type of starch

6. Heat must be applied before the dry starch granule can begin to absorb liquid.
7. The source (type) of the starch will determine
    a. The temperature required for gelatinization
    b. The degree of thickening (consistency)
    c. Stability of starch paste on thawing after freezing
8. Gelatinized starch granule loses its thickening property as a result of
    a. Hydrolysis by acid
    b. Rupturing of granule by mechanical means (overstirring)

COMPARISON OF QUALITY CHARACTERISTICS OF SELECTED STARCHES

U.S.A. Measurements

Ingredient	Variable Number						
	1	**2**	**3**	**4**	**5**	**6**	**7**
*Water	7/8 cup	7/8 cup	7/8 cup	7/8 cup	3/4 cup		7/8 cup
*Lemon juice					2 T.		
*Milk						7/8 cup	
Cornstarch	1 T.			1 T.	1 T.	1 T.	
Flour		2 T.					
Tapioca			1 1/2 T.				
Sugar				3 T.			
Flour, browned							1/4 cup

*This quantity of liquid is used to give a gel structure within a 2-hour laboratory period.

Metric Measurements

Ingredient	Variable Number						
	1	**2**	**3**	**4**	**5**	**6**	**7**
*Water	200 ml	200 ml	200 ml	200 ml	170 ml		200 ml
*Lemon juice					30 ml		
*Milk						200 ml	
Cornstarch	15 ml			15 ml	15 ml	15 ml	
Flour		30 ml					
Tapioca			25 ml				
Sugar				45 ml			
Flour, browned							60 ml

*This quantity of liquid is used to give a gel structure within a 2-hour laboratory period.

A more typical gel structure is evident if the gels can stand for 3–4 hours before testing. The changes in gel structure due to treatment are still evident up to 24 hours after preparation.

1. For each variable, combine the starch with the cold liquid. Stir until the starch granules are separated and the mixture is homogeneous.
2. Allow variable 3 to stand for 15 minutes before cooking.
3. For each of the remaining variables, place the saucepan containing the starch mixture over direct heat. With continuous stirring, bring to a boil and boil for 1 minute. Pour into a glass custard cup.
4. For variable 3, after the 15-minute soaking period, place the saucepan over the direct heat. With continuous stirring, bring to a boil and remove *immediately* from the heat. Pour into a glass custard cup. After 5 minutes, stir mixture gently with a fork so tapioca completes gelatinization evenly.
*5. Allow all gel samples to come to room temperature before comparing.
6. For variable 7 put flour in saucepan. Place pan over direct heat. Stir constantly until flour is dark brown. Cool, add cold water, and cook as indicated in Step 3.

*Note: Evaluation sheet is on page 125.

EFFECT OF WATER TEMPERATURE ON STARCH DISPERSION
(Demonstrated by the instructor)

Cold Water

1. Stir 1 tablespoon (15 ml) of cornstarch into a glass of cold water.
   Record observations:

2. Allow glass to stand, undisturbed, for 10 minutes.
   Record observations:

Boiling Water

Bring 1 cup (250 ml) of water to a boil in a 1-quart (1-L) saucepan. Add 1 table-spoon (15 ml) of cornstarch or flour to the boiling water. Stir vigorously.
Record observations:

CHARACTERISTICS OF HIGH-QUALITY WHITE SAUCES

Appearance: White to creamy (dependent on type and amount of fat used); opaque.

Consistency: Smooth; even starch distribution and gelatinization.
Thin: Like "thin cream"; flows freely.
Medium: Fluid, but thick; flows slowly; like "whipping cream" before whipping.
Thick: Thick; holds imprint of spoon or slightly "mounds" on stirring.
Very thick: Will not flow; holds cut edge, even while warm.

Flavor: Very bland, mild; fat used may affect the flavor.

CHARACTERISTICS OF HIGH-QUALITY CHOCOLATE PUDDINGS

Appearance: Moist and shiny. Film will form on top of a cooked pudding as it cools.

Consistency: Pudding should "mound" slightly. However, the pudding may be firm enough to form a mold.

Flavor: Distinct chocolate; slightly sweet, well-rounded flavor; not bitter.

WHITE SAUCE—U.S.A. MEASUREMENTS

Type	Milk	Flour	Fat	Salt	Uses
Thin	1 cup	1 tablespoon	1 tablespoon	1/4 teaspoon	soups
Medium	1 cup	2 tablespoons	2 tablespoons	1/4 teaspoon	sauces; gravies
Thick	1 cup	3 tablespoons	3 tablespoons	1/2 teaspoon	souffles
Very thick	1 cup	4 tablespoons	4 tablespoons	1/2 teaspoon	croquettes

WHITE SAUCE—METRIC MEASUREMENTS

Type	Milk	Flour	Fat	Salt	Uses
Thin	250 ml	15 ml	15 ml	1 ml	soups
Medium	250 ml	30 ml	30 ml	1 ml	sauces; gravies
Thick	250 ml	45 ml	45 ml	2 ml	souffles
Very thick	250 ml	60 ml	60 ml	2 ml	croquettes

METHODS OF PREPARATION (SEE PAGE 123 FOR MICROWAVE METHOD)

Method I. Saucepan or Frying Pan

1. Melt fat in saucepan or heavy frying pan.
2. Add flour and salt. Blend until smooth.
3. Remove from heat.
4. Add milk in small portions and blend thoroughly after each addition until all milk has been added.
5. Place over direct heat. Stir constantly. Bring to a boil and boil for 1 minute.
6. Record total working time: _____ minutes.

Method II. Double Boiler

1. Melt fat in the upper part of the double boiler. Have the upper section of the double boiler over hot water.
2. Add flour and salt. Blend until smooth.
3. Add milk gradually. Stir thoroughly after each addition of milk.
4. Continue heating with occasional stirring until the mixture has thickened. Heat an additional 5 minutes after the sauce has thickened to ensure gelatinization of the starch.
5. Record total working time: _____ minutes.

Method III. Used When a Low-Fat Product Is Desired

1. Blend the flour and salt with 1/4 cup (60 ml) cold milk. Stir until all lumps of flour have been separated.
2. Add the remaining milk. Stir thoroughly.
3. Place the mixture in a saucepan over direct heat. Stir constantly until the mixture boils. Boil for 1 minute.
*4. As the mixture boils, add approximately half the indicated amount of fat for type of sauce being prepared. Stir thoroughly until the fat is blended into the sauce.
5. Record total working time: _____ minutes.

*Fat may be omitted entirely if desired. This method is not recommended when the full amount of fat is to be used; it is extremely difficult to emulsify the full amount of fat.

Chocolate Pudding

*Chocolate	1/2 square	1/2 square
Milk	1 cup	250 ml
Sugar	3 tablespoons	45 ml
Cornstarch	1 tablespoon	15 ml
Salt	few grains	few grains
Vanilla	1/2 teaspoon	2 ml

1. Cut the chocolate into several pieces. Place the chocolate and 3/4 cup (175 ml) milk in the upper part of a double boiler. Heat over hot water until the chocolate melts and blends with the milk. Cover during the first part of heating to avoid excess loss of moisture.
2. Mix sugar, cornstarch, salt, and remaining cold milk together until smooth.
3. Add the starch mixture to the scalded milk-chocolate mixture while stirring continuously.
4. Place the upper part of the double boiler over the direct heat. While stirring continuously bring the mixture to a boil and boil 1 minute. Remove from heat.
5. Add vanilla. Pour into two dessert dishes.
6. Record total working time: _____ minutes.

*Two tablespoons (30 ml) cocoa may be substituted for the chocolate. Replace Steps 1–3 with the following:
1. Scald 3/4 cup (185 ml) milk in upper part of double boiler.
2. Mix together cocoa, cornstarch, sugar, salt, and remaining cold milk. Add this mixture to the scalded milk.
3. Continue at Step 4 above.

Pregelatinized Starch Pudding

Instant chocolate pudding mix	1 package	1 package
Milk	2 cups	500 ml

1. Combine ingredients according to directions on package.
2. Allow pudding to stand at least 30 minutes before evaluating.

High Amylopectin Starch Pudding

Canned chocolate pudding	1 can

1. Open can and transfer pudding to a serving dish for evaluation.
2. Optional: chill can of pudding before evaluating.

White Sauce (Microwave)

Flour, all-purpose	2 tablespoons	30 ml
Margarine or butter	2 tablespoons	30 ml
Salt	1/4 teaspoon	1 ml
Milk	1 cup	250 ml

1. Put butter or margarine into a 1-quart (1-L) glass measuring cup. Microwave at high power for 30 seconds or until fat has melted.
2. Add flour and salt. Stir until thoroughly blended. Add milk gradually and stir continuously to evenly disperse the flour.
3. Microwave at *high* power for 30 seconds. Stir thoroughly to prevent starch from settling to the bottom of container. Microwave for 30 seconds at *high* power. Stir thoroughly. Microwave for 30 seconds. Stir thoroughly. If the sauce has not boiled, heat an additional 30 seconds or more until the sauce does boil. If the sauce has been cooked sufficiently, it will have the consistency of a medium white sauce.
4. Record total working time: _____ minutes.
5. Refer to page 120 for characteristics of high-quality white sauce.

Cheese Sauce (Microwave)

Cheddar cheese, grated	1/2 cup	125 ml
Medium white sauce as prepared (above)		

1. After the white sauce has boiled as indicated in Step 3, allow the sauce to cool for 2 or 3 minutes. Add the grated cheese. Blend cheese thoroughly.
2. If the cheese does not melt completely, microwave at *medium* power (50%) for 10 seconds. Stir. If more heat is necessary, continue heating for short intervals.
3. Record total working time: _____ minutes.
4. Refer to page 230 for characteristics of a high-quality cheese sauce.

Chocolate Pudding (Microwave)

Chocolate	1/2 square	1/2 square
Water	1 tablespoon	15 ml
Milk	1 cup	250 ml
Cornstarch	1 tablespoon +	
	1 teaspoon	20 ml
Sugar	3 tablespoons	45 ml
Salt	few grains	few grains
Vanilla	1/2 teaspoon	2 ml

1. In a 1-cup (250-ml) glass measure, put water and chocolate broken into several pieces. Microwave at *high* for 30 seconds. Thoroughly stir until a smooth paste forms. Add approximately 1/4 of the milk. Stir until evenly blended. There should not be lumps of chocolate at this stage.

2. In a 1-quart (1-L) glass measure, combine the cornstarch, sugar, salt, and remaining milk. Stir until evenly blended. There should not be lumps of unblended cornstarch at this stage.

3. Add the chocolate-milk mixture to the starch mixture. Stir until thoroughly blended. Microwave at *high* for 30 seconds; stir.

4. Microwave for 30 seconds at *high* power 4 more times (for 2 minutes). Stir after each 30-second heating period. If the pudding has boiled up in the cup during the last 30-second heating period and the pudding appears to be thick, no further cooking is necessary. If the pudding has not boiled or does not appear thick, microwave at *high* power until the pudding does boil. If more cooking is necessary, heat the pudding for 15 seconds for these final stages of heating.

5. Add vanilla to the cooked pudding. Stir until blended. Pour pudding into 2 serving dishes.

6. Record total working time: _____ minutes.

7. Refer to page 120 for characteristics of a high-quality chocolate pudding.

COMPARISON OF QUALITY CHARACTERISTICS OF SELECTED STARCH GELS

Variable Number	Treatment	Appearance*	Consistency and Texture	Tenderness	Flavor
1	Cornstarch Water				
2	Flour Water				
3	Tapioca Water				
4	Cornstarch Water Sugar				
5	Cornstarch Lemon juice Water				
6	Cornstarch Milk				
7	Flour, browned Water				

*Note: Transparent, translucent, opaque.

Rice, Pasta Products, and Cereals

OBJECTIVES

1. To prepare products of high starch content.
2. To continue the study of the behavior of starch in cookery where starch is the major component of the main food ingredient.
3. To demonstrate a method of cookery which retains the nutrients added to enriched rice and pasta products.
4. To show volume increase in these starch-containing foods as a result of cooking.
5. To demonstrate methods of cereal cookery.

PRODUCTS TO BE PREPARED TO ILLUSTRATE PRINCIPLES

Rice pilaf
Hamburger skillet meal
Plain cooked rice, spaghetti, macaroni, noodles
Spaghetti with meat sauce
Baked macaroni in tomato sauce
Macaroni salad
Selected cereals

PRINCIPLES

*1. Water and heat must be present for gelatinization of starch.
2. Melted fat aids in separation of starch foods as well as in separating dry starch granules.
3. Gelatinized starch in cereals, rice, and pasta products tends to be sticky (adhesive properties of cooked starch). Starch from ruptured starch granules can be removed by washing cooked rice or cooked pasta products.
4. Gelatinization of starch in cereals, rice, and pasta products causes an increase in volume.
5. Dextrinization of starch reduces amount of gelatinization.
6. Products high in starch tend to be bland in flavor.
7. Vitamins and minerals used to enrich rice, cereals, and pasta products are water soluble.

*Ratio of water to starch is important.

CEREALS

Bulgur wheat (sometimes called *parboiled wheat*): whole wheat that has been cooked, dried, partly debranned, and cracked into coarse, angular fragments. It originated in the Near East.

1. Prepare following directions on package.
2. Record working time: _____ minutes.

Farina (granulated wheat endosperm): made from wheat other than durum with the bran and most of the germ removed. It is prepared by grinding and sifting the wheat to a granular form.

1. Prepare following directions on package.
2. Record working time: _____ minutes.

Oatmeal (rolled oats): made by rolling the groats (oats with hull removed) to form flakes. Regular oats and quick-cooking oats differ only in thinness of flakes. For quick-cooking oats, the finished groats (edible portion of the kernel) are cut into tiny particles which are then rolled into thin, small flakes. Instant oatmeal has been precooked.

1. Prepare following directions on package.
2. Record working time: _____ minutes.

Hominy grits (corn grits, grits): prepared from either white or yellow corn from which the bran and the germ have been removed. The remaining edible portion is ground and sifted. Grits are coarser than cornmeal.

1. Prepare following directions on package.
2. Record working time: _____ minutes.

Corn meal: prepared by grinding cleaned white or yellow corn to a fineness specified by federal standards. Corn meal may be *bolted* (further decreases size of granule). It may be *degerminated* (remove germ portion of kernel, thus removing fat). It may be *enriched* (adds specified amounts of thiamine, riboflavin, niacin, and iron—optional: calcium and vitamin D).

1. Prepare following recipe on page 129.
2. Record working time: _____ minutes.

CHARACTERISTICS OF HIGH-QUALITY COOKED CEREALS (*CEREALS TO BE EVALUATED WHILE HOT*)

Appearance: Distinct particles, granules, or flakes.

Consistency: Thick; somewhat viscous (without gumminess).

Flavor: Bland (cooked starch); typical for grain (wheat, corn, oats); well-rounded (no raw starch).

Tenderness: Not evaluated for this product.

Mouth Feel: Particles remain discrete; soft.

Corn Meal Mush

Corn meal	1/2 cup	125 ml
Water, cold	1/2 cup	125 ml
Water, boiling	1 1/2 cups	375 ml
Salt	1/2 teaspoon	2 ml

1. Bring 1 1/2 cups (375 ml) water to boiling.
2. Blend the corn meal, salt, and cold water together.
3. Remove saucepan of boiling water from heat. Spoon or pour the corn meal and cold water mixture into the hot water, stirring until evenly blended.
4. Return saucepan to heat and bring corn meal mixture to a boil and boil for 5 minutes. Stir constantly. Be careful the hot cereal does not boil so vigorously that it spatters.
5. Reduce heat to lowest temperature. Cover saucepan and allow mush to heat for 10 minutes more.
6. Serve hot as a cereal or transfer cooked mush to small aluminum loaf pan to cool completely for fried mush. Cover.
7. Refrigerate until fried.
8. Record total working time: _____ minutes.

Fried Mush

Cooked mush slices	5 or 6	5 or 6
Hydrogenated shortening	1 tablespoon	15 ml

1. Heat a heavy frying pan until it is moderately hot. (A few drops of water will evaporate in 2 or 3 seconds). Spread melted fat evenly over the bottom of the frying pan. *Do not allow fat to smoke!*
2. Cut mush into slices 1/4 to 3/8 inch (0.6 to 1.0 cm) thick. Place slices in hot frying pan. Reduce heat to medium temperature. Fry mush until it is crisp and golden brown; this may take 10–15 minutes for each side.
3. Use pancake turner to turn slice. Add more shortening if necessary. Fry mush on second side until crisp and golden brown.
4. For class evaluation do not use syrup on mush.
5. Record total working time: _____ minutes.

CHARACTERISTICS OF HIGH-QUALITY FRIED CORN MEAL MUSH

Appearance: Slices are golden brown on each side. Surfaces appear fairly dry.

Texture:
Exterior: Crust is crisp.
Interior: Soft; thickness of slice determines degree of softness.

Flavor: Toasted corn; very slightly sweet.

Rice*

Rice, long grain	1/3 cup	75 ml
Water	7/8 cup	200 ml
Salt	1/4 teaspoon	1 ml
Margarine or butter	1/2 teaspoon	2 ml

1. Bring water to a boil. Add the salt and the butter.
2. Add the rice. Stir to make sure rice is not clumped together. (Stir with a fork.)
3. Reduce heat. Tightly cover saucepan. Finish cooking at a simmering temperature. Stir occasionally with a fork.
4. Cook until a rice kernel can be mashed between the fingers—approximately 20 minutes. Do not rinse the rice before serving.
5. Measure the cooked rice to obtain increase in volume:
   1/3 cup raw rice yields _____ cup(s) cooked rice.
   75 ml raw rice yields _____ ml cooked rice.
6. Record total working time: _____ minutes.

*Plain cooked rice is served with Pork Chop Suey, page 181, and Japanese Vegetables with Chicken and Shrimp, page 229.

One-half cup (125 ml) uncooked rice can be substituted for the 3 ounces (625 ml) dry noodles in the Hamburger Skillet Meal, page 132.

CHARACTERISTICS OF HIGH-QUALITY COOKED RICE

Appearance: Grains intact; white, translucent.

Texture: Grains firm, but tender; fluffy.

Flavor: Bland.

Basic Rice Pilaf**

Rice, long grain, uncooked	1/2 cup	125 ml
Margarine	2 teaspoons	10 ml
Liquid (chicken broth, water, tomato juice)	1 1/2 cups	375 ml
Salt	1/4 teaspoon	1 ml

1. Melt fat in saucepan. Add dry rice. Stir rice constantly with a fork until very lightly browned—more creamy than brown.
2. Add liquid and salt. Bring to a boil. Boil about 2 minutes. Reduce heat to low.
3. Cover saucepan tightly. Cook 25–30 minutes or until rice is tender and has absorbed the liquid. Stir occasionally with a fork.
4. Record total working time: _____ minutes.

**Bulgur wheat may be substituted for the rice.
Either Rice or Bulgur Pilaf can be used as a substitute for potatoes in a meal.

Macaroni, Spaghetti, Noodles (Pasta)

Macaroni (elbow) or spaghetti	1/2 cup	57 g
Noodles	1/2 cup	33 g
Water	2 cups	500 ml
Salt	1/2 teaspoon	2 ml
Margarine	1 teaspoon	5 ml

1. Place water in a 2-quart (2-L) saucepan. Add salt and margarine. Heat to boiling.
2. Add one of the pasta products to the boiling salted water. Keep the product boiling vigorously during the cooking period. Stir with a fork every 3 to 4 minutes to keep pasta from sticking to saucepan. Cook with saucepan uncovered.
3. Cook until pasta is tender—approximately 15 minutes.
4. Drain pasta through strainer. Rinse with hot tap water.
5. Measure the cooked pasta to measure increase in volume:

Pasta Product	Uncooked (Dry) Volume	Cooked Volume
Macaroni	1/2 cup	_____ cup(s)
	125 ml	_____ ml
Spaghetti	1/2 cup	_____ cup(s)
	125 ml	_____ ml
Noodles	1/2 cup	_____ cup(s)
	125 ml	_____ ml

6. Record total working time: _____ minutes.

CHARACTERISTICS OF HIGH-QUALITY PASTA

Appearance: Distinct strands or pieces.

Tenderness: Tender; little resistance to bite.

Flavor: Bland; noodles may have a slight egg flavor.

Hamburger Skillet Meal

Ground beef	1/2 pound	250 ml
Margarine	1 tablespoon	15 ml
Onion, medium	1/2	1/2
Green pepper	1/2	1/2
Tomatoes, canned	1 cup	250 ml
Worcestershire sauce	1/2 teaspoon	2 ml
Salt	1/2 teaspoon	2 ml
Pepper	few grains	few grains
Noodles, dry, 3 inch (8 cm) lengths*	3 ounces	625 ml
Water	1 cup	250 ml
Tomato juice	1 cup	250 ml

1. Melt the fat in an electric frying pan. Add the beef and cook until brown, stirring occasionally.
2. Remove the dry skin from the onion. Wash, dry, and chop the onion.
3. Wash the green pepper and remove the center core. Rinse center cavity, dry, and chop into medium-size pieces.
4. Add the onion, pepper, and all the other ingredients except the tomato juice and noodles to the browned meat. Mix thoroughly.
5. Spread the uncooked noodles over the top of the meat and vegetable mixture. Pour the tomato juice evenly over the mixture; stir and heat to boiling. Cover tightly, reduce the heat, and simmer for 30 minutes or until the noodles are tender and have absorbed most of the liquid. Stir occasionally.
6. Record total working time: _____ minutes.

*One-half cup (125 ml) uncooked rice may be substituted.

Spaghetti with Meat Sauce

Ground beef	3/4 pound	375 ml
Olive oil or shortening	2 tablespoons	30 ml
Mushrooms, canned	4 ounces	125 ml
Garlic clove	1	1
Onions, large	2	2
Salt	1/2 teaspoon	2 ml
Pepper	1/8 teaspoon	0.5 ml
Tomato paste	1/2 cup	125 ml
Tomato juice	1 1/2 cups	375 ml
Bay leaf	1/2	1/2
Spaghetti, dry, 3 inch (8 cm) lengths	4 ounces	375 ml
Italian type cheese, grated	1/2 cup	125 ml

1. Remove dry skin from onion. Wash, dry, and chop.
2. Remove dry skin from garlic clove. Wash, dry, and impale with half a toothpick.
3. Melt fat in the bottom of a heavy frying pan. Add ground beef, mushrooms, onions, salt, pepper, and garlic. With constant stirring, cook until meat is brown.
4. Add tomato paste, tomato juice, and bay leaf; stir. Simmer until thick. Remove bay leaf and garlic.
5. Boil spaghetti in 2–3 quarts (2–3L) of boiling, salted water (1 teaspoon salt/quart water or 5 ml/L water) in an uncovered pan. Cook until tender. Pour off cooking water and rinse spaghetti in hot water. Drain.
6. Place drained spaghetti on a large, heated platter. Pour sauce over the top. Serve with grated Italian type cheese (Parmesan or Romano).
7. Record total working time: _____ minutes.

Baked Macaroni in Tomato Sauce

Macaroni, elbow	4 ounces	300 ml
Tomatoes, canned	1 cup	250 ml
Onion, small	1/2	1/2
Peppercorns	2	2
Bay leaf	1/4	1/4
Salt	1/2 teaspoon	2 ml
Tomato paste	2 tablespoons	30 ml
Cheddar cheese, shredded	1 cup	250 ml
Fine bread crumbs	1/3 cup	75 ml
Margarine	2 tablespoons	30 ml

1. Preheat oven to 350°F (175°C).
2. Boil macaroni in 2–3 quarts (2–3 L) of boiling, salted water (1 teaspoon salt/quart water or 5 ml salt/L water) in an uncovered pan. Cook until tender. Pour off cooking water and rinse macaroni in hot water. Drain. Place in a well-greased casserole.
3. Remove dry skin from onion. Wash, dry, and slice onion into several thin slices.
4. Simmer tomatoes with onion, peppercorns, and bay leaf for 5 minutes. Rub through a sieve. Add salt and tomato paste. Stir.
5. Pour sauce over macaroni. Add grated cheese. Lightly stir with fork.
6. Melt margarine in small pan, add crumbs, and stir. Sprinkle evenly over macaroni mixture.
7. Bake in a 350°F (175°C) oven 20–30 minutes or until crumbs are browned.
8. Record total working time: _____ minutes.

Macaroni Salad

(Main course salad, see page 266.)

Shell macaroni, uncooked	6 ounces	375 ml
Water	2 cups	500 ml
Salt	1/2 teaspoon	2 ml
Margarine, oil, or butter	1/2 teaspoon	2 ml
Cider vinegar	1 tablespoon	15 ml
Broccoli florets	3/4 cup	185 ml
Celery, finely chopped	1/2 cup	125 ml
Carrots, grated	1/4 cup	60 ml
Green pepper, finely chopped	1/4 cup	60 ml
Red pepper, fresh, finely chopped	2 tablespoons	30 ml
Scallions, finely chopped	2 tablespoons	30 ml
Eggs, hard-cooked, used for garnish	2	2

Dressing:

Salad dressing, mayonnaise type	1/2 cup	125 ml
Lemon juice	1 tablespoon	15 ml
Milk, 2%	1 tablespoon	15 ml
Tabasco sauce	4–6 drops	4–6 drops
Mustard, Dijon type	1 teaspoon	5 ml
Italian seasoning	1/2 teaspoon	2 ml
Sour cream	1 tablespoon	15 ml

1. Bring water to a boil in a 3-quart (3-L) saucepan. Add salt, margarine, and macaroni shells. Cook approximately 15 minutes or to *al dente* stage of tenderness.
2. Drain and rinse in *hot* water. Drain thoroughly and transfer to a 2–3 quart (2–3 L) bowl. Add vinegar to *hot* pasta. Toss lightly with 2 forks to evenly distribute vinegar. Chill thoroughly.
3. Prepare hard-cooked eggs as directed on page 155.
4. Steam broccoli florets for 3 minutes. Rinse in cold water, drain thoroughly, and set aside.
5. Prepare the remaining vegetables. Lightly toss all vegetables together before adding to the cooked macaroni. *Do not* combine vegetables with cooked macaroni until the dressing has been prepared and is ready to combine.
6. Blend together all dressing ingredients before adding to cooked macaroni shells and vegetables. Use 2 forks to lightly combine all ingredients.
7. Remove shells from the hard-cooked eggs, rinse under cold water, and blot dry. Quarter each egg and add as garnish to the salad.
8. Record total working time: _____ minutes.

Note: Flavor is enhanced if salad can be refrigerated 2–4 hours before serving.

REVIEW QUESTIONS

1. Define or explain each of the following terms:
   - a. Starch
   - b. Dextrins
   - c. Maltose
   - d. Glucose (dextrose)
   - e. Amylose
   - f. Amylopectin
   - g. Dextrinization
   - h. Hydration
   - i. Hydrolysis
   - j. Pregelatinized starch
   - k. Waxy starch
   - l. Modified starch
2. a. Give the ratio of ingredients in each of the four types of white sauce.
   b. List the use(s) for each type of white sauce.
3. Explain each of the following procedures in terms of the principles of starch cookery:
   - a. Mixing starch with melted fat
   - b. Heating to boiling over direct heat
   - c. Constant stirring when cooking on direct heat
   - d. In a lemon pie filling, adding the lemon juice as the last step
4. Give reasons why the following statement cannot be true: An undercooked starch pudding can be brought to optimum thickness by cooling in the refrigerator.
5. On the following scale, rate the clarity of the pastas made from the three different starches with water.

   Opaque ◄···············► Translucent ◄···············► Transparent

6. Why is pasta rinsed with hot water after cooking?
7. Describe the characteristics of high quality for the following:
   - a. Chocolate pudding
   - b. Noodles
   - c. Rice
8. Enriched rice is cooked in a small amount of water and is not rinsed after cooking. Explain why this procedure must be followed.
9. If you had to prepare a cooked cereal for breakfast, what principles of starch cookery would be applicable?
10. The following was taken from an evaluation sheet of samples of brown gravy:

    Appearance—2, lumpy
    Consistency—2, thin and lumpy
    Flavor—4, starchy

    What principles were not observed to account for the poor quality of this gravy?
11. Explain the effect of dry heat on starch
    - a. On the color
    - b. On the thickening properties
12. a. If 2 tablespoons (30 ml) of flour and 1 cup (250 ml) of milk will make a medium white sauce, how much browned flour will be needed to make a gravy of the same thickness using 1 cup (250 ml) of milk?
    b. What factor would affect your answer to 12(a)?
13. Explain your observations made on the effect of boiling water on cornstarch or flour.
14. Why is the dry corn meal mixed with cold water in making corn meal mush?
15. a. Why is a high temperature, 425°F (220°C) used to fry corn meal mush?
    b. How does this influence the choice of fat used for frying?
16. What is the relationship between the amount of stirring and the quality of oatmeal? Explain.
17. Why do "instant" cereals require so little preparation time?

Milk

OBJECTIVES

1. To acquaint students with various selected factors which affect the stability of proteins:
   a. Homogenization process
   b. Heat
   c. Acid
   d. Enzymes
   e. Salts
2. To get students to appreciate the fact that stability of milk proteins may be both desirable and undesirable.

PRODUCTS TO BE PREPARED TO ILLUSTRATE PRINCIPLES

Variety of milk products
Heated fresh, fluid milk
Acidified fresh, fluid milk
Enzyme coagulation of milk
Heated, sweetened condensed milk
Acidified, sweetened condensed milk
Cream of tomato soup

PRINCIPLES

1. Casein is coagulated (precipitated) by the action of acid and/or the rennet enzyme.
2. Lactoglobulin and lactalbumin are coagulated (precipitated) by the action of heat.
3. Lactose caramelizes at a relatively low temperature.
4. Starch "buffers" the action of acid on milk protein.
*5. Commercial processing methods for production of dried milk solids and evaporated milk require heating of milk to a temperature at which enzymes in milk are inactivated and bacteria in milk are destroyed.

*While dried milk powder may be free of bacteria as produced, great care must be taken by the manufacturer not to reintroduce microorganisms during subsequent handling and packaging. The user must also handle dried milk powder in a sanitary way to avoid reintroduction of microorganisms.

CHARACTERISTICS OF MILK AND CREAM

Product	*Percentage Water	*Percentage Fat	*Percentage Protein	Appearance	Consistency	Flavor
Reconstituted dry milk solids	90	0.1	3.6			
Fresh skim milk	90	0.1	3.6			
Fresh 1% milk	90	1.0	3.3			
Whole milk, plain or homogenized	87	3.0–4.0	3.5			
Evaporated milk	74	not less than 7.9	10.0			
Sweetened condensed milk	26	not less than 8.5	8.1			
Half-and-half	80	11.5	3.1			
Heavy whipping cream	58	36.0	2.2			

*Typical composition.

Coagulation of Fresh Fluid Milk—By Heat

Milk   1/2 cup   125 ml

1. Place milk in a flameproof glass saucepan. Place over low heat.
2. Heat slowly to 212°F (100°C). *Do not stir.* Remove from heat.
3. Observe and identify constituent(s) of milk involved in each change:
    a. Formation of film on surface of milk

    b. Precipitation on surface of saucepan

    c. Caramelization on surface of saucepan

Coagulation of Fresh Fluid Milk—By Acid

| Milk | 1 cup minus 1 tablespoon | 235 ml |
| Vinegar or lemon juice | 1 tablespoon | 15 ml |

1. Measure the milk in a glass measuring cup.
2. Measure the pH of plain milk with special tape: pH _____.
3. Add the vinegar or lemon juice. Stir quickly to blend the two liquids.
4. Allow the mixture to stand at least 5 minutes before testing for curd formation.
5. Measure the pH of the mixture with special tape: pH _____.
6. Observe and identify constituent(s) in milk involved in curd formation.

Coagulation of Fresh Fluid Milk—By Enzyme

		Milk Temperature		Measure of Milk		Rennet Tablet	Water (cold)	
1.	From refrigerator	42°F	6°C	1 cup	250 ml	1/2	1 teaspoon	5 ml
2.	Heated to	110°F	43°C	1 cup	250 ml	1/2	1 teaspoon	5 ml
3.	Heated to	212°F	100°C	1 cup	250 ml	1/2	1 teaspoon	5 ml

1. Set out 5 custard cups for each temperature of milk.
2. Dissolve tablet in cold water.
3. If milk is to be heated, heat to temperature indicated.
4. Add rennet solution to milk. Stir quickly to thoroughly blend.
5. Pour mixture immediately into 5 custard cups.
6. Allow to stand at room temperature for 10 minutes.
7. Refrigerate for 1 hour before evaluating.
8. Observe and record the following:
    a. Which sample(s) form a gel structure?

    b. Why did some sample(s) not form a gel structure?

    c. Which protein is involved in the formation of the gel?

Coagulation of Sweetened Condensed Milk—By Heat

Sweetened condensed milk   1 can

*1. Pour the sweetened condensed milk into the upper section of a 1 1/2 quart (1.5 L) double boiler.
2. Put water into lower section of double boiler. Place upper section over water and cover.
3. Heat to boiling. Continue boiling for 3 hours or until the sweetened condensed milk has formed a gel and has become caramel in color. Add boiling water to lower section as necessary. *Do not let lower section become dry!*
4. Observe:
   a. Browning

   b. Heat coagulation

   *Alternate method:
   1. Remove one end of the can. Tightly cover the milk by pressing aluminum foil down over the top of the can.
   2. Place can in a pan of water. Water should be at half the height of the can. Cover the pan.
   3. Place pan over medium heat. Heat to boiling. Continue boiling for 3 hours or until the milk has become caramel in color. Do not let pan become dry. Add boiling water as necessary.

Coagulation of Sweetened Condensed Milk—By Acid

Sweetened condensed milk	1/2 can	1/2 can
Lemon juice	1/4 cup	60 ml

1. Gradually stir lemon juice into the sweetened condensed milk.
2. Allow the mixture to stand at least 10 minutes before cutting into it.
3. Observe:
   a. Thickening of milk during addition of lemon juice

   b. Firmness of gel after standing

Cream of Tomato Soup

Margarine or butter	1 tablespoon	15 ml
Flour	1 tablespoon	15 ml
Salt	1/4 teaspoon	1 ml
Milk	1/2 cup	125 ml
Tomato paste	1 tablespoon	15 ml
Tomato juice	2/3 cup	150 ml
Peppercorn, whole	1	1
Bay leaf	1/4	1/4
Onion, thin slice	1	1

1. Simmer together for 5 minutes the tomato juice, peppercorn, bay leaf, and onion. Strain into glass measuring cup. Add tomato juice to bring to 2/3 cup (150 ml). Add tomato paste. Blend.
2. Make a white sauce by melting the fat in a saucepan, adding the flour and salt, and blending until smooth.
3. Add the milk gradually with constant stirring to form a smooth paste. Do not have over heat while adding the milk.
4. Return mixture to heat. Bring to a boil with constant stirring.
5. Add the tomato juice to the white sauce.
6. Heat to serving temperature, but *do not boil.*
7. Record total working time: _____ minutes.

CHARACTERISTICS OF HIGH-QUALITY TOMATO SOUP

Appearance: Pale red-orange. All ingredients appear well blended.

Consistency: Comparable to "thin" cream; smooth throughout.

Flavor: Mild tomato should predominate. Spice flavors should be noticeable but not strong enough to be identified.

Cheese

OBJECTIVES

1. To study factors inherent in production of a natural cheese.
2. To recognize the relationship between *natural cheese* and *process cheese*.
3. To recognize that the term *process* identifies a specific cheese product and is also a part of the name of several other processed cheese products.
4. To give students the opportunity to compare quality characteristics for selected natural cheeses and process cheese products.
5. To demonstrate the effect of emulsifiers on fat stability of cheeses exposed to heat.
6. To demonstrate the effect of heat
   a. On the protein in cheese
   b. On the milk sugar

PRODUCTS TO BE STUDIED TO ILLUSTRATE PRINCIPLES

Natural cheeses: Cottage, Cream, Camembert, Blue, Swiss, Cheddar
Process cheeses: Process Cheese, Process Cheese Food, Process Cheese Spread
Imitation cheese
Light cheese
Open-faced grilled cheese sandwiches

PRINCIPLES

1. Casein is precipitated from milk by the interaction of rennet enzymes, acid, and calcium salts. Mild heat is required for the reaction.
2. The character of natural cheese is determined by
   a. Moisture content of the finished cheese
   b. Length of aging period
      (1) Unripened cheese—not aged
      (2) Ripened cheese—type of organism used
         (a) Bacteria—some produce gas holes
         (b) Mold—the mold becomes an integral part of the cheese
3. Complex casein molecule is peptized during the ripening of natural cheese.
4. The distinctive flavor of each type of natural cheese is due to one or more of the following factors:
   a. The microorganisms used in ripening
   b. Length of aging period
   c. Heat and humidity during aging
   d. Breakdown of protein and/or fat
   e. Production of specific chemicals

5. All process cheese products contain added emulsifiers to help hold milk fat in dispersion during the cooking of the cheese products.
6. Addition of water, milk, and/or milk products to process cheese products reduces the distinctive cheese flavor of the natural cheese used in the production of the process cheese product.
7. Cheese protein can be toughened or made rubbery by overheating during the cooking of cheese products.
8. There are no Standards of Identity for Light (Lite) cheeses; therefore, the labels must have an ingredient list.

CHEESE CLASSIFICATIONS WITH STANDARDS OF IDENTITY FOR SEVERAL TYPES

1. Natural cheese
   a. Moisture content (*soft*—high moisture; *hard*—low moisture)
   b. Unripened or ripened
   c. Type of bacteria or mold used in ripening to produce specific characteristics of appearance, texture, or flavor
2. Process cheese products
   a. Moisture content
   b. Milk fat content
   c. Addition of emulsifiers
   d. Addition of other ingredients
3. Imitation process cheese spread
   a. No Standards of Identity have been written for this product.
   b. Any ingredient can be used as long as it is properly declared on the label.
   c. The term *IMITATION* must appear on the label along with a complete ingredient list.
   Note: Since there is no Standard of Identity for these products, any food materials may be used and the complete list of ingredients must appear on the label. Following is an ingredient list typical of this type of product: water, partially hydrogenated soybean oil, casein, modified whey, calcium caseinate, whey, sodium citrate, salt, natural flavoring, lactic acid, sodium phosphate, calcium phosphate, sorbic acid (added as a preservative), citric acid, buttermilk, blue cheese, vitamin A palmitate, riboflavin, artificial color.
4. Light (or Lite) Pasteurized process cheese product.
   a. No Standards of Identity have been written for these products; however, the following Standards of Identity would apply to the manufacture of light cheese products: 133.167 Pasteurized blended cheese where the word *blended* has replaced the word *processed* and 133.189 Skim milk cheese for manufacturing. Following is the ingredient list for a typical product: skim milk cheese, water, swiss cheese (cultured milk and skim milk, salt, and enzymes), American cheese, sodium phosphate, natural flavors, salt, sodium citrate, whey, calcium phosphate, sorbic acid (a preservative), acetic acid. The ingredient list must appear on the package.

STANDARDS OF IDENTITY—CODE OF FEDERAL REGULATIONS: TITLE 21: PART 133 DATED APRIL 1, 1993

Type	Moisture (%)	Fat (% on solids basis)	Special Information
Natural Cheeses			
Cottage	Not more than 80	Not less than 4	Salt, an acid, and a stabilizer may be added
Cream	Not more than 55	Not less than 33	May contain not more than 0.5% of specified emulsifier*
Camembert	No standard set	No standard set	—
Blue	Not more than 46	Not less than 50	Not less than 60 days old
Swiss	Not more than 41	Not less than 43	Not less than 60 days old
Cheddar	Not more than 39	Not less than 50	Not less than 60 days old; held at not more than 35°F.
Process Cheese Products			
Process	Not more than 43	Not less than 47	†Emulsifier
Process cheese food	Not more than 44	Not less than 23	†Emulsifier, milk, and/or milk products; spices, flavorings, or other ingredients such as fruits, vegetables, or meats.
**Process cheese spread	More than 44 but *not* more than 60	Not less than 20	†Emulsifier, milk, and/or milk products; spices, flavorings, or other ingredients such as fruits, vegetables, or meats.

*Where a Standard of Identity has been written for a product, no ingredient list is required *unless* the optional ingredients are used; in which case ingredients must be listed on the label.

†Weight of solids of emulsifier cannot be more than 3% of the weight of the process cheese product. Emulsifiers may be one or a mixture of disodium phos-phate, sodium or potassium citrate, or others as listed.

**Product must be spreadable at 70°F.

CHEESE EVALUATION

Date: _____

Name	Natural or Processed	Moisture Content	Not Ripened or Ripened	Mold or Bacteria	Added Ingredients	Tenderness	Texture	Flavor	Comments

EFFECT OF HEAT ON NATURAL CHEESE AND PROCESS CHEESE PRODUCTS

Open-Faced Grilled Cheese Sandwiches

Bread—1 slice for each cheese product tested.
*Cheese slices—cut equally thick for each type; sufficient to cover bread.

1. Place a slice of bread for each cheese to be tested on a baking sheet. Arrange so that each slice of bread will receive equal heat from the broiler.
2. Arrange slices of cheese of one type on a slice of bread. Each sandwich may be cut into four pieces after broiling so each group member will have his or her portion for evaluation from the same basic sample.
3. Have the surface of the cheese 6–8 inches (15–20 cm) below the broiler element (or gas flame).
4. Broil the tray of sandwiches until the sample of process cheese is just melted.
5. Remove tray from heat.
6. Cut samples for evaluation.

*Use following types of cheese: natural cheddar, process cheese, process cheese food, process cheese spread, imitation process cheese spread.

CHARACTERISTICS OF HIGH-QUALITY OPEN-FACED GRILLED CHEESE SANDWICHES

Appearance: Bread—golden brown, even color; cheese—just barely melted; little or no browning.

Texture: Cheese—smooth, even.

Tenderness: Cheese—tender.

Flavor: Cheese—typical natural cheddar cheese—slightly tart, yet sweet flavor.

REVIEW QUESTIONS FOR MILK AND CHEESE

1. a. List the main constituents of milk (those constituents which contribute to its functional properties). Include the specific names of the three most important milk proteins.
   b. What action does the application of heat have on the carbohydrate and proteins?
   c. How does the addition of an acid affect the stability of each of the three proteins?
2. a. What are the optimum conditions for preparation of rennet desserts?
   b. Explain what happens if a rennet dessert is prepared using milk at 150°F (65.5°C).
   c. Explain what happens if the milk is too cold.
3. List some food products containing milk in which the coagulation of milk is
   a. Undesirable
   b. Desirable or essential
4. a. Why does sweetened condensed milk turn brown when heated?
   b. What happened to the consistency of the sweetened condensed milk when heated? Explain why this happened.
5. List and discuss the factors that determine the characteristics of natural cheese.
6. a. What happened to the cheddar cheese when it was heated in making the open-face grilled cheese sandwich?
   b. Explain the observations in part (a).
   c. Which samples had the greatest tendency to brown?
   d. From your knowledge of the constituents of process cheese, explain your observations in part (c).
7. Define or explain the following terms:
   a. Sol
   b. Gel
   c. Gelation
   d. Syneresis
   e. Natural cheese
   f. Process cheese
   g. Standards of Identity
   h. Peptization
   i. pH (hydrogen ion concentration)
   j. Light cheese

Eggs and Custards

OBJECTIVES

1. To illustrate and discuss quality characteristics of shell eggs:
   a. Fresh eggs
   b. Frozen in the shell
2. To illustrate selected methods for cooking.
3. To illustrate selected factors which affect the coagulation of egg protein.
4. To acquaint students with differences between stirred (soft) and baked custards.
5. To acquaint students with egg substitutes.

PRODUCTS TO BE PREPARED TO ILLUSTRATE PRINCIPLES

Fresh eggs (in shell and broken onto plate)
Egg frozen in shell
Baked custard
Stirred custard
Fried eggs
Scrambled eggs
Hard-cooked eggs
French (or plain) cheese omelet

PRINCIPLES

1. Quality characteristics of shell eggs
   a. Deteriorate with aging
   b. Are dependent on storage conditions
   c. Deteriorate with freezing in the shell
2. Egg protein coagulates to form a gel structure by application of
   a. Heat
   b. Mechanical treatment
3. Coagulation temperature of egg protein is affected by
   a. Dilution
   b. Sugar
   c. Acid
   d. Homogenization treatment of milk
   e. Rate of heating
4. Excessive heat treatment of the egg protein results in
   a. Curdling
   b. Syneresis
   c. Toughening of the protein

Basic Custard

Milk	1 cup	250 ml
*Egg, blended**	1 whole + 2 tablespoons	1 whole + 30 ml
***Sugar	2 tablespoons	30 ml
Salt	few grains	few grains
Vanilla	1/4 teaspoon	1 ml

Nutmeg, if desired—a few grains on top of each custard to be baked

1. Preheat oven to 400°F (220°C).
2. Put 1 small custard cup in refrigerator to use in Step 12.
3. Blend together the milk, egg, sugar, and salt. Do not beat until the mixture becomes foamy. (The mixture may be strained before heating to remove chalazae.)

Baked Custard

4. Pour part of the mixture into one of the smallest custard cups. Cup should be filled to 1/2 inch (1.3 cm) from the top. Add 1/8 teaspoon (0.5 ml) vanilla. Blend by stirring. Sprinkle a few grains of nutmeg on the top if desired.
5. Place the custard cup in a pan of warm water. The water in the pan should be of the same depth as the custard in the custard cup. (For class several students can put custards in one baking pan.)
6. Place the pan of custards in the oven. Reduce heat to 350°F (175°C).
7. Bake until a knife inserted near the center comes out clean (about 45 minutes).
8. Record total working time: _____ minutes.

Stirred Custard

9. Put the custard mix remaining after Step 3 in the upper part of a double boiler. Have water in the lower part of the double boiler hot but not boiling. Do not allow the water to boil during the cooking period.
10. Stir custard constantly with a wooden spoon during cooking. Custard must be cooked *slowly*, 15–25 minutes.
11. Cook until the custard coats a metal spoon. (At this stage the custard clings to the spoon in a coating about half the thickness of a chocolate coating on a candy bar.)
12. Pour the cooked custard *immediately* into a cold serving dish. It is essential to stop the cooking process quickly to prevent the custard from curdling.
13. Add 1/8 teaspoon (0.5 ml) vanilla. Stir until well blended.
14. Record total working time: _____ minutes.

*Egg substitutes may be used in place of fresh eggs; use conversion factor shown on package.
**Quantity of egg has been increased to reduce baking time to accommodate a 110 minute laboratory period. One egg + 1 cup (250 ml) milk will form a firm gel structure but require a longer baking period.
***Any synthetic sweetener made with Acesulfame–K may be substituted for sugar using the conversion factors shown on the package.

CHARACTERISTICS OF HIGH-QUALITY BAKED CUSTARDS

Appearance: Pale golden brown surface.

Consistency: Even gel structure that holds a clear, sharp cut edge.

Flavor: Nutmeg may mask slight egg flavor.

CHARACTERISTICS OF HIGH-QUALITY STIRRED CUSTARDS

Appearance: Pale yellow, dependent on color of egg yolks.

Consistency: Consistency of heavy cream before the cream is whipped; smooth.

Flavor: Bland, slightly sweet, slight egg flavor; vanilla may mask egg flavor.

Observations of Quality of Raw Eggs out of Shell

Eggs as available—1 egg per student
1. Break egg out onto a flat plate 6–7 inches (15–18 cm) in diameter, white plate preferred. Before discarding the shell, observe the depth of the air cell in the large end of the egg shell as an indication of deterioration: the larger the air cell, the greater is the degree of deterioration.
2. Avoid moving the egg around on the plate as much as possible to minimize damage to the egg before it can be evaluated for quality.
3. If models of graded eggs are available, compare the fresh egg with the models; otherwise, compare the fresh egg with photographs of graded eggs.

CHARACTERISTICS OF HIGH-QUALITY RAW EGGS OUT OF SHELL*

Appearance
Yolk: Will stand up high and firm above the egg white; diameter will be relatively small; yolk should be fairly well centered in the egg white.
White: Will have a high ratio of thick, firm, white; thick white will also stand up; white will be free from meat spots or blood spots; white may be somewhat translucent.

Odor: Mild egg aroma.

*Where possible, compare egg out of shell with grade models of eggs and/or marketing charts depicting characteristics of egg quality.

Frozen Egg in the Shell

1. Place one or more shell eggs in a freezer. The shell is apt to crack, so the eggs should be placed in a container during freezing. The eggs must remain in the freezer long enough to be thoroughly frozen (24 hours).
2. Remove the frozen eggs from the freezer several hours before the eggs are to be observed and discussed. Place the eggs in a glass custard cup so the amount of leakage during thawing can be observed.
3. Observe crack in the shell and leakage of egg white before breaking egg out onto a plate.
4. Break egg out onto a plate 6–7 inches (15–18 cm) in diameter, white plate preferred. Observe the following:

Egg white
a. Physical breakdown of egg white
b. White is thin, watery, and breaks away from the egg yolk.
c. Whipping properties, however, have not been affected.

Egg yolk
a. Firmness, rubberiness, and pastiness are a result of chemical "binding" of water during freezing.
b. Yolk loses its ability to blend with other ingredients.

Hard-Cooked Eggs

Eggs, room temperature—4 or 5

1. Use enough water in saucepan so the water completely covers the eggs in the shell during the cooking period.
2. Bring the water to a boil.
3. Place the eggs in the shell on a tablespoon to set into the boiling water. At the time eggs are added, heat should be reduced so water is no longer actively boiling.
*4. Cook the eggs at a simmering temperature, 185°–200°F (85°–93°C) for about 20–25 minutes. Original temperature of the eggs, number of eggs cooked at one time, and the temperature at which the eggs are cooked will all influence the time necessary to produce a high-quality hard-cooked egg.
5. At the end of the cooking period, allow cold tap water to flow over the eggs until the eggs feel cool, about 5 minutes.
6. Remove eggs from water. Dry shells. Remove shells.
7. Record total working time: _____ minutes.

   *To compare the effect of temperature of cooking on the quality of hard-cooked eggs, prepare a second sample at a rolling boil for as long as the first sample is simmered.

CHARACTERISTICS OF HIGH-QUALITY HARD-COOKED EGGS

Appearance: Yolk should be evenly centered in the egg white; yolk should have the same color on its exterior surface and its interior cut edge (no dark ring); yolk should have even consistency throughout—it appears mealy and dry.

Texture: Yolk should be dry and mealy.

Tenderness: White is firm enough to hold together, yet is only slightly resistant to bite.

Flavor: Mild to bland egg flavor.

Fried Eggs

Egg	1	1
Butter or margarine	1 teaspoon	5 ml
Water	1 tablespoon	15 ml

1. Melt butter or margarine in small frying pan.
2. Break the egg out of its shell onto a small saucer. Slide the egg into the hot (but not smoking) fat.
3. Add the water. Cover frying pan immediately with a tight-fitting lid.
4. Allow to steam until the white is opaque and the yolk is coagulated.
5. Record total working time: _____ minutes.

CHARACTERISTICS OF HIGH-QUALITY FRIED EGGS

Appearance: Yolk is covered with film of coagulated egg white; coagulated egg white is opaque and shiny.

Consistency: Egg yolk should be firm; the egg white has coagulated to form a firm gel structure.

Tenderness: Egg white is tender and shows very little resistance to cutting or chewing.

Flavor: Mild egg flavor; if butter has been used, butter flavor may enhance the egg flavor.

Note: Recent research indicates the egg yolk should be cooked to the firm stage to avoid the possibility of salmonella food poisoning.

Scrambled Eggs

*Eggs	2	2
Milk	2 tablespoons	30 ml
Butter or margarine	1 teaspoon	5 ml
Salt	1/4 teaspoon	1 ml
Pepper, white (if desired)	few grains	few grains

1. Place the eggs in a bowl. Add the milk and seasonings.
2. Blend ingredients with a rotary beater until well blended but not foamy.
3. Melt the butter or margarine in a heavy frying pan.
4. Add the egg mixture to the hot (not smoking) fat.
5. Use a pancake turner to stir the egg mixture occasionally. *Do not overcook.* The eggs continue to cook slightly after they are removed from the frying pan.
6. Record total working time: _____ minutes.

Variation: Replace the 2 fresh eggs with the equivalent quantity of an egg substitute; the equivalent will be shown on the package. *Do **not** add the milk shown in Step 1.* Follow the remaining directions.

Scrambled Eggs (Microwave)

Eggs	2	2
Milk	2 tablespoons	30 ml
Salt	1/8 teaspoon	0.5 ml
Butter or margarine	1 teaspoon	5 ml

1. Place butter or margarine into a 2-cup (500-ml) microwave cooking container. Microwave at *high* for 15 seconds or until fat is melted.
2. In a small bowl combine eggs, milk, and salt. Beat until egg yolks and whites are thoroughly blended but not foamy. Pour into melted fat.
3. Microwave at *high* for 30 seconds. Stir. Microwave for another 30 seconds at *high* power. Stir.
4. Microwave for another 30 seconds at *high*. At this point the eggs will appear moist and slightly creamy. They are servable as the eggs will continue to cook for a short time. However, the eggs can be cooked to a greater degree of doneness by heating at 5-second intervals. Care must be used to avoid overcooking.
5. Record total working time: _____ minutes.

CHARACTERISTICS OF HIGH-QUALITY SCRAMBLED EGGS

Appearance: Egg masses appear slightly moist and creamy; usually egg masses are large.

Consistency: Even, firm consistency throughout. All liquid is held by coagulated protein.

Tenderness: Egg masses are tender and have little resistance when cut or chewed.

Flavor: Mild egg flavor; butter flavor will enhance egg flavor.

French (or Plain) Cheese Omelet

*Eggs	2	2
Milk	2 tablespoons	30 ml
Butter or margarine	2 teaspoons	10 ml
Salt	1/4 teaspoon	1 ml
Pepper, white (if desired)	few grains	few grains
Sharp cheddar cheese, grated**	2 tablespoons	30 ml

1. Place eggs in a bowl with milk and seasonings.
2. Beat with a rotary beater until blended, but not foamy.
3. Melt butter in a 6- or 8-inch (15–20 cm) omelet pan or frying pan.
4. Add egg mixture to hot (not smoking) fat.
5. As the egg begins to coagulate around the edges of the pan, gently lift the eggs with a metal spatula to allow liquid egg to flow onto the surface of the frying pan. Do not break up the coagulated mass. Keep working uncooked portion of egg onto the omelet pan. Keep heat low enough so egg does not burn on bottom. Surface of egg will appear quite moist, although coagulated.
6. Sprinkle grated cheese over half the top of the omelet.
7. Gently fold remaining half of omelet over the cheese.
8. Ease the folded omelet onto a serving plate.
9. Record total working time: _____ minutes.

   *Variation: Replace the 2 fresh eggs with the equivalent quantity of an egg substitute; the equivalent will be shown on the package. *Do **not** add the milk shown in Step 1.* Follow the remaining directions.
   **Finely chopped, cooked ham could be substituted. A cooked vegetable such as asparagus, spinach, or broccoli could be substituted for the cheese and a cheese sauce, pages 223 and 230, could be served over the omelet. Combinations of these vegetables may also be used.

CHARACTERISTICS OF HIGH-QUALITY FRENCH OR PLAIN CHEESE OMELET

Appearance: Surface of omelet is golden brown. Omelet retains its shape.

Consistency: Surface is firm; center egg mass is slightly moist and creamy; cheese may not be completely melted.

Tenderness: Surface may show slight resistance when cut. Center portion has little resistance when cut or chewed.

Flavor: Mild egg flavor blended with distinct cheese flavor (or a distinct ham or vegetable used as a substitute).

Egg Foams

OBJECTIVES

1. To prepare selected food products based on egg white foam structure.
2. To illustrate and discuss stages of foam formation.
3. To illustrate selected factors that affect the following:
   a. Rate of foam formation
   b. Stability of egg white foams

PRODUCTS TO BE PREPARED TO ILLUSTRATE PRINCIPLES

Angel cake
Sponge cake
Demonstration of stages of foam formation
Jelly roll
Cheese souffle
Prune whip
Floating island

PRINCIPLES

1. Foam structure depends on a gas (air) to be dispersed throughout a liquid that contains a third constituent having the ability to become rigid at the gas/liquid interface (point of contact).
2. Egg white protein gives rigidity to the foam structure as a result of partial coagulation.
3. Temperature of egg white affects the amount of work necessary for foam formation.
4. Stability of egg white foam depends on
   a. Quality of eggs
   b. Degree of beating
   c. Addition of sugar
      (1) Amount added
      (2) Time of addition of sugar in relation to stage of beating
   d. Addition or presence of fat
   e. Addition of acid
      (1) Time of addition of acid in relation to stage of beating
      (2) Amount of acid added

STAGES OF FRESH EGG WHITE FOAM FORMATION

1. **Foamy**
   a. Bubbles form on the surface, but not all of the white is broken up.
   b. Foam is extremely unstable.
   c. Air cells are variable in size but are generally quite large.
   d. Mixture is still fluid.
   e. Mixture starts to become opalescent.
   Acid, cream of tartar, salt, and vanilla are added at this stage.

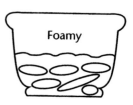

2. **Soft Peaks**
   a. Air cells are medium fine; all of the white exists as foam.
   b. Foam is fairly stable; slight drainage upon short standing.
   c. Mixture is shiny; flows readily in bowl.
   d. Mass is elastic.
   e. Soft peaks fall over to near the base of the foam as beater is lifted from foam.
   To obtain optimum volume, sugar is added gradually, but quickly, to prevent peptization of egg albumen by sugar at this stage and to reduce the possibility of overbeating.

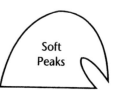

3. **Stiff Peaks**
   a. Air cells are fine, especially if acid has been added at the foamy stage; mixture is very white and opaque.
   b. Foam is quite stable (even if plain egg whites); some drainage will occur with prolonged standing.
   c. Mixture is shiny; flows slowly in bowl.
   d. Mass is still elastic.
   e. Peaks are still quite soft, but only the tip of the peak falls over as the beater is pulled from the foam.
   Egg whites for souffles and omelets are beaten to this stage. Egg whites and sugar are beaten to this stage for angel cakes and pie meringues in order to retain elasticity.

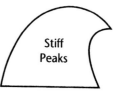

4. **Dry**
   a. Air cells are very fine; mixture is extremely white.
   b. Foam is not stable; drainage occurs rapidly on standing.
   c. Mixture is dull; it has lost its ability to flow in the bowl.
   d. Mass is brittle and inelastic; peaks remain in rigid points.
   This stage is generally to be avoided for products using fresh egg whites.
   Reconstituted, dehydrated egg whites must be beaten to this stage for all products, including commercial angel cake mixes.

Angel Cakes

Egg whites, 2	1/4 cup	60 ml
Cream of tartar	1/8 teaspoon	0.5 ml
Salt	1/8 teaspoon	0.5 ml
Sugar	1/4 cup + 1 tablespoon	75 ml
Cake flour	1/4 cup	60 ml
Vanilla	1/8 teaspoon	0.5 ml

1. Preheat oven to 350°F (175°C).
2. Sift 1 tablespoon (15 ml) of sugar with the flour.
3. Beat egg whites until foamy.
4. Add cream of tartar, salt, and vanilla. Continue beating until soft peaks form.
5. Add remaining sugar in approximately 5 portions to the beaten egg whites. Beat 6–8 revolutions of the beater after each addition of sugar. Use a hand mixer. *Do not overbeat.* The egg white–sugar mixture should have the consistency of a pie meringue with stiff peaks.
6. Add the flour mixture in 4 approximately equal portions to the egg white–sugar mixture. The flour will fold in easier if it is sifted over the top of the egg white meringue. Fold the flour into the egg whites using a metal spatula. *Do not overblend.*
*7. Use the rubber spatula to push the batter into an ungreased baking pan approximately 5 × 3 1/4 × 2 1/2 inches (12 × 8 × 6 cm).
8. Bake for 25 to 30 minutes in an oven preheated to 350°F (175°C). The top will spring back when lightly pressed with the finger.
9. Invert cake on rack to cool.
10. Record total working time: _____ minutes.

*If pans the size described are unavailable, the recipe above can be doubled and baked in a 6- or 7-inch (15- or 18-cm) tube pan. Students may find it easier to work with the larger quantities; however, baking time will be increased.

CHARACTERISTICS OF HIGH-QUALITY ANGEL CAKES

Appearance: Top crust is slightly rounded; top crust is golden brown to medium brown; surface may be rough and slightly cracked.

Texture: Air cells may vary in size from small to medium; cell walls should be fairly thin.

***Tenderness:** Crumb is tender; the crumb "melts" in the mouth—very little resistance to bite.

Flavor: Flavor is slightly sweet; vanilla and/or almond flavor may be detected. Small cakes baked and evaluated within a 2-hour period may have a distinct eggy flavor. This eggy flavor is lost as the cake stands for several hours.

*In foam cakes, tenderness is a more important characteristic than texture (size of air cells).

Sponge Cake (Make 1 1/2 times these quantities.*)

Eggs, separated	4	4
Sugar	2/3 cup	150 ml
Lemon juice	2 teaspoons	10 ml
Water	2 tablespoons	30 ml
Salt	1/4 teaspoon	1 ml
Lemon rind, grated	1/2 teaspoon	2 ml
Cake flour	2/3 cup	150 ml

1. Preheat oven to 350°F (175°C).
2. The sugar is to be divided into approximately three equal portions. One portion will be added at Step 3, one portion at Step 6, and the last portion at Step 8.
3. Sift one portion of the sugar with the cake flour and salt.
4. Combine the water and the lemon juice.
5. In a small bowl beat the egg yolks with an electric mixer until the yolks are very thick and lemon colored. Soft peaks should begin to form. Add lemon rind.
6. With continuous beating add one of the portions of sugar, about 1 teaspoon (5 ml) at a time, alternately with the lemon juice–water mixture (1 teaspoon or 5 ml at a time). After each addition of sugar or liquid, beat the egg yolks back to a light foam before further additions. Peaks will remain quite soft, but the yolk-sugar mixture should have the consistency of mayonnaise dressing.
7. Add the flour-sugar mixture a tablespoon (15 ml) at a time by folding it in with a metal spatula. *Do not overblend.*
8. Use a hand beater to beat the egg whites until soft peaks form. Gradually add the last portion of sugar about 1 teaspoon (5 ml) at a time, turning the handle of the beater 6 to 8 times after each addition. *Do not overbeat.* The egg white–sugar mixture should be beaten until stiff peaks are formed.
9. Add the egg yolk–flour mixture to the egg white meringue. Fold the two mixtures together with a metal spatula. *Do not overblend.*
10. Use the rubber spatula to push the batter into an ungreased tube pan 7 inches (18 cm) in diameter.
11. Bake for 25–30 minutes in an oven preheated to 350°F (175°C). The top crust should spring back when lightly pressed with the finger.
12. Invert cake on cake rack for cooling.
13. Record total working time: _____ minutes.

*Students may find it easier to work with these larger quantities; however, baking time will be increased.

CHARACTERISTICS OF HIGH-QUALITY SPONGE CAKES

Appearance: Top is slightly rounded; top crust is light golden brown; surface may be rough and slightly cracked.

Texture: Air cells are fairly small and uniformly distributed; cell walls are fairly thin.

***Tenderness:** Crumb is tender with slight resistance to bite.

Flavor: A delicate lemon flavor should predominate when grated lemon rind and fresh lemon juice are used. A slight egg flavor can be detected if the lemon rind and lemon juice are not used. A slightly sweet flavor is apparent.

*In foam cakes, tenderness is a more important characteristic than texture (size of air cells).

Jelly Roll

Eggs, separated	3	3
Sugar	1 cup	250 ml
Water	1/4 cup	60 ml
Vanilla	1 teaspoon	5 ml
Cake flour	1 cup	250 ml
Baking powder	1 teaspoon	5 ml
Salt	1/4 teaspoon	1 ml
Confectioner's sugar	1/2 cup	125 ml
Raspberry jam	3/4 cup	175 ml

1. Preheat oven to 375°F (190°C).
2. Sift together cake flour, baking powder, salt, and 2 tablespoons (30 ml) of the sugar.
3. Blend water and vanilla.
4. In a small bowl beat the egg yolks with an electric mixer until the yolks are very thick and lemon colored. Soft peaks should begin to form.
5. With continuous beating add about 7 tablespoons (100 ml) of remaining sugar, 1 teaspoon (5 ml) at a time, alternately with 1 teaspoon (5 ml) vanilla-water mixture. After each addition of sugar or water, beat the egg yolks back to a light foam before further additions. Peaks will remain quite soft, but the yolk-sugar mixture should have the consistency of mayonnaise dressing.
6. Sift one-fourth of the flour mixture over the egg yolk mixture. Fold in with approximately 15 strokes using a metal spatula.
7. Repeat Step 6 until all of the flour has been added.
8. Beat egg whites until soft peaks form.
9. With continuous beating add last of sugar, approximately 7 tablespoons (100 ml), gradually but quickly to the beaten egg whites. Beat until stiff peaks are formed. *Do not overbeat egg whites after the addition of the sugar.*
10. Pour the egg yolk–flour mixture over the beaten egg white–sugar mixture. Fold the two mixtures together lightly until ingredients are just blended.
11. Grease a 15 1/2 × 10 1/2 inch (39 × 26 cm) jelly roll pan (bottom only). Line the bottom with brown paper. Grease the brown paper.
12. Pour the batter into the prepared baking pan. Bake in a 375°F (190°C) oven for 12–15 minutes or until the top springs back when lightly touched.
13. Sift confectioner's sugar on a clean towel the dimensions of the baking pan.
14. As soon as the cake is removed from the oven, loosen edges, then turn cake out onto the confectioner's sugar. Carefully remove the paper. Trim 1/2 inch (1.5 cm) off all four sides. Use serrated cake knife with a sawing motion.
15. While the cake is still hot, starting at the narrow end, roll cake and towel together. The towel should hold the cake in position until the cake has cooled.
16. When the cake is cold, carefully open up the towel and unroll the cake. If the cake is warm when the filling is added, the filling will soak into the cake.
17. Carefully spread the cake with filling (red raspberry jam). *Do not* spread filling on the last inch (2.5 cm) of the narrow end of the cake toward which the cake will be rolled. The jam tends to spread out as the cake is rolled, so filling will fill this area. Be sure the filling is at the edges of the cake on the long sides of the cake. The filling should be soft, easily spreadable, but not wet or syrupy.
18. Carefully reroll the cake. Cut into 1-inch (2.5-cm) slices for serving.
19. Record total working time: _____ minutes.

CHARACTERISTICS OF HIGH-QUALITY JELLY ROLLS

Appearance: Cake evenly browned; crumb lemon yellow (depending on color of egg yolk); any frosting or covering evenly distributed; filling even.

Texture: Air cells small (slightly larger than sponge cake), evenly distributed; cell walls fairly thin.

Tenderness: Crumb tender, slightly resilient to bite (a bit elastic—not "short").

Flavor: Cake—sweet and slightly eggy. Filling—evenly balanced; typical of the food product used.

Cheese Souffle

Flour, all-purpose	2 tablespoons	30 ml
Salt	1/4 teaspoon	1 ml
Milk	2/3 cup	150 ml
Margarine	1 tablespoon	15 ml
Cheddar cheese, shredded	3/4 cup	175 ml
Cayenne pepper	few grains	few grains
Eggs, separated	2	2

1. Preheat oven to 350°F (175°C).
2. Blend the flour, salt, and cayenne pepper together in a saucepan. Add the cold milk gradually and stir until the flour is evenly dispersed.
3. Place on heat and bring quickly to a boil with constant stirring. Boil 1 minute, until the sauce is thick. Remove from heat.
4. Add the butter and shredded cheese to the hot sauce. Stir until the cheese has melted. (This mixture should appear well blended.)
5. Add the unbeaten egg yolks to the sauce. Stir until eggs are well blended.
6. Beat the egg whites until they begin to form stiff peaks—the peaks should still bend *slightly.* Have the egg whites in a bowl large enough to add the sauce mixture.
7. Add the sauce mixture to the egg whites. Fold with a metal spatula until all ingredients are blended. *Fold lightly. Do not overblend.*
*8. Lightly butter the *bottom* of a small (1-quart or 1-L) baking dish. Pour in souffle mixture. Set the dish in a pan of warm water—the water should be the same depth as the amount of souffle in its baking dish.
9. Place in a 350°F (175°C) oven and bake until a knife inserted in the center comes out "clean."†
10. Record total working time: _____ minutes.

*For class, bake these products in individual glass baking dishes (lightly butter the *bottom* of 4 or 5 of the smallest size glass baking dishes). Bake in pans of water as indicated above.

†Approximate baking times: small cups, 30–35 minutes; quart baking dish, 50 minutes.

CHARACTERISTICS OF HIGH-QUALITY CHEESE SOUFFLES

Appearance: Dark golden brown top crust; top is generally uneven.

Texture: Even distribution of medium-small gas cells; medium thick to fine cell walls; mixture is homogeneous.

Tenderness: Very little resistance when cut; "melts" in the mouth.

Flavor: Mild cheese.

Baked Prune Whip

*Prune pulp	1/2 cup	125 ml
Sugar	3 tablespoons	45 ml
Salt	1/8 teaspoon	0.5 ml
Lemon juice	2 teaspoons	10 ml
Egg whites	2	2

1. Preheat oven to 350°F (175°C).
2. Stewed prunes should be drained and pitted. The pulp should be rather dry. Cut the pulp into several pieces for each prune. Place in a bowl large enough for all ingredients after beating.
3. Add the egg whites, salt, and lemon juice. Beat with an electric mixer until stiff peaks are formed.
4. Add the sugar gradually with continued beating.
**5. Pile lightly into a baking dish (butter the bottom only). Set dish in pan of warm water.
6. Bake in a 350°F (175°C) oven for 45 minutes or until the center is firm to the touch when pressed lightly with the forefinger.
7. Prune whip may be served with soft (stirred) custard (page 152).
8. Record total working time: _____ minutes.

*Apricots could be stewed and used in place of prunes.
**For class, bake these products in individual glass baking dishes (lightly butter the bottom of 4 or 5 small glass baking dishes). Bake in pans of water as indicated above.

CHARACTERISTICS OF HIGH-QUALITY BAKED PRUNE WHIP

Appearance: Dark golden brown to light brown top crust; top is generally uneven with some peaks.

Texture: Even distribution of medium–small gas cells; medium thick to thin cell walls; pieces of prune pulp may be evident.

Tenderness: Top crust may be slightly tough to cut through; interior is tender; little resistance to cutting or chewing.

Flavor: Mild prune with possible suggestion of lemon flavor; slightly sweet.

Floating Island

Meringue:*

Egg whites	2	2
Sugar, finely granulated	1/4 cup	60 ml
Vanilla	1/4 teaspoon	1 ml

1. Preheat oven to 350°F (175°C).
2. Place egg whites into small bowl. Add vanilla. Beat with rotary beater until the whites will form soft peaks as the beater is pulled from the foam.
3. Add the sugar gradually, beating only enough after each addition to blend sugar with foam. At the end of the beating period, the egg whites should form fairly stiff peaks that bend over slightly at the tips.
4. Place 1/2 inch (1.5 cm) of hot water in a 9 × 13 inch (22 × 32 cm) pan.
5. Place the meringue on the hot water using a teaspoon to form 10 "islands."
6. Bake in a 350°F (175°C) oven until the meringue is set and the tips are golden brown— approximately 20 minutes.
7. Use a slotted pancake turner to remove "islands" from the hot water onto a plate for cooling.
8. Place cooled "islands" on cooled soft custard for serving.
9. Record total working time: _____ minutes.

   *This recipe may be used for the meringue on cream pies. Stop after Step 3. Spread meringue on cooled pie filling. Brown meringue in 350°F (175°C) oven for 15–20 minutes.

Custard†:

Milk	1 1/2 cups	375 ml
Egg yolks	2	2
Egg, whole	1	1
Sugar	1/4 cup	60 ml
Vanilla	1/2 teaspoon	2 ml

Prepare a stirred custard from the custard ingredients (page 152).

   †The color of the custard will be more yellow and the consistency will be softer when egg yolks are used.

CHARACTERISTICS OF HIGH-QUALITY FLOATING ISLANDS

Stirred Custard

See page 153.

Meringue

   Appearance: Top is golden brown with peaks slightly darker; top surface is uneven.

   Texture: Even distribution of small gas cells; cell walls are thin.

   Tenderness: Top crust may be slightly tough to cut through; interior is easily cut with a knife and leaves a clean-cut edge.

   Flavor: Mild, sweet.

REVIEW QUESTIONS

1. a. List the factors upon which eggs are graded for quality.
   b. Describe the characteristics of a high-quality raw egg when it is broken out on a plate.
2. a. Describe the characteristics of the egg white and egg yolk from the egg frozen in the shell.
   b. Explain what happens to the constituents of the yolk and white to account for your observations.
3. Define and/or identify each of the following terms:
   a. Semipermeable membrane
   b. Air cell
   c. Vitelline membrane
   d. Chalazae
   e. Curdling
   f. Syneresis
   g. Ferrous sulfide
4. Write the recipe for a basic custard mix.
5. How would each of the following changes affect the coagulation temperatures of a custard? Explain your answer.
   a. Increase the amount of sugar in the recipe.
   b. Substitute two egg yolks for one whole egg.
   c. Increase the amount of milk in the recipe.
6. a. Describe the changes in state (physical changes) of a stirred custard as it is heated.
   b. Differentiate between rate of heating and coagulation temperature.
   c. How will the rate of heating affect the coagulation temperature in making a stirred custard?
7. Why are baked custards, souffles, and whips baked with the container placed in a pan of water?
8. Why does a beaten whole egg give less volume than the egg white alone?
9. Formation of egg white foams
   a. List the four stages of beating a fresh egg white foam.
   b. At what stage is cream of tartar added? Why?
   c. At what stage is sugar added? Why?
10. Foam-type cakes
    a. What is the leavening agent in cakes of this type?
    b. What are the structural ingredients?
    c. How does the term *extensible protein* apply to these cakes?
    d. How does the temperature of the egg white affect foam formation?
    e. What are the functions of cream of tartar in the angel cake recipe?
    f. Why are foam cakes cooled in the inverted position?
    g. How is it possible to overdevelop gluten in preparing an angel cake?
11. Why should foams be beaten only at the time they are to be used?

12. One student evaluated his products as shown in the following evaluation table. Explain the treatment each product received to account for this student's evaluations.

Quality Characteristic	Fried Egg	Angel Cake	Stirred Custard	Hard-Cooked Eggs
Appearance	3 Dark brown around edges	4 Slightly dark	5	3 Raw in center
Consistency or Texture	3 White is lacy; yolk O.K.	2 Many large air cells; cell walls thick	2 Like milk	3 Center of yolk not coagulated
Tenderness	3 White tough; yolk O.K.	2 Tough	—	3 Too tender
Flavor	4 Slightly burned	4 Sweet; sugary	4 Eggy	4 Raw
Overall Eating Quality	3	2	2	3

Starch-Egg Combinations

OBJECTIVES

1. To combine selected principles of starch cookery with selected principles of egg protein cookery in the preparation of a food product.
2. To review principles of starch cookery.
3. To review principles of egg protein cookery.
4. To relate temperature of coagulation of egg protein to temperature of maximum gelatinization of starch in preparation of a pudding or cream pie filling.

PRODUCTS TO BE PREPARED TO ILLUSTRATE PRINCIPLES

Creamy tapioca pudding
Lemon pudding or pie filling
Creamy cornstarch pudding or pie filling
Fruit salad dressing (see page 279)

PRINCIPLES

1. Starch granules are separated by dry ingredients and cold liquid for even gelatinization.
2. Starch mixtures are stirred constantly during cooking for even gelatinization of starch granules.
3. Starch mixtures are heated to boiling temperature to obtain maximum gelatinization.
4. Gelatinized starch may be hydrolyzed when boiled with acid, resulting in loss of thickening properties.
5. Temperature of coagulation of egg protein may be 27–45°F (15–25°C) lower than temperature for maximum gelatinization of starch.
6. Egg protein acts as a thickening agent.
7. Egg protein may be peptized when boiled with acid.

Lemon Pudding

Water	1 cup	250 ml
Sugar	1 cup	250 ml
Cornstarch	3 tablespoons	45 ml
Salt	1/8 teaspoon	0.5 ml
Egg yolk	1	1
Margarine or butter	1 tablespoon	15 ml
Lemon juice	3 tablespoons	45 ml
Lemon rind, grated	1 teaspoon	5 ml

1. Set out 4 small custard cups or one 6-inch (15-cm) baked pie shell.
2. Combine approximately 3/4 of both water and sugar in a 1–1 1/2 quart (1–1.5 L) saucepan.
3. Add grated lemon rind.
4. Bring mixture to a boil. Boil 1 minute. Stir until sugar is dissolved.
5. Blend cornstarch and salt with remaining sugar. Add remaining water. Blend.
6. Blend 1 tablespoon (15 ml) of the hot water-sugar mixture with the cornstarch-sugar mixture. Repeat 2 times.
7. Add all of starch mixture to remaining hot water mixture. Blend.
8. Place over heat and bring to boil. Boil 1 minute, stirring constantly. Remove from heat.
9. Place egg yolk in a pint (500 ml) bowl. Stir with fork until blended.
10. Add approximately 1 tablespoon (15 ml) hot starch paste to egg yolk. Blend thoroughly. Repeat 2 times.
11. Add egg mixture to remaining starch mixture. Blend thoroughly. Observe shiny quality due to raw egg.
12. Carefully heat egg-starch mixture over medium heat for 3 to 4 minutes with constant stirring. *This mixture must not boil.* When egg has coagulated the mixture will not be as shiny as at Step 11. Stir in the lemon juice and margarine and continue stirring until mixture is smooth.
13. Pour into serving dishes.
14. This recipe serves 4 as a pudding or will make filling for one 6-inch (15-cm) pie.
15. Record total working time: _____minutes.

Lemon Meringue or Cream Pie

1 6-inch (15-cm) baked pastry shell	Page 100
1 Recipe Lemon or Creamy Cornstarch Pudding	Pages 170 or 171
1/2 Recipe Meringue	Page 166

1. Pour cooled filling into a cold, baked pastry shell.
2. Spread meringue to completely cover filling and touch edge of pastry.
3. Bake in a 350°F (175°C) oven for 20–30 minutes or until meringue is golden.

Pie should be evaluated on High-Quality Characteristics for Pastry Shell (page 101), Starch-Egg Products (page 172), and Meringues (page 167), as well as for its Overall Eating Quality.

Creamy Cornstarch Pudding

Milk	1 cup	250 ml
Sugar	1/4 cup	60 ml
Salt	1/8 teaspoon	0.5 ml
Cornstarch	1 1/2–2 tablespoons	23–30 ml
Egg yolk	1	1
Margarine or butter	1 tablespoon	15 ml
Vanilla	1/2 teaspoon	2 ml

1. Set out two small custard cups or one 6-inch (15-cm) baked pie shell.
2. Blend cornstarch, sugar, and salt in a 1 or 1 1/2 quart (1–1.5 L) saucepan.
3. Add milk in portions. Stir after each addition until mixture is free of lumps.
4. Place saucepan over medium heat and stir constantly. Bring to a boil and boil 1 minute. Remove from heat.
5. Place egg yolk in a 2 or 3 cup (500–750 ml) bowl. Blend with a fork.
6. Add 1 tablespoon (15 ml) hot starch mixture to egg yolk. Blend thoroughly. Repeat 3 more times.
7. Pour egg-starch mixture into remaining starch paste. Blend thoroughly. Observe shiny appearance due to raw egg.
8. Place saucepan over medium heat. Stir constantly and heat egg-starch mixture for 3 to 4 minutes or until mixture loses its glossy appearance. *Do not let mixture boil.* Stir in butter or margarine and vanilla. Stir until mixture is well blended.
9. Pour into serving dishes.
10. Recipe yields 2 servings of pudding or filling for one 6-inch (15-cm) pie.
11. Record total working time: _____minutes.

Variations

1. **Coconut Cream:** Gently fold in 2 tablespoons (30 ml) flaked or finely chopped coconut before serving.
2. **Banana Cream:** Use 1/2 of cooled pudding for bottom layer. Slice 1/4 ripe banana onto pudding in each serving dish or 1/2 banana over layer of pudding in baked pastry crust. Top with remaining cooled pudding.
3. **Pineapple Cream:** Gently fold in 1/4 cup (60 ml) thoroughly drained crushed pineapple before serving.
4. **Nut or Date Cream:** Gently fold in 2 tablespoons (30 ml) chopped nuts or chopped dates before serving.

Cream Pie

(See page 170).

Creamy Tapioca Pudding

Milk	1 cup	250 ml
Tapioca	1 1/2 tablespoons	25 ml
Sugar	2 1/2 tablespoons	40 ml
Salt	few grains	few grains
Egg, separated	1	1
Vanilla	1/2 teaspoon	2 ml

1. Set out three small custard cups.
2. Combine milk, tapioca, sugar, and salt in a 1–1 1/2 quart (1–1.5 L) saucepan. Allow the mixture to stand at least 5 minutes.
3. In a 2–3 cup (500–700 ml) bowl, beat whole egg until foamy.
4. Place saucepan over medium heat. Bring the mixture to a boil with constant stirring. Remove from heat.
5. Gradually add the hot tapioca mixture to the beaten egg. Return to heat and bring to boiling with constant, slow stirring. Remove pan from heat immediately. Add the vanilla.
6. Pour into serving dishes and allow to cool.
7. Record total working time: _____minutes.

CHARACTERISTICS OF HIGH-QUALITY STARCH-EGG PRODUCTS

Appearance: Puddings or cooked fruit salad dressing have a shiny surface. Film forms on top as cooked mixture cools.

Consistency: Puddings will "mound" on serving spoon or, as a pie filling, be firm enough to retain a firm, clear-cut edge. Smooth.

Flavor:
   Creamy Cornstarch Pudding: Sweet with *slight* vanilla flavor.
   Creamy Tapioca Pudding: Sweet with *slight* egg and *slight* vanilla flavor.
   Lemon Pudding: Tart lemon.
   Fruit Salad Dressing: Well balanced fruit flavor; tart.

*See page 279 for Fruit Salad Dressing recipe.

REVIEW QUESTIONS

1. What special considerations arise when starch and egg are to be combined in a single food product?
2. Discuss the need for close temperature control in preparing the fruit salad dressing.
3. What variations could be made starting with cream pudding?
4. Discuss the role of acid in starch-egg cookery.

Meat and Poultry (Tender Cuts): Dry Heat Methods

OBJECTIVES

1. To illustrate dry heat methods of cooking tender cuts of meat and poultry.
2. To discuss and illustrate factors that determine the tenderness of a cut of meat or poultry before cooking.
3. To discuss the effect of cooking on the quality characteristics of the cooked meat or poultry.
4. To discuss characteristic differences in fat, bone, muscle color, and texture in meat cuts from different animals.
5. To acquaint students with selected variety cuts included as tender cuts of meat.
6. To acquaint students with poultry classified as *tender* and to discuss typical quality characteristics of tender birds.

PRODUCTS TO BE PREPARED TO ILLUSTRATE PRINCIPLES

Hamburger patties (pan-broiled and microwave)
Liver (baby beef or calf)
Chicken breasts (fried and oven-baked)
Bacon (pan-broiled and microwave)
Pork chop suey
Pork chop (broiled)

PRINCIPLES

1. Tender cuts of meat contain small amounts of collagenous connective tissue as a result of less exercise of the muscle area. In poultry, age of the bird is also a factor.
2. The degree of hydrolysis of collagen depends on the cooking time and temperature.
3. Muscle fiber protein becomes tough with extended application of heat.
4. Some less tender muscles are tenderized by mechanical treatment of grinding. Such ground meat can then be considered and used as a "tender" cut.
5. Bone structure of a young animal or bird
   a. Porous since calcification is not completed.
   b. Reddish: blood cells carry nutrients into the bone structure and are trapped in the bone at the time of slaughter.
   c. In poultry the degree of calcification of the keel bone is an indication of the age of the bird.

6. Age of the animal or bird influences the
    a.   Amount of fat deposited
    b.   Color of the fat
    c.   Firmness of the fat
7. Firmness of the fat is related to the chemical composition (fatty acids) of the fat as determi
    by
    a.   Inherent animal characteristics
    b.   Diet of the animal
8. Flavor of muscle fiber protein of both animals and birds is influenced by
    a.   Age
    b.   Amount of exercise of muscle
    c.   Degree of marbling
    d.   Feed
9. Diameter of the muscle fiber and the size and number of muscle fibers forming the fascicul
    determine the texture of meat.
10. Color of muscle fiber protein is an inherent characteristic of the species of animal or fish, t
    color will also relate to the amount of exercise of the specific muscle. This condition is esp(
    noticeable in poultry.
11. Advanced breeding and production techniques for pigs have resulted in a more tender mea
    mitting dry heat cookery methods to be used for certain selected cuts.
12. Poultry must be well cooked in order to kill any salmonella bacteria which may be present.

DIRECTIONS FOR DRY HEAT METHODS

Broiling

Meat is directly exposed to the source of heat.
1. If pieces of meat are very lean, the broiler rack should be lightly greased to make it easier tc
    clean.
2. Place cuts of meat on the broiler rack.
3. Place rack under the broiler so the cut surface of the meat is approximately 4 inches (10 cm
    from the source of heat. Distance from the source of heat depends on the thickness of the (
    thicker cuts are placed farther away.
4. Cook the meat for approximately half of the total cooking time before turning. The total cc
    time will depend on
    a.   Thickness of the cut
    b.   Degree of coagulation desired—rare, medium, or well done for beef. Most other cuts are
         cooked well done.
5. Salt meat lightly. Serve on a well-heated plate or platter.

Pan Broiling

Heavy metal of frying pan transfers heat to meat.
1. Lightly grease a heavy frying pan. Heat, but do not allow the fat to smoke.
2. Meat may be browned by cooking at a higher temperature for about 2 minutes on each side
    the piece of meat. Heat may then be reduced until meat has reached desired stage of donen
    See Step 4 in directions for broiling.
3. Fat should be removed from the frying pan as it accumulates. Put these drippings in a smal
    custard cup.
4. Salt the meat lightly (exception—ham slices and sausage). Serve on a well-heated plate or p

Pan Frying

Heavy metal of frying pan transfers heat to meat and to a thin layer of fat in the frying pan.

1. Pan frying differs from pan broiling primarily in the amount of fat used in the frying pan. For pan broiling all excess fat is removed during the cooking period. For pan frying a small amount of fat is kept in the frying pan during the entire cooking period.
2. Where cuts of meat have been coated with flour, as in the case with some chicken and fish cuts, pan frying is more practical than pan broiling, so the coating does not stick to the frying pan.

Stir Frying (Flash Cooking)

Wok or frying pan transfers heat to a small quantity of oil and to the food (meat and/or vegetables).

1. More fat is used here than in pan frying; vegetable oil is traditionally used.
2. All food must be cleaned and cut into proper shape before the cooking is started. All pieces are small or thinly sliced in order to cook quickly.

Deep-Fat Frying

Heat is transferred to the meat through the medium of heated fat or oil. Relatively large amounts of fat or oil are used. The food product may be breaded before frying.

Roasting (Baking)

Meat is in an *uncovered* pan; meat is heated by heated air.

1. Meat is placed on a rack in the baking pan with the fat side up.
2. A meat thermometer will give the most accurate means of determining degree of "doneness" for the cooked piece of meat. The bulb of the meat thermometer should be inserted in the center of the largest muscle of the roast.

PREPARATION OF FRESH MEAT AND POULTRY FOR COOKING

Steaks, Chops, and Roasts

1. Small pieces of bone may adhere to the cut surface of the meat. Gently scrape the cut surface with a knife to remove the loose pieces of bone. Wipe each piece of meat with a damp cloth.
2. Steaks and chops usually have a layer of fat on the exterior side. Cut through this fat layer to the muscle, but *do not cut into the muscle*. Make these cuts about 1 inch apart. This is termed *scoring* the cut. Scoring is done to reduce curling of the cut during cooking.
3. *Do not salt* the meat before cooking because salt draws juices from the muscle fibers through the process of osmosis.

Poultry

1. Trim off inedible portions from either the skin side or the interior wall.
2. Wash entire piece under cold, running tap water.
3. Dry each piece of chicken with paper toweling before cooking.

Pan-Broiled Ground Beef Patties

| *Ground beef or hamburger | 4 ounces | 120 g |
| Shortening | 1/2–1 teaspoon | 2–5 ml |

1. Shape the ground meat into one patty 3/4–1 inch (2–2.5 cm) thick.
2. Melt the shortening in a heavy frying pan. Use only enough fat to prevent sticking. The fat should be hot but not smoking.
3. Place the patty on the greased portion of the fry pan. Cook the patty 4 to 5 minutes on each side depending on thickness of the patty.
4. If hamburger is used and is quite fat, remove excess fat from frying pan as the patty cooks. Fat should not be allowed to accumulate in the frying pan.
5. The patty can be turned more than once during cooking. However, *do not* press patty against dry pan with spatula or turner—this presses juices out of the patty, resulting in a dry product.
6. Ground beef patties should be cooked to the well-done stage.
7. The ground beef patties will be evaluated without added salt and pepper. However, in the normal preparation, seasonings would be added at this time.
8. Record total working time: _____minutes.

*Ground beef or hamburger with textured vegetable protein may be used here.

Ground Beef Patty (Microwave)

| Ground beef | 4 ounces | 120 g |
| Liquid margarine | 1 teaspoon | 5 ml |

1. Preheat browning grill for 8 minutes at *high* power in the microwave oven. Do not heat longer than 8 minutes.
*2. While grill is heating, shape meat into a patty 3/8–1/2 inch (1 cm–1.3 cm) thick. Add about half the fat to the surface of patty being browned.
3. Place patty on heated grill. turn patty when it appears well browned (about 2 minutes); add remaining fat. Brown patty on second side. Time for browing depends on the temperature of the meat as well as the number of patties being cooked at one time.
4. Microwave at *high* power to complete cooking, approximately 30 seconds for 1 patty.
5. Record total working time: _____minutes.
6. Refer to pages 178–179 for characteristics of high-quality cooked meat.**

*If no browning grill is available, microwave at *high* power for 1 1/2 minutes on each side for 1 patty.

**Patty not cooked on heated browning grill will have characteristics of steamed meat.

Pan-Broiled Liver

Baby beef or calf liver	4 to 5 ounces	120 to 150 g
*Shortening	1 teaspoon	5 ml
Flour	2 tablespoons	30 ml
Salt	1/4 teaspoon	1 ml
Pepper	few grains	few grains

1. Prepare bacon or onion first if either is to be served with the liver.
2. Remove any outer membrane that may be on the slice of liver. Snip out veins with scissors.
3. Blend salt and pepper with flour. Have the flour mixture on a piece of waxed paper or on a flat plate.
4. Dip the liver in the flour mixture. Coat liver on each side. Do not have an excess of flour clinging to the meat.
5. Melt fat in heavy frying pan. Have fat hot but not smoking.
6. Brown liver on each side.
7. *Do not overcook.* A total of 5 minutes cooking time may be enough.
8. Liver should be cooked only long enough to bring about a color change in the interior of the meat.
9. Record total working time: _____minutes.

*Fat may be derived by frying one slice of bacon in the frying pan in which the liver is to be cooked.

Sautéed Onions (Can be included in Vegetable Cookery, page 228. Make 3 times recipe.)

Onion, thin slices	2 or 3	2 or 3
Shortening, margarine, or butter for flavor	1 tablespoon	15 ml

1. Place shortening in a heavy frying pan. Heat until fat is melted.
2. Add onion slices. Heat slowly until the onion is tender (approximately 10 minutes).
3. Remove onion to plate. Add more fat if necessary to pan broil liver.
4. Record total working time: _____ minutes.

Fried Chicken Breasts

Whole chicken breasts	2	2
Margarine or butter	1 tablespoon	15 ml
Flour	1/4 cup	60 ml
Salt	1/2 teaspoon	2 ml
Pepper (optional)	few grains	few grains

1. Trim and clean chicken breasts as necessary. Rinse in clear water. Drain on paper towels. Cut each breast in half to give 4 pieces. Bone if desired.
2. Blend flour with seasonings on flat dinner plate, on waxed paper, or in a paper bag.
3. Coat each piece of chicken with the seasoned flour. Lightly shake off excess flour.
4. Melt fat in a heavy frying pan. Heat electric frying pan to 350°F (175°C). Fat should be hot but not smoking as the pieces of chicken are added.
5. Brown each piece of chicken. Fat should never be so hot as to smoke.
6. Reduce heat and continue to cook in fat for approximately 25 minutes or more, depending on thickness of the chicken breasts. Fillets cook in a shorter time.
7. Record total working time: _____ minutes.

Oven-Baked Chicken Breasts

Whole chicken breasts	2	2
Margarine or butter	1 tablespoon	15 ml
Flour	1/4 cup	60 ml
Salt	1/2 teaspoon	2 ml
Pepper (optional)	few grains	few grains

1. Preheat oven to 425°F (200°C).
2. Trim chicken breasts as necessary. Wash in clear water. Dry with paper towels. Cut each breast in half to give 4 pieces. Bone if desired.
3. Blend flour with seasonings.
4. Melt butter in pan in which the chicken is to be baked. Dip each piece of chicken in the melted fat. Arrange in the baking pan with the skin side up. Carefully dredge (dust) each piece of chicken with the flour mixture.
5. Bake uncovered in an oven preheated to 425°F (200°C) for 45–60 minutes. Baste with the fat in the pan twice during the baking period. Do this quickly. Do not allow oven to cool off while basting. Fillets will bake in a shorter time.
6. Record total working time: _____ minutes.

CHARACTERISTICS OF HIGH-QUALITY MEAT AND POULTRY

Appearance: All cooked meat is opaque and moist. Color of cooked meat—*Outside:* rich brown; *Interior:* beef, from deep red or pink (rare meat) through a light pink (medium) to a light gray or brown (well done); pork, from almost white to light gray with certain muscles being light brown; veal, predominately light gray. Color of cooked poultry varies from a creamy white in light meat to a light to medium brown in dark meat.

Texture: Determined by the diameter of the muscle fibers and the diameter of the fasciculi; cuts having fibers and fasciculi of small diameter are fine grained, while cuts having fibers and fasciculi of large diameter are coarse grained (see Texture of Meat in next section).

Tenderness: Some resistance to chewing, but sample should be easily masticated.

Juiciness: Free-flowing juice in cuts cooked to rare stage changing to noticeable moistness in cuts cooked to the well-done stage.

Flavor: Typical for cut of meat; meat flavor characteristic of breed should predominate.

TEXTURE OF MEAT

Fine-grain meat: Cuts from rib and loin of beef, pork, and lamb; veal; white meat of broilers.

Medium-fine-grain meat: Top round steak; ham.

Medium-coarse-grain meat: Bottom round steak; blade and arm steaks of beef; dark meat of poultry.

Coarse-grain meat: Flank steak; stewing hen; duck.

Note: Ground meat is usually coarse. Texture of ground meat is determined by the diameter of the holes in the grinder plate and the number of times the meat is put through the grinder rather than by the diameter of the fibers and fasciculi.

Pan-Broiled Bacon

*Bacon—2 slices

1. Place bacon strip in *cold* frying pan. Heat pan slowly so the bacon will not curl. Broil until crisp but not brittle. Turn as needed during the cooking period.
2. Remove bacon to paper towel to drain off excess fat.
3. Use bacon dripping for pan broiling liver.
4. Record total working time: _____ minutes.

*Substitute turkey bacon (optional).

Bacon (Microwave)

Bacon, sliced   1 or 2 slices

1. If bacon fat is to be used at a later time, place bacon slices on a trivet or on the bottom of a microwave dish.
2. If bacon fat is not to be saved, place bacon strips on a double layer of paper toweling placed on a ceramic plate suitable for microwave cooking.
3. In either Step 1 or Step 2 lay a piece of paper toweling on top of the bacon to avoid spattering as the bacon cooks.
4. Microwave at *high* power for 3/4–1 minute for each slice of bacon.
5. Total cooking time: _____ minutes.

CHARACTERISTICS OF HIGH-QUALITY BACON

Appearance: Slices lie flat on plate; are evenly browned.

Tenderness: Crisp-tender when bitten.

Flavor: Slightly salty; slightly sweet; slightly smoky.

Stir-Fry Pork Chop Suey

Oil	2 tablespoons	30 ml
Pork, fresh	1/4–1 cup	60–250 ml
Chinese cabbage, shredded	1/2 cup	125 ml
*Celery, 1/2 inch rounds	1/4 cup	60 ml
*Green pepper, shredded	1	1
*Green onions, minced	3	3
Bean sprouts, rinsed	1/2 cup	125 ml
Beef (or chicken) stock	1 cup	250 ml
Salt (optional)	1/2 teaspoon	2 ml
Soy sauce	2 tablespoons	30 ml
Cornstarch	1 tablespoon	15 ml
Water, cold	3 tablespoons	45 ml

  1. Clean the pork in the prescribed manner (see page 175). Cut the pork into thin, narrow strips (1/8" x 3/8" x 2")(0.3 cm x 1 cm x 5 cm).

  2. Mix the cornstarch and water.

  3. Clean all the vegetables in the prescribed manner.

**4. Set the ingredients by the wok in the order listed. Do not start to cook until all of the ingredients have been prepared and set in place.

  5. Set the wok thermostat on high (400°F), add the oil, and heat to temperature.

  6. Add the sliced pork and stir-fry for 45 seconds.

  7. Add the cabbage, celery, and green peppers. Stir-fry for 1 minute.

  8. Add the green onions and bean sprouts. Stir-fry for 3 minutes.

  9. Push all of the ingredients up on the sides of the wok.

10. Slowly pour the beef (or chicken) stock into the center of the wok. Add the soy sauce and the cornstarch mixture. With continuous stirring, cook until the starch gelatinizes and becomes clear.

11. Mix thoroughly with the cooked vegetables. Serve immediately in a heated dish.

12. Record total working time: _____ minutes.

*Cleaning vegetables: Scrub with vegetable brush and cold water. Trim as necessary.

**Note: This recipe may be stir-fried in an electric fry pan (Teflon ® coated if a wok is not available). Rice may be served with this recipe; see page 130.

Pork Chops, Broiled

Pork loin chops, cut 1 inch thick	2
Nonstick pan spray	As required
Salt and pepper	To taste

1. Trim excess fat and prepare pork chops for cooking.
2. Preheat the pork chops in the microwave oven by cooking for 2 minutes on each side at full power. Prepare the broiler pan by spraying both the rack and the inside of the pan with the nonstick spray.
3. Insert the oven rack so it is 6 inches (15 cm) below the broiler unit. The top of the pan should be 4–5 inches (10–13 cm) below the broiler unit. Set the oven controls to "broil."
4. Place the pork chops in the center of the rack and place the rack under the broiler unit.
5. Broil until the chops are golden brown on the outside, about 8–10 minutes. Turn the chops over and broil the second side until golden brown, about 6–8 minutes. *Do not overcook.*
6. Remove the broiler tray from the oven and cover with foil. Hold for 5 minutes to finish the cooking.
7. Remove the chops to a heated platter, garnish, and serve.
8. Record the total preparation time: _____ minutes.
   Note: At Steps 4 and 5, 1/2 teaspoon of solid or liquid margarine may be added to the top of each pork chop to help retain moisture.

Name: _____

Date: _____

EVALUATION OF PRODUCTS
(MEAT)

Score System

Points	Quality
7	Excellent
6	Very good
5	Good
4	Medium
3	Fair
2	Poor
1	Very poor

Directions:
1. Place the numerical score in the box in the upper left-hand corner.
2. Comments should justify the numerical score. Comments must be brief.
3. Evaluation of the food products must be on an *individual* basis.

Products

Quality Characteristic					
Outside Appearance					
Interior Appearance					
Tenderness					
Juiciness					
Flavor					

Meat and Poultry (Less-Tender Cuts): Moist Heat Methods

OBJECTIVES

1. To illustrate moist heat methods of cooking less-tender cuts of meat.
2. To review the factors that cause a cut of meat to be considered "less tender."
3. To illustrate that collagenous tissue will hydrolyze in the presence of heat and moisture.
4. To illustrate principles applied in the breading of a meat, fish, or poultry product.
5. To illustrate the effectiveness of the mechanical treatment of pounding to break down collagenous connective tissue.
6. To acquaint students with selected variety meats considered less-tender meats.
7. To acquaint students with the principles and the use of the pressure saucepan.

PRODUCTS TO BE PREPARED TO ILLUSTRATE PRINCIPLES

Swiss steak
Braised pork chop
Braised chicken thighs

Spiced tongue
Veal rosemary (optional)
Lamb stew (optional)

PRINCIPLES

1. Hydrolysis of collagen is a function of
   a. Temperature—time
   b. Pressure
   c. Addition of acid
2. Both collagen and elastin can be broken down by mechanical means to increase the tenderness of the cut of meat.
   a. Pounding or "Swissing"
   b. Grinding
3. Excessive heat toughens muscle fiber protein.
4. Cooking losses increase with an increase in temperature and pressure.
5. Breading may be used as a means of retaining moisture.

Chicken Thighs*

(Use pressure cooker)

Chicken thighs	3 or 4	3 or 4
Flour	1/4 cup	60 ml
Salt	1/2 teaspoon	2 ml
Pepper (optional)	few grains	few grains
Margarine or butter	2 tablespoons	30 ml

  1. Trim and clean chicken thighs as necessary. Rinse in clear water. Drain and dry with paper toweling.
  2. Blend together the flour, salt, and pepper. Place on a flat plate, on waxed paper, or in a paper bag.
  3. Coat the chicken thighs with flour. Lightly shake off excess flour.
  *4. Melt fat in a *pressure saucepan*. Fat should not be so hot that it separates or smokes.
  5. Add the floured chicken thighs. Brown to deep golden brown on both sides.
  6. Remove thighs from pressure saucepan. Insert rack and place thighs on rack.
  7. Add 1 cup (250 ml) of water or enough water to have water the depth of the rack. Pieces of chicken should not lie in water.
  8. Position cover on pressure saucepan. Heat until steam flows in a steady stream through lid vent for 2 minutes.
  9. Position pressure gauge on vent. Count cooking time from the time the gauge registers 10 pounds pressure. Regulate heat controls to keep pressure constant for the 15-minute cooking period.
  10. Place the pressure saucepan under cold running water for 2 minutes. *Do not let water run over the pressure gauge.* When pressure is at 0, remove the pressure gauge and then the lid. *Use caution in removing the lid.* (Use lid as a screen between you and any steam that may still be in the saucepan.)
  11. Gravy may be made with the drippings. Use 2 tablespoons (30 ml) flour for each cup of drippings. (Apply principles of starch cookery.)
  12. Record total working time: _____ minutes.

  *Chicken thighs could be braised. Use of the pressure saucepan is included here to give students additional experience with this method of cookery.

Breaded Braised Pork Chop or Steak*

Pork chop or steak	1	1
Egg	1	1
Water	2 tablespoons	30 ml
Crumbs, fine, sifted	1/4 cup	60 ml
Shortening	1 tablespoon	15 ml
Salt	1/4 teaspoon	1 ml

1. Add the water to the egg. Blend with a fork or beater until yolk and white are just blended—egg should not be foamy. Pour blended egg into a flat dish or plate so the chop or steak will lie flat in the egg. Dip the meat in the egg so each side of the meat is covered with egg. (Score outer covering of chop before dipping in egg.)
2. Add the salt to the crumbs. Place the crumbs on a piece of waxed paper. Place the egg-coated meat in the crumbs. Turn so both sides become coated with crumbs.
3. If a heavy coating of crumbs is desired, the meat may be dipped in the egg a second time and then in the crumbs again. Usually one coating is sufficient.
4. Melt the fat in a heavy frying pan (#5 for class use). Brown the meat on each side. Do not have the fat too hot—the fat should not smoke.
5. Reduce heat. Add about 1 tablespoon (15 ml) of water. Cover frying pan with a tight-fitting cover. Simmer for 3/4 to 1 hour or until meat is tender.
6. It may be necessary to add additional water during the cooking period.
7. Record total working time: _____ minutes.

*Chops and cutlets (of any type) may be braised without breading. Start at Step 4.

Swiss Steak

Round steak	4–5 ounces	120–150 g
Flour	2 tablespoons	30 ml
Salt	1/4 teaspoon	1 ml
Pepper	few grains	few grains
Shortening	1 tablespoon	15 ml
Onion slices (1/4 inch or 0.6 cm thick)	2–3	2–3
Canned tomatoes, tomato juice, or hot water	1/2 cup	125 ml

1. Steak would usually be cut approximately 1 1/2 inches (3.8 cm) thick. For class work it will be approximately 1 inch (2.5 cm) thick to speed cooking time.
2. Blend together the flour and seasonings. Put the flour onto a sheet of waxed paper large enough to hold the meat. Rub the flour into each side of the meat. Then pound meat with the side of a plate or with a Swissing iron. Almost all of the flour should be held by the meat by the time the meat is pounded. Turn meat during pounding so flour is distributed on each side of the meat.
3. Melt fat in a heavy (#5 for class) frying pan. Have fat hot but not smoking. Add meat and brown meat on each side.
4. Add tomatoes and onion slices. Cover with a tight-fitting lid. Simmer until tender. Add more liquid (water or tomato juice) as needed.
5. This may be baked for approximately 1 1/2 hours in a 350°F (175°C) oven. Place in oven after covering in Step 4.
6. At the end of the cooking period, there should be some thickened sauce on the meat.
7. Record total working time: _____ minutes.

Spiced Veal Tongue

Veal tongue	1	1
*Water	1 cup	250 ml
Salt	1 teaspoon	5 ml
Celery	1 stalk	1 stalk
Onions, small, sliced	2	2
Cloves, whole	6	6
Bay leaf	1	1
Peppercorns, whole	6	6
Cornstarch	2 tablespoons	30 ml
Brown sugar	1/2 cup	125 ml
Vinegar	1/4 cup	60 ml

1. Remove dry skin from onions. Wash, dry, and slice into 1/4 inch (0.6 cm) thick slices. Wash and dry celery stalk. Cut into 1 inch (2.5 cm) thick slices.
†2. Rinse tongue under cold tap water. Place tongue, water, salt, celery, cloves, bay leaf, peppercorns, and onions in a pressure saucepan.** Cover saucepan. Heat until a steady stream of steam is produced. Place pressure gauge on steam vent. Allow pressure to reach 15 pounds. Cook for 30 minutes at 15 pounds pressure.
3. At the end of the cooking period, stand covered saucepan under cold running water until the pan feels cool. Remove pressure gauge and open saucepan.
4. Remove skin from tongue and slice meat into 1/4 inch (0.6 cm) thick slices.
5. Strain meat broth. Blend cornstarch with brown sugar and vinegar. Add this mixture to 1 cup (250 ml) of the strained meat broth and bring to a boil.
6. Reduce heat to a simmer and add meat slices. Simmer meat in sauce for 5 minutes.
7. Serve meat slices with a small amount of the sauce.
8. Record total working time: _____ minutes.

*Water should just cover rack on bottom of pressure saucepan.

†The rack should be in place in the bottom of the pressure saucepan before food is added.

**A pressure saucepan is used for this product to reduce the cooking time so the product can be prepared in a two-hour laboratory period.

Braised Veal Rosemary

Veal round or veal cutlet	1 pound	450 g
Flour	1/4 cup	60 ml
Salt	1 teaspoon	5 ml
Pepper	1/8 teaspoon	0.5 ml
Paprika	2 teaspoons	10 ml
Shortening	3 tablespoons	45 ml
Onions, medium, sliced	2	2
Rosemary	1/4 teaspoon	1 ml
Water	1/3 cup	75 ml
Sour cream	3/4 cup	175 ml

1. Blend flour with all of the seasonings except the rosemary.
2. Cut veal into bite-size pieces. Rub each piece with seasoned flour.
3. Melt 2 tablespoons (30 ml) of the fat in a heavy frying pan. Add pieces of veal and brown the veal on each side.
4. Remove dry skin from onions and wash. Slice into 1/4 inch (0.6 cm) thick slices. In a separate, small frying pan melt the remaining fat. Add onion slices. Cook onions slowly until lightly golden in color.
5. Arrange the meat so each piece can be sprinkled with a portion of the rosemary. Arrange the onion slices over the seasoned pieces of veal.
6. Add water. Tightly cover the frying pan. Simmer slowly for about 1 hour or until the veal is tender. (*Do not overbrown the meat.* Do not let the meat scorch during the final cooking period.) Remove meat to a warm serving plate.
7. Blend sour cream with liquid in the pan just before serving. Do not boil sour cream. Pour over meat.
8. Record total working time: _____ minutes.

Lamb Stew

Boneless lamb shoulder	1 pound	450 g
Flour	1/4 cup	60 ml
Salt	1 teaspoon	5 ml
Pepper	1/8 teaspoon	0.5 ml
Shortening	2 tablespoons	30 ml
Water, boiling	3 cups	750 ml
Onions, small	6	6
Carrots, medium large	2	2
Potatoes, medium large	2	2
Peas, frozen, thawed	1 cup	250 ml
Parsley, minced	1 tablespoon	15 ml

1. Blend the flour, salt, and pepper. Cut the lamb into approximately 1 inch (2.5 cm) cubes. Place flour on a plate or waxed paper. Roll each piece of lamb in flour mixture. Shake off excess flour. (Save excess flour to thicken gravy later, if needed. See Step 7.)

*2. Melt fat in the bottom of a pressure saucepan; have fat hot but *not* smoking. Add lamb pieces. Brown on all sides.

3. Add 1 cup (250 ml) boiling water to meat. Lock pressure saucepan cover in place. Heat until a steady stream of steam comes through the vent. Place pressure gauge over vent. Cook at 10 pounds pressure for 30 minutes.

4. Remove dry skins from onions and wash. Use vegetable peeler to pare carrots and potatoes, then wash. Cut carrots into 1 inch (2.5 cm) lengths. Cut each potato into 6–8 pieces. To the remaining 2 cups (500 ml) of boiling water, add the whole onions and the carrots. Boil (with saucepan partially covered) for 10 minutes. Add potatoes and boil an additional 10 minutes or until vegetables are barely tender. *Do not overcook the vegetables.* Have vegetables cooked by the time the stew meat is ready. Save cooking liquid to add to meat, if desired.

5. At the end of the 30-minute cooking period, hold the pressure saucepan under a stream of cold tap water to reduce the pressure (2 minutes under cold running water). Remove pressure gauge and then remove lid.

6. Carefully transfer the cooked vegetables to the meat. Add frozen peas. Add liquid from vegetables if additional liquid is necessary. Heat meat and vegetables for about 5 minutes or until peas are cooked.

7. If liquid needs to be thickened, blend 2 tablespoons (30 ml) of flour (use seasoned flour remaining from Step 1) with 1/2 cup (125 ml) cold water. Add a portion of the hot liquid to the starch paste and then add all the flour mixture to the stew. This mixture must be brought to a boil to cook the starch. Do not overstir the stew mixture during the final stages of preparation.

8. Garnish with minced parsley. Wash and thoroughly drain parsley before mincing.

9. Record total working time: _____ minutes.

*Remove browned meat; insert rack in pan; return meat. Proceed to Step 3.

EVALUATION OF PRODUCTS
(MEAT)

Name: _____

Date: _____

Score System

Points	Quality
7	Excellent
6	Very good
5	Good
4	Medium
3	Fair
2	Poor
1	Very poor

Directions:
1. Place the numerical score in the box in the upper left-hand corner.
2. Comments should justify the numerical score. Comments must be brief.
3. Evaluation of the food products must be on an *individual* basis.

Products

Quality Characteristic					
Outside Appearance					
Interior Appearance					
Tenderness					
Juiciness					
Flavor					

REVIEW QUESTIONS

1. List and explain the factors considered in the grading of meat.
2. a. What does the federal inspection of meat and poultry indicate to the consumer?
   b. Is meat shipped interstate required to be federally inspected?
   c. How does the law affect meat that is not shipped in interstate trade?
3. a. Define *rigor mortis.*
   b. What role does rigor mortis play in the tenderness of cooked meat?
4. a. What effect does aging (ripening) have on the quality characteristics of meat?
   b. What types of meat are normally given a ripening period?
5. How can bone and fat be used to indicate the age of an animal or a bird?
6. a. Name three proteins found in muscle fibers.
   b. Name the two proteins that constitute the connective tissue.
   c. What happens to each of the five proteins [in (a) and (b)] when they are heated during the cooking process?
7. Briefly discuss the relationships between the amount of connective tissue in a piece of meat and the proper cooking method for the piece of meat.
8. Hamburger frequently is prepared from one of the less-tender cuts of beef, yet it is frequently pan broiled or broiled. Why?
9. a. What factors determine the texture of meat?
   b. Name some retail cuts of meat that have a fine texture.
   c. Name some retail cuts of meat that have a coarse texture.
10. Why are "time per pound" tables only an approximation rather than a definite guide to degree of doneness?
11. Discuss the relationship of oven temperature during roasting (baking) to the tenderness and juiciness of the finished roast.
12. Discuss the relationship of internal temperature to which a roast is cooked to tenderness and juiciness.
13. What is the function(s) of each of the following ingredients in the preparation of the product indicated?
    a. Tomato in Swiss steak
    b. Bread crumbs on pork chop
14. a. Why does the use of a pressure saucepan reduce the cooking time?
    b. List the important steps to consider to ensure the safe use of a pressure saucepan.
15. List and discuss factors which will affect the flavor of meat and poultry.
16. In poultry, how does the amount of exercise of the specific muscle relate to each of the following:
    a. Color of the muscle
    b. Tenderness of the muscle
    c. Texture of the muscle
    d. Flavor of the muscle
17. a. List the various classifications of poultry and indicate the proper cooking procedure for each class of bird.
    b. Explain why some types of poultry are normally cooked by dry heat methods of cooking.
18. a. Compare the nutritive value of meat and poultry.
    b. What is the relationship between method of preparation and nutritive value?

19.   The products listed in the table were evaluated as indicated. What was done to these products to account for such an evaluation?

Quality Characteristic	Ground Beef Patty		Chicken Thigh		Veal Tongue	
Outside Appearance	5	Well browned	3	Overbrowned	3	Sauce too thin
Interior	3	Red	3	Stringy	5	
Tenderness	5		5		6	
Juiciness	5		4	Interior dry	5	
Flavor	3	Raw	4	Lacks flavor	3	Too tart

20.   Explain why a pork chop may be oven broiled if the meat is cut from the newer type of pork (less fat).

Fish and Shellfish

OBJECTIVES

1. To illustrate factors to be considered in the selection of fish and shellfish.
2. To illustrate different types of fish and shellfish.
3. To illustrate different market forms (cuts) of fish.
4. To demonstrate factors affecting the cooking of several types of fish and shellfish.

PRODUCTS TO BE PREPARED TO ILLUSTRATE PRINCIPLES

Shrimp
Pan-fried perch
Broiled salmon steaks
Baked scallops
Clam chowder (microwave)

Fish poached in court boullion
Whole baked fish
"Oven-fried" fillets
Salmon cakes

PRINCIPLES

1. Biology
   a. The chemistry of living organisms is geared to the environment in which the organism exists.
   b. The bodily processes are regulated by enzymes, which in fish function at lower temperatures than the enzyme systems of mammals such as cows, hogs, or sheep.
   c. An increase of temperature causes the enzyme systems to function more rapidly, which in the case of fish and shellfish has important practical considerations for storage and handling.

2. Storage
   a. Storage of fish and shellfish at higher than refrigeration temperature, 42°–50°F (6°–10°C), will cause rapid deterioration of the flesh, rendering the flesh inedible.
   b. Even at low temperature, fish and shellfish can be stored for only a short time.
   c. Prolonged storage requires some method of preservation such as freezing, canning, brining, smoking, or a combination of these methods.
   d. Fish and shellfish should be kept tightly covered or wrapped when stored because of their distinctive odors, which are readily absorbed by other foods.

3. Cookery
   a. Fish and shellfish contain little connective tissue so they can be cooked by any method of cookery.
   b. Because most fish contain small amounts of fat, some fat is generally added during the cooking process.
   c. Dry heat methods of cookery are usually preferred. Dry heat methods develop more flavor.
   d. Fish to be cooked by moist heat methods of cookery is frequently wrapped in parchment or cheesecloth to hold the flesh together as the fish cooks.
   e. As purchased, fish and shellfish usually require washing and some cleaning before being cooked.
   f. Shrimp, especially, should be washed, peeled, deveined, and rinsed before cooking.
   g. Fish and shellfish must be cooked to the well-done stage to be palatable and to be bacteriologically safe.
   h. Fish flesh is sufficiently cooked when the flesh separates easily into flakes.
   i. Overcooked fish and shellfish are tough and rubbery.
   j. High cooking temperatures and long cooking times are generally to be avoided.
   k. Smoked fish, dried fish, and salted fish may be soaked in water prior to cooking to
      (1) Rehydrate muscle tissue
      (2) Reduce smoke flavor in cooked fish
      (3) Reduce salt flavor in cooked fish
   l. Poaching is a moist heat method of cookery most appropriate for preparing fish.

DIRECTIONS FOR POACHING

Poaching may be done in a special poaching pan, which has a rack and a lid, or it may be done in a frying pan or electric skillet which can be covered. A fish may be poached whole if it is dressed (fins, gills, and internal organs removed). Whole fillets may be cooked or the fish may be cut into serving-size pieces before cooking. Any type of fish or shellfish may be poached. Some of the best are haddock, sea bass, tuna, orange roughy, trout, bass, perch, pike, shrimp, lobster, mussels, and clams.

There is a wide latitude in selecting the cooking liquid; any one of the following may be used: water, milk, beer, wine, canned clam juice, canned chicken broth, or something more exciting, a court boullion. There are as many different court boullions as there are cooks on the planet.

A court boullion can be as simple as slices of a fresh lime in water. Celery tops, chopped green onions, sliced carrots, and white wine can be added to the cooking water. A recipe for a court boullion will be included in the recipe for poaching the fish.

The fish is just covered with the cooking liquid and heated to simmering temperature until the flakes separate when tested with a fork. Drain the fish well before placing on a heated serving platter. The fish may be simply garnished or a sauce may be added. The best part of this method is that no fat need be added to the fish.

Shrimp

Shrimp, fresh or frozen, thawed in the shell
  (Number to cook will be assigned)

1. Peel off the shell of fresh or frozen, thawed shrimp.
2. With a sharp knife, cut along the outside of the center back deep enough only to expose the sand vein. (This is the intestinal tract.)
3. Remove the sand vein, which may vary in color from light tan to black depending on contents.
4. Wash the shrimp in running, cold tap water. Hold in cold tap water until it is ready to cook.
5. Add 3/4 teaspoon (3 ml) salt to each cup of water used for cooking shrimp.
6. Bring the water to a boil.
7. Add the cleaned shrimp to the boiling water. *Reduce heat.*
*8. Cook at simmering temperature, 185°–200°F (85°–90°C), for 5 minutes or until the meat becomes opaque and some portions of the outer surface become light coral pink.
9. Drain. Put the shrimp into ice water to chill if they are to be served cold. Do not serve in cocktail sauce for class evaluation.
10. Record total working time: _____ minutes

*To determine the effect of overcooking, leave one or two of the shrimp in the cooking water and boil, 212°F (100°C), these shrimp for 10 minutes. Observe the shrinkage during the cooking period. Compare with the simmered shrimp for *tenderness.*

CHARACTERISTICS OF HIGH-QUALITY COOKED SHRIMP

Appearance: Opaque white with salmon-colored (pink-orange) striations.

Texture: Firm (does not flake).

Juiciness: Slightly moist to very slightly dry.

Tenderness: Very slight resistance to chewing.

Flavor: Very mild, typical; should not have any fishy flavor.

Pan-Fried Ocean Perch

Perch fillets	2	2
Milk	2 tablespoons	30 ml
Salt	1/4 teaspoon	1 ml
Flour	2 tablespoons	30 ml
Pepper (optional)	few grains	few grains
Shortening or butter or margarine	1 tablespoon	15 ml

1. Blend seasonings with the flour. Place on a piece of waxed paper.
2. Dip perch fillet in milk and then in seasoned flour.
3. Melt fat in heavy frying pan. *Do not overheat,* especially if butter or margarine is used. Add flour-coated perch fillets. Fry until fillets are golden brown on each side. The flesh will tend to flake.
4. Serve with Tartar Sauce, page 207.
5. Record total working time: _____ minutes.

Broiled Salmon Steak*

Salmon steak, 3/4 inch (2 cm) thick	1	1
Margarine or butter	1 tablespoon	15 ml
Lemon juice (optional)	1 tablespoon	15 ml
Lemon wedge	1	1

1. Preheat broiler.
2. Arrange salmon steak directly on a broiler pan or on an ovenglass serving platter. (Broiler rack may be lightly greased.)
3. Melt butter or margarine. Add lemon juice (if used). Spoon half the mixture over surface of steak.
4. Place the broiler pan so the surface of the fish is 3–4 inches (8–10 cm) below the broiler unit. Broil until the surface of the fish is browned—about 10 minutes. If the fish does not appear thoroughly cooked (when the surface is browned), bake in a 350°F (175°C) oven until the fish flakes.
5. Spoon remaining lemon-butter sauce over fish as it broils or at the end of the cooking period. Do not serve in pools of butter.
6. Serve with wedge of lemon.
7. Record total working time: _____ minutes.

*Other fat-fleshed fish such as halibut or swordfish may be broiled.

"Oven-Fried" Fish Fillets or Steaks

Haddock fillets or steaks	1 pound	450 g
(Steaks cut 1/2–3/4 inch or 1–2 cm thick)		
Half and Half	1/2 cup	125 ml
Salt	3/4 teaspoon	3 ml
Pepper	few grains	few grains
Paprika	1/4 teaspoon	1 ml
Margarine or butter	3 tablespoons	45 ml
Bread crumbs, dry, fine, sifted	1 cup	250 ml

1. Preheat oven to 550°F (290°C)
2. Add the seasonings to the Half and Half.
3. Melt butter or margarine.
4. Mix 1 tablespoon (15 ml) melted butter with the crumbs.
5. Cut fish fillets into serving portions. Dip fish portions into Half and Half, then into the crumbs. Have an even coating of crumbs on each portion of fish.
6. Arrange the prepared pieces of fish 2 inches (5 cm) apart in a shallow baking pan. Drizzle the remaining melted butter evenly over the fish.
7. Place the baking pan on the top rack, about 4 inches (10 cm) from the top of the oven, preheated to 550°F (290°C). Bake until the top surface of the fish is well browned.
8. If the fish is not completely cooked by the time the surface has browned, reduce the oven temperature to 350°F (175°C) and continue baking until the flesh flakes easily when tested with a fork. Total cooking time may be 8–12 minutes depending on the thickness of steaks or fillets.
9. Serve with Tartar Sauce, page 207.
10. Record total working time: _____ minutes.

Baked Scallops

Scallops	4 to 6	4 to 6
Milk	1/4 cup	60 ml
Salt	1/2 teaspoon	2 ml
Flour	1/4 cup	60 ml
Egg	1	1
Water	2 tablespoons	30 ml
Bread crumbs, dry, fine, sifted	1/2 cup	125 ml
Margarine or butter	2 tablespoons	30 ml

1. Preheat oven to 350°F (175°C).
2. Add the salt to the milk. Stir until salt is dissolved.
3. Dip scallops in the seasoned milk.
4. Dip into flour and coat evenly with flour. (Put flour on a piece of waxed paper.)
5. Stir egg until yolk and white are blended. Add the water. Blend. (Egg and water may be blended with a beater, but do not beat until foamy.)
6. Dip the flour-coated scallops into the egg.
7. Place the sifted crumbs on a piece of waxed paper. Place the egg-covered scallops in the crumbs. Coat with crumbs.
8. Lightly butter the bottom of a shallow baking dish. Place the crumb-coated scallops in the baking dish.
9. Evenly drizzle the melted fat over the scallops.
10. Bake in a 350°F (175°C) oven until the crumbs are golden brown. The interior of the scallops becomes clear white. Baking time: approximately 30 minutes.
11. Record total working time: _____ minutes.

Salmon Cakes with Sauce

Salmon, 1 pound (454 gm) can	1 can	1 can
Crackers, saltine, low-salt	1/2 cup	125 ml
Eggs	2	2
Milk	2 tablespoons	30 ml
Vegetable oil, butter flavor	2 tablespoons	30 ml
Pepper	1/4 teaspoon	1 ml

For white sauce:		
Milk	1 cup	250 ml
Flour, all-purpose	2 tablespoons	30 ml
Peas, frozen	3/4 cup	175 ml
Celery salt and Tabasco, each	1/8 teaspoon	0.5 ml

1. Directions for preparing ingredients:
   a. Drain all liquid from the salmon. Remove skin and vertebra; small bones may be used. Flake meat with a fork.
   b. Place crackers in a plastic bag, seal, and use rolling pin to reduce to fine crumbs.
   c. In a 2–3 quart (2–3 L) bowl, beat eggs until thoroughly blended.
2. To the beaten eggs add salmon, 2 tablespoons milk, cracker crumbs, and pepper. Stir thoroughly with a fork. Form into 4 cakes about 1/2 inch (1.2 cm) thick.
3. Prepare medium white sauce by Method III, page 121. Add peas which have been boiled 3 minutes, then drained. Heat to boil.
4. Add oil to a hot frying pan. Add salmon cakes and fry 3 minutes on each side. Blot off fat with paper towels.
5. Serve each cake with 2–3 tablespoons (30 ml) sauce.
6. Record total working time: _____ minutes.

Whole Baked Fish

*White fish, whole	2–3 pounds	1–1.5 kg
Bread cubes, 1/2 inch (1.3 cm) dice, soft	1 quart	1 L
Butter or margarine, melted	1/2 cup	125 ml
Salt	1 teaspoon	5 ml
Pepper	1/8 teaspoon	0.5 ml
Onion, finely chopped	1 tablespoon	15 ml
Parsley, finely chopped	1 tablespoon	15 ml
Pickle relish, sweet	1 tablespoon	15 ml
Butter, melted (additional), for use at Step 7	2 tablespoons	30 ml

1. Preheat oven to 450°F (230°C).
2. Thoroughly wash fish. Remove any scales which may remain on the skin. The head may be removed.
3. Starting at the head end, carefully remove the backbone and rib bones the length of the fish. This makes the serving of the baked fish much easier.
4. Make the dressing from the remaining ingredients. Place the bread cubes in a bowl. Carefully stir in the melted fat with a fork. Add other ingredients. *Do not overstir.*
5. Lightly salt the interior of the fish. Arrange the stuffing in the cavity.
6. Hold the sides of the fish together with skewers or heavy toothpicks. Hold skewers in position by lacing with heavy cord.
7. Arrange on an ovenglass baking dish. Spoon 1–2 tablespoons (15–30 ml) melted butter over the surface of the fish.
8. Reduce oven setting to 350°F (175°C) when placing stuffed fish in oven for baking. Bake in oven for about 1 hour. Fish will easily separate into flakes when done.
9. Serve with Drawn Butter Sauce, page 207.
10. Record total working time: _____ minutes.

*Two fillets of 1 pound (450 g) each may be used here. Skewer or sew together loosely 1 side and 2 ends of the fillets. Fill cavity with dressing and complete closure.

CHARACTERISTICS OF HIGH-QUALITY COOKED FISH

Appearance: Typical for method of cookery; boiled and poached products will not have a browned surface. Surface of fish cooked by broiling, baking, or frying will generally have a golden brown surface.

Texture: Fish easily separates into flakes.

Juiciness: Flakes of fish will appear moist.

Tenderness: Some resistance to chewing, but sample should be easily masticated.

Flavor: Typical of variety of fish or seafood but not a distinct fishy flavor or aroma.

Fish Poached in Court Bouillon

Court Bouillon

Options 1 and 2

Water or Milk	*Enough to cover fish.	

Option 3

Milk	*Enough to cover fish.	
Lime, whole	1	1
Salt	1/2 teaspoon	2 ml
Pepper	1/4 teaspoon	1 ml

1. Scrub the skin of the lime under warm water, then dry.
2. Heat the lime in the microwave oven for 25 seconds on full power.
3. Cut the lime into 1/8 inch thick slices.
4. Add all of the slices to the cooking water.

Options 4 and 5

**Water	*Enough to cover fish.	
Scallions (green onions)	6 thinly sliced	6
Celery tops and celery	1/2 cup, chopped	125 ml
Carrots	2 thinly sliced	2 thinly sliced
Salt	1 teaspoon	5 ml
Peppercorns	1/2 teaspoon	2 ml

*See directions that follow for poaching of fish.

**May use 1/2 water and 1/2 white wine.

Note: The preceding options are good examples of court bouillons. Many other vegetables, fruits, spices, or herbs may be used. Examples are lemons, cinnamon, allspice, red pepper, bay leaf, garlic, onions, marjoram, and thyme.

Poaching Directions

Preparation of Fish

Whole fish
1. Cut off all of the fins.
2. If not already done, open the abdominal cavity and remove all of the viscera. Using a sharp knife, open the cavity by making a slit from tail to head. The viscera are removed by hand, using the knife if necessary.
3. Rinse well under cold water. If there is blood present, rub salt throughout the entire cavity and again rinse well with cold water.
4. Drain and blot dry.

Fillets
1. Rinse well under cold water; drain.
2. Remove any visible bones. (A pair of small pliers may be necessary.) Rinse again with cold water and blot dry.
3. Cut the fillets into serving-size pieces.

Poaching of either whole fish or fillets
1. Select the cooking utensil. The best equipment to use is a special poaching pan, an electric skillet, or a 12-inch (31 cm) regular skillet.
2. Place the cleaned, prepared fish in the cooking utensil and add just enough liquid to cover the fish.
3. Add the other ingredients if using a court boullion and stir.
4. Heat to the simmering temperature (185°F, 89°C).
5. Continue cooking until the fish flakes when tested with a fork.

New England Clam Chowder (Microwave)

Bacon, chopped into 1/4 inch pieces	2 slices	2 slices
Potatoes, peeled, cut in 3/8 inch cubes	1 1/2 cups	375 ml
Onion, medium	1/2 cup	125 ml
Minced clams	1 can	1 can
Flour, all-purpose	2 tablespoons	30 ml
Milk, divided	1 cup	250 ml
Pepper, black	1/8 teaspoon	0.5 ml
Half and Half	1/3 cup	80 ml

1. Drain the clams and reserve the liquid.
2. Place the bacon pieces in a 3-quart (3-L) casserole. Cover and microwave on *high* for 3 minutes.
3. Remove all but 2 tablespoons of bacon fat. Add the potatoes and onions to the casserole. Pour the reserved clam liquid into the casserole, cover, and microwave on *high* 7 to 9 minutes or until the potatoes are fork tender, stirring once during heating.
4. Thoroughly mix the flour in 1/4 cup (60 ml) of the milk.
5. Add the flour mixture, the remaining milk, salt, and pepper to the casserole. *Do not cover.*
6. Microwave on *high* 8 to 10 minutes, or until thickened, stirring three times during the cooking.
7. Stir in clams and Half and Half and microwave on *high* for 2 to 4 minutes or until heated through.
8. Record total working time: _____ minutes.

Cocktail Sauce

Catsup	2 tablespoons	30 ml
Lemon juice	1 tablespoon	15 ml
Salt	1/4 teaspoon	1 ml
Horseradish (freshly grated for best flavor)	1 teaspoon	5 ml
Worcestershire sauce	1/4 teaspoon	1 ml
Tabasco sauce	1–2 drops	1–2 drops

1. Blend together all ingredients.
2. Chill for best flavor.
3. Serve as accompaniment to cooked shrimp.

Tartar Sauce

Salad dressing, mayonnaise type	1/3 cup	75 ml
Sour cucumber pickles, minced	2 teaspoons	10 ml
Green olives, minced	2 teaspoons	10 ml
Capers	1/2 teaspoon	2 ml
Green onion or chives, minced	1/2 teaspoon	2 ml
Parsley, minced	1/2 teaspoon	2 ml
Tarragon vinegar	1/2 teaspoon	2 ml

1. Mix all ingredients together.
2. Serve cold.

Drawn Butter Sauce

Margarine or butter	3 tablespoons	45 ml
Flour	1 1/2 tablespoons	25 ml
Salt	1/4 teaspoon	1 ml
Cayenne	few grains	few grains
Water, boiling	1 cup	250 ml

1. Melt 2 tablespoons (30 ml) of the fat in the upper part of the double boiler.
2. Add the flour and stir until well blended.
3. Add the boiling water gradually. Stir until smooth after each addition of water.
4. Bring to a boil over direct heat with continuous stirring.
5. Stir in the remaining butter just before serving. Serve hot.

REVIEW QUESTIONS

1. a. Explain why fish must be stored at refrigerator temperatures.
    b. Compare keeping quality of fish and red meat, both being held at refrigerator temperature.
    c. List some other methods of preservation which can be used to extend the keeping quality of fish.
2. Distinguish between a fish steak and a fish fillet.
3. a. Compare the quantity of connective tissue in a fish with the amount of connective tissue in a chicken breast.
    b. Relate the amount of connective tissue in fish to the methods used in cooking fish.
4. Why is smoked and/or salted fish soaked in fresh cool water before cooking?
5. What principles were violated to account for the evaluations given in the following table?

Quality Characteristic	Shrimp	Poached Cod	Salmon Steak
Outside Appearance	2 Black stripe down center back	1 Disintegrated	2 Overbrowned
Interior Appearance	5	1 Disintegrated	5
Tenderness	2 Tough, stringy, rubbery	5	5
Juiciness	4	2 Dry	5
Flavor	2 Bitter	5	5

EVALUATION OF PRODUCTS
(FISH; SEAFOOD)

Name: _____

Date: _____

Score System

Points	Quality
7	Excellent
6	Very good
5	Good
4	Medium
3	Fair
2	Poor
1	Very poor

Directions:
1. Place the numerical score in the box in the upper left-hand corner.
2. Comments should justify the numerical score. Comments must be brief.
3. Evaluation of the food products must be on an *individual* basis.

Products

Quality Characteristic					
Outside Appearance					
Interior Appearance					
Tenderness					
Juiciness					
Flavor					

Vegetables

OBJECTIVES

1. To study selected vegetables for quality characteristic changes caused by
   a. Method and time of cooking
   b. Addition of acid
   c. Addition of baking soda
2. To study the relationship between varietal characteristics and quality characteristics for selected varieties of potatoes.
3. To further illustrate principles of cooking by preparing selected vegetable dishes.

PRODUCTS TO BE PREPARED TO ILLUSTRATE PRINCIPLES

Various methods of cooking carrots, red cabbage, onions, broccoli, and spinach

Harvard beets
Creamed green beans
Baked potatoes, white and sweet
Fried vegetables
Japanese-style vegetables with
    chicken and shrimp
Broccoli

Cauliflower with cheese sauce
Savory spinach
Buttered vegetables
Sweet and sour cabbage
Stuffed zucchini
Squash in cream sauce

PRINCIPLES

1. Pigments
   a. Classified by solubility
      (1) Water insoluble (fat soluble)
          (a) Chlorophyll
          (b) Carotenoid group
              (i) Carotene
              (ii) Lycopene
              (iii) Xanthophyll
      (2) Water soluble (fat insoluble)
          (a) Anthocyanins
          (b) Anthoxanthins (flavones)
   b. Color changes caused by
      (1) Acid (plant acids, vinegar, cream of tartar)
      (2) Alkali (baking soda)
      (3) Minerals (iron, copper, zinc)
      (4) Enzymes
      (5) Tannins
      (6) Heat

2. Tenderness
   a. Reactions of cellulose, hemicellulose, lignocellulose
      (1) Heat plus moisture
      (2) Effect of acid
      (3) Effect of alkali
   b. Change in pectic compounds (protopectin, pectin, pectic acid)
      (1) Maturation
      (2) Heat plus moisture
      (3) Effect of acid
      (4) Effect of alkali
      (5) Effect of calcium
3. Texture
   a. Sloughing—varietal differences; effect of alkali (*see* Change in pectic compounds).
   b. Effect of acid—retention of structure and shape (*see* Change in pectic compounds).
   c. Effect of varietal differences, especially in potatoes, lima beans, and tomatoes.
4. Flavor
   a. Sulfur compounds
      (1) Sinigrin—a glycoside (combination with a sugar) broken down to allylisothiocyanate and then to hydrogen sulfide by action of water and heat, resulting in an unpleasant flavor, which increases as cooking is extended.
      (2) Allyl sulfide—decomposes and dissipates, giving a milder flavor.
   b. Carbohydrates (sugar and starch)
      (1) Maturation—as vegetables mature, sugar is converted to starch, resulting in a bland flavor.
      (2) Storage temperature—especially important in potatoes, sweet corn, lima beans, and parsnips. As vegetables are held in cold storage, carbohydrate is retained as sugar, resulting in sweet flavor. Sweetness is desirable in nearly all vegetables except white potatoes.
   c. Organic acids
      (1) Oxalic acid
      (2) Other plant acids
   d. Other compounds
      (1) Solanin
      (2) Organic compounds (aldehydes, alcohols, esters) occur in very small amounts; many are volatile and may be lost during cooking.
5. Method of cooking
   a. Boiling water
      (1) Loss of water-soluble nutrients
      (2) Loss of some water-soluble pigments
   b. Steaming
      (1) Increases length of cooking time
      (2) Change in chlorophyll pigment
      (3) Possibly better retention of shape
      (4) Better retention of nutrients.
   c. Baking
      (1) Possibly highest retention of nutrients
      (2) Development of different type of flavor

PREPARATION OF SELECTED VEGETABLES FOR COOKING

Beans, green	Trim off blossom and stem ends of each bean. (Discard brown, spotted, and/or wilted beans.) Wash thoroughly. Lift out of last wash water. Drain. Cut into 1–1 1/2 inch (2–4 cm) lengths.
Beets	Cut off stems and leaves 3 inches (7.5 cm) above the bulb. Brush bulb with vegetable brush, holding the beets under running tap water. Do not remove the 3-inch (7.5 cm) portion of stem or root and do not peel the bulb before cooking. After beets have been cooked, drain off boiling water. Add cold water to quickly cool cooked beets. When beets are cool enough to handle with your fingers, slip off the skin of the beets (as you might peel a tangerine). Trim off long roots. Beets tend to "bleed" when cooking, so they are peeled after cooking.
Broccoli	Cut off approximately 1/4 inch (0.6 cm) slice from the stem end. Cut off coarse leaves. If outer portion of stem end is woody, strip off the woody outer portion up to the stem portion of the bud-blossom portion. Cut the stalk into two portions so the bud-blossom portion is 3–4 inches (7–10 cm) in length. (The heavier stem portion can be brought to a boil before the bud portions are added.) Wash thoroughly. Lift from last wash water.
Brussels Sprouts	Trim off outer leaves if bruised or wilted. Look closely at stem end for insects; discard any infested sprouts. Wash trimmed sprouts thoroughly. To speed cooking, a 1/2 inch (1.3 cm) cut into the center of the sprout may be made at the stem end. Cut should almost bisect sprout but not allow sprout to cook apart during the cooking period.
Cabbage	Trim off outer leaves if they are wilted. Wash cabbage thoroughly. For experimental work, cut into four equal wedges so each portion is held together by a portion of the heart of the cabbage. Cuts are made from stem end to top of cabbage.
Carrots and Parsnips	Remove a thin outer portion of the skin with a vegetable peeler. Trim off root end and stem end if necessary. Do not use any green portion from the stem end—this is bitter. Wash vegetable. For experimental work, cut carrots into disks approximately 1/4 inch (0.6 cm) thick. It is important that the thickness of the disks be standardized for the experimental work.
Cauliflower	Trim off outer leaf and/or vein portions. Wash thoroughly. Separate into floweret portions of about the same size.
Onions, dry	Remove outer layers of dry skin. Trim off root portion. For experimental work, all pieces should be of equal size. For small onions to be left whole, make a cut across the diameter of the onion at the stem end, about 1/2 inch (1.3 cm) toward the bottom of the onion. This allows for more rapid and even cooking. If onions are halved or quartered, retain a portion of the root section on each part to help hold the onion together.
Potatoes	*Baking*—hold potatoes under cold, running tap water and scrub with a vegetable brush. Dry skin with paper towels. *Boiling*—rinse unpeeled potatoes in cold water. Remove a thin layer of skin with a vegetable peeler. Any green portion should be cut away and discarded. Cut out discolored eyes. Wash peeled potatoes. Cut into approximately 1/2 inch (1.3 cm) cubes for rapid cooking in boiling water. Hold peeled potatoes in water to cover until ready to place in boiling water for cooking.
Rutabaga and Turnips	Use vegetable peeler to remove outer skin. Do not use any green portion. Cut approximately 1/2 inch (1.3 cm) cubes for cooking.
Spinach	Trim off heavy stem ends (and roots, if any). Place spinach leaves in a large panful of water. Rinse each leaf separately through the first wash water. Wash through at least two wash waters. Lift leaves out of water.
Zucchini	Thoroughly wash zucchini or other summer squash. Sand tends to cling to the zucchini skin. The zucchini is then ready to slice for sautéing or to parboil to stuff and bake.

PROCEDURES FOR BOILING SELECTED FRESH VEGETABLES

Vegetable	Size of Piece†	Amount of Water	Use of Cover	Boiling Time(Min)†
Asparagus	young, whole stalks	to barely cover	uncovered	10–15
Beans, green or yellow wax	2 inch (5 cm)	to barely cover	green—uncovered yellow wax—covered	15–20
Beets	whole	1 inch (2.5 cm) more than vegetable	covered	45–60
Broccoli	4 inch (10 cm)	1 inch (2.5 cm) more than vegetable	uncovered	10–15
Brussels sprouts	whole	1 inch (2.5 cm) more than vegetable	uncovered	10–15
Cabbage, green or red*	2 inch (5 cm) wedge	2 inches (5 cm) more than vegetable	uncovered	8–15
Carrots	1/4 inch (0.6 cm) disks	to barely cover	covered	10–20
Cauliflower*	2 inch (5 cm) flowerets	2 inches (5 cm) more than vegetable	uncovered	8–15
Corn on the cob	whole ear	1 inch (2.5 cm) more than vegetable	covered	3–5
Onions*	1 inch (2.5 cm) dia.	1 inch (2.5 cm) more than vegetable	uncovered	10–15
Parsnips	3–4 inch (7–10 cm) lengths; halve or quarter each length depending on diameter	to barely cover	covered	10–20
Peas	whole	to barely cover	uncovered	10–15
Potatoes, white*	1 inch (2.5 cm) cubes	to barely cover	covered	10–15
Rutabaga	3/4 inch (2 cm) cubes	1 inch (2.5 cm) more than vegetable	uncovered	10–20
Spinach	leaves	1/2 inch (1.3 cm) deep in saucepan	covered for 3 min.; then remove cover	5–8
Squash, summer varieties**	1/4 inch (0.6 cm) disks	1/2 inch (1.3 cm) deep in saucepan	**covered or **uncovered	5–8
Turnips*	3/4 inch (2 cm) cubes	1 inch (2.5 cm) more than vegetable	uncovered	10–20

Note: Use 1/4 teaspoon (1 ml) salt per cup (250 ml) water. Add cleaned vegetable to boiling water. Count time when water returns to boil.

†Total cooking time is always related to size of piece.

*May add 1/8–1/4 teaspoon (0.5–1 ml) cream of tartar for better color.

**Yellow and white—covered; green—uncovered.

Vegetables—Effect of Cooking Treatment

Red cabbage—1/2 medium head
Carrots—8 medium
Broccoli—1 bunch
Onions—8 medium
Spinach, fresh—2 10-ounce packages (500 g)
Cream of tartar
Soda
Vinegar

1. Put 1 quart (1 L) cold water in a 2-quart (2-L) saucepan and bring to a boil. Start one pan for each treatment.
2. Clean vegetables.
3. Divide carrots, red cabbage, onions, and spinach into four equal portions. Divide the broccoli into five equal portions.
4. For each cooking treatment listed below, cook one portion of vegetable. Add vegetables to boiling water.
5. It may be necessary to add more hot water if substantial amounts of water are lost by evaporation. Do not let the vegetable boil dry.
6. At the end of the cooking period, drain the vegetable by placing it in a strainer. Collect part of the cooking liquid in a glass custard cup. Put the cooked vegetable on a white plate for evaluation. (It is important that all samples of one vegetable be on the same type of plate for comparative evaluation.)
*7. Evaluation and discussions should include both the cooked vegetable and the cooking liquid.
8. Record observations in the tables on the following pages.

*To illustrate reversibility of anthocyanin pigment in presence of acid, put two or three leaves of red cabbage cooked by treatments 1, 2, or 3 on a small white plate. Evenly spread 1 tablespoon (15 ml) of vinegar over leaves. Allow to stand 5–10 minutes. Note the increase in redness.

*Cooking Treatments***

1. Boil for 15 minutes. Count time after water returns to a boil.
2. Boil for 30 minutes. Count time after water returns to a boil.
3. Add 1/2 teaspoon (2 ml) baking soda after adding the water. Boil for 15 minutes after water returns to a boil.
4. Add 1 teaspoon (5 ml) cream of tartar after adding the water. Boil for 15 minutes after water returns to a boil.
5. For the fifth sample of broccoli, place a lid on the saucepan after the water has been added. Boil for 30 minutes after water returns to a boil.

**In this particular lesson, cooking treatments have been standardized so that direct comparisons on the effect of treatment can be made. Length of cooking time is a more objective method to achieve standardization than the degree of tenderness ("cook until crisp tender"). Cover saucepan for cooking carrots; use uncovered saucepan for all other samples.

Steaming Vegetables*—General Directions

1. Place 1–2 inches (2–5 cm) of water in lower section of steamer. Enough water must be used to produce steam for entire cooking time.
2. Place cleaned vegetable in steamer basket and position over water. Tightly cover pan.
3. Bring water quickly to boiling over high heat. When water is boiling, reduce heat to keep water boiling slowly.
4. Cooking time for steaming vegetables is approximately 50% longer than if the vegetable is boiled in water.

*Caution: When opening steamer, tilt the lid so it prevents steam from rising in your face.

Baked Potatoes* (Conventional)

1. Preheat oven to 400°F (200°C). If time is an important factor, a higher oven temperature, up to 450°F (230°C), may be used. However, potatoes must be carefully checked so they do not get too hot. The oven can be preheated to 450°F (230°C) and heat can be lowered to 400°F (200°C) after 10 minutes cooking.
2. Place washed, dried potatoes on a shallow baking pan. Do not crowd potatoes on the baking sheet.
3. Bake until the potatoes can be pierced readily with a fork. Medium-sized potatoes in a 400°F (200°C) oven may require 1–1 1/2 hours to bake
   a. If potato skins are to be eaten, a small amount of fat can be rubbed over the surface of the potato skin to give a more tender skin on the baked potato.
   b. If potatoes are freshly harvested, they may have a high water content. These potatoes tend to explode in the oven. If these potatoes are pricked with a fork about halfway through the baking period, they will have less tendency to explode in the oven.
4. As soon as potatoes are removed from the oven, the potatoes should be split open to allow steam to escape and prevent the potatoes from becoming soggy.
5. Record total working time: _____ minutes.

   *We suggest using a high-solids variety (Russet), a low-solids variety (Red Pontiac), and a sweet potato or yam for baking.

Baked Potatoes (Microwave)

Baking potatoes, medium   3

1. Thoroughly wash potatoes. Use vegetable brush to scrub dirt from skin. Rinse and dry.
2. Prick through skin of potatoes 4 or 5 times on each side. Use a fork.
3. Arrange potatoes in a circular pattern on a microwave tray or on a piece of paper toweling.
4. Microwave at *high* power for 3 minutes. Rearrange potatoes on tray and turn them over so the side that had been on top becomes the underside. Microwave at *high* power for 3 minutes. Rearrange potatoes on tray. Microwave at *high* power for 3 minutes. Check for degree of tenderness. Potatoes will cook for a short time after being removed from oven. Continue microwaving at *high* power as needed for 30-second or 1-minute intervals.
5. Record total working time: _____ minutes.

Note: Evaluation sheet for baked potatoes is on page 219. The characteristics of high-quality baked potatoes are on page 221.

OBSERVATIONS ON VEGETABLES

Vegetable	Treatment Number	Color		Texture	Flavor
		Juice	Vegetable		
Red cabbage Pigment: Flavor constituent:	(1) 15 minutes				
	(2) 30 minutes				
	(3) soda				
	(4) acid				
Onions Pigment: Flavor constituent:	(1) 15 minutes				
	(2) 30 minutes				
	(3) soda				
	(4) acid				
Carrots Pigment: Flavor constituent:	(1) 15 minutes				
	(2) 30 minutes				
	(3) soda				
	(4) acid				

OBSERVATIONS ON VEGETABLES (Continued)

Vegetable	Treatment Number	Color Juice	Color Vegetable	Texture	Flavor
Broccoli Pigment: Flavor constituent:	(1) 15 minutes uncovered				
	(2) 30 minutes uncovered				
	(3) soda uncovered				
	(4) acid uncovered				
	(5) 30 minutes covered				
Spinach Pigment: Flavor constituent:	(1) 15 minutes				
	(2) 30 minutes				
	(3) soda				
	(4) acid				

BAKED POTATOES

Variety	Appearance	Moistness and Texture	Flavor

CHARACTERISTICS OF HIGH-QUALITY BAKED WHITE POTATOES

Appearance: White; opaque or slightly translucent depending on variety.

Texture: Cell structure is friable; mealy; light.

Moistness: Dry.

Flavor: Bland, yet slightly sweet.

CHARACTERISTICS OF HIGH-QUALITY BAKED SWEET POTATOES

Appearance: Yellow to orange; slightly translucent.

Texture: Solid or compact.

Moistness: Moist to wet depending on variety.

Flavor: Sweet; may be slightly caramelized.

Stuffed Zucchini (Microwave)

Zucchini squash, medium	2	2
Onion, small, chopped	1	1
Sausage, bulk	1/2 pound	225 g
Mushrooms, fresh, coarsely chopped	1 cup	250 ml
Celery, chopped	1/2 cup	125 ml
Tomato, fresh, medium, chopped	1	1
Margarine or butter	1 tablespoon	15 ml
Soda cracker crumbs	3/4 cup	187 ml
Egg, blended	1	1
Cheddar cheese, grated	1/2 cup	125 ml
Parmesan cheese, grated	2 tablespoons	30 ml
Salt	1/2 teaspoon	2 ml
Pepper	1/8 teaspoon	0.5 ml
Paprika	1/2 teaspoon	2 ml

1. Cut zucchini in half lengthwise. Scoop out pulp leaving 1/4-inch (0.6-cm) shell.
2. Chop the pulp coarsely. In a 1 1/2–2 quart (1.5–2 L) casserole combine with onion, mushrooms, celery, and tomatoes.
3. Cover and microwave on *high* for 4 to 6 minutes or until tender, stirring once during cooking. Drain thoroughly.
4. Add cracker crumbs, egg, cheddar cheese, parmesan cheese, salt, and pepper.
5. Mound 1/4 of the filling in each zucchini shell. Sprinkle with paprika.
6. Arrange the stuffed zucchini on the rack of a microwave baking dish. Cover with a plastic wrap and vent.
7. Microwave on *high* for 5 to 7 minutes, or until filling is set and the zucchini is fork tender. Rotate the dish 1/2 turn and rearrange the zucchini after one half of the cooking time.
8. Record total working time: _____ minutes.

Buttered Vegetables

1. Cook vegetable according to directions on page 214.
2. Allow 1/2–1 teaspoon (2–5 ml) butter or margarine for each serving.
3. Place the hot, cooked, and drained vegetable in its serving dish. Add the butter or margarine.
4. Stir lightly so the fat melts evenly throughout the vegetable.*
5. Do not have the vegetable swimming in fat.
6. Record total working time: _____ minutes.

*For four or more servings, the butter or margarine can be melted before it is added to the hot, cooked vegetable.

Creamed Vegetables

Vegetable, cooked 2 cups (500 ml)	1/2 pound	225 g
Milk	1 cup	250 ml
Margarine or butter	2 tablespoons	30 ml
Flour	2 tablespoons	30 ml
Salt	1/4 teaspoon	1 ml

1. Cook vegetable according to directions on page 214.
2. Melt fat in a saucepan. Add flour and salt. Stir thoroughly to blend.
3. Remove from heat. Add milk gradually. Stir well after each addition to get a smooth paste.
4. Bring to a boil over direct heat. Boil for 1 minute with constant stirring.
5. Add cooked, drained vegetable. Add more salt if necessary.
6. Heat to serving. Sauce should have consistency of whipping cream before whipping. Add more milk if necessary to obtain the correct consistency.
7. Record total working time: _____ minutes.

Cauliflower or Broccoli with Cheese Sauce
(See page 123 for microwave method.)

Cauliflower or broccoli, cooked	1/2 pound	225 g
Milk	1 cup	250 ml
Margarine or butter	2 tablespoons	30 ml
Flour	2 tablespoons	30 ml
Salt	1/4 teaspoon	1 ml
Cheddar cheese, grated	1/2 cup	125 ml

1. Cook vegetable according to directions on page 214. Drain thoroughly.
2. Melt fat in saucepan. Add flour and salt. Blend thoroughly.
3. Remove from heat. Add milk in portions. Stir thoroughly after each addition to form a smooth paste.
4. Bring to a boil over direct heat. Boil for 1 minute with constant stirring.
5. Remove from heat. Add grated cheese. Stir until blended.
6. Place the hot, cooked cauliflower or broccoli in a warm serving dish. Pour hot cheese sauce over the vegetable. Use only sufficient sauce to cover vegetable. Do not drown vegetable in sauce.
7. Record total working time: _____ minutes.

Harvard Beets

Beets, cooked or canned	2 cups	500 ml
Liquid from beets (or water)	1/2 cup	125 ml
Cornstarch	1 tablespoon + 1 teaspoon	20 ml
Sugar	2 tablespoons	30 ml
Salt	1/2 teaspoon	2 ml
Vinegar	1/4 cup	60 ml
Margarine or butter	1 tablespoon	15 ml

1. Blend together the liquid, cornstarch, sugar, and salt in a saucepan.
2. Bring to a boil over direct heat with constant stirring. The mixture should boil until it is clear.
3. Remove from heat. Add margarine and vinegar. Stir to blend. Add cooked beets.
4. Heat over low heat until the beets are heated through.
5. Record total working time: _____ minutes.

Sweet-Sour Red Cabbage

Red cabbage, finely shredded (not grated)	1 pound	450 g
Apple, tart, medium size, chopped fine	1	1
Brown sugar	3 tablespoons	45 ml
Vinegar	3 tablespoons	45 ml
Cornstarch	2 teaspoons	10 ml
Caraway seeds (optional)	1/2 teaspoon	2 ml
Cooking liquid or water	1/2 cup	125 ml

1. Place shredded cabbage and chopped apple together in a saucepan. Add boiling water for approximately 1/2 inch (1.3 cm) water in pan. Cook rapidly, uncovered, until cabbage is crisp tender. Add more boiling water as necessary. Stir through cabbage with a fork for even cooking. Drain.
2. Combine brown sugar and cornstarch. Add cold water or cooled cooking liquid. Bring mixture to a boil and boil 1 minute. Add vinegar. Blend. Add to cooked cabbage. Heat to serving temperature. If caraway seeds are used, add for this last heating period.
3. Record total working time: _____ minutes.

Savory Spinach

Spinach, fresh, cooked, drained raw weight	1 1/2 pounds	675 g
Bacon	4 slices	4 slices
Onion, small, thinly sliced	1	1
Sweet pickle relish	2 tablespoons	30 ml

1. Cook vegetable according to directions on page 214.
2. Cut bacon into small pieces with scissors. Place in an electric frying pan. Add the onion slices. Cook over low heat until the bacon is crisp and the onion is tender.
3. Stir in the sweet pickle and the cooked, drained spinach. Reheat if necessary.
4. Record total working time: _____ minutes.

Savory Spinach (Microwave)

Leaf spinach, frozen	1 package	1 package
Bacon slices	4	4
Onion, medium	1	1
Sweet pickle relish	2 tablespoons	30 ml

1. Cut each bacon slice into 6–8 pieces. Place pieces in a 2-quart microwave casserole and cover with wax paper. Microwave at *high* power 2–3 minutes or until bacon is crisp. Remove bacon pieces from fat.
2. Remove dry skin from onion. Wash, dry, and cut into coarse dice. Add onion to bacon fat. Cover casserole with waxed paper. Microwave at *high* power until onion is translucent, 2–3 minutes.
3. Defrost spinach—follow package directions or defrost at *medium* power for 3–5 minutes. Place frozen spinach directly on top of cooked onions in casserole dish. If dish will not tolerate freezing as well as boiling temperatures, defrost the spinach in a separate container.
4. Add the defrosted spinach to the casserole containing the cooked onions. Cut through the spinach 6–8 times with scissors to facilitate serving. Cover casserole. Microwave at *high* power for 5 minutes or until the stems of the spinach are tender.
5. Add pickle relish. Microwave at *high* power for 15–20 seconds to heat relish.
6. Top with crisp bacon pieces for serving.
7. Total cooking time: _____ minutes.
8. Refer to page 229 for characteristics of high-quality cooked vegetables.

Squash in Cream Sauce (Microwave)

Yellow summer squash, cut in 1/4-inch slices	1 pound	450 g
Water	2 tablespoons	30 ml
Margarine or butter	1 tablespoon	15 ml
Flour, all-purpose	1 tablespoon	15 ml
Parsley, fresh (or dry)	1/2 teaspoon	2 ml
Chives, fresh (or dry)	1/2 teaspoon	2 ml
Sugar	1/2 teaspoon	2 ml
Pepper, white or black	dash	dash
Salt	1/2 teaspoon	2 ml
Half and Half	1/2 cup	125 ml

1. In a 1 1/2-quart (1.5-L) casserole combine squash and water. Cover and microwave on *high* 5 to 7 minutes, or until fork tender. Drain well and set aside.
2. In a small bowl or a 2-cup (500-ml) Pyrex-type cup, melt the margarine or butter by microwaving for 15 to 30 seconds on *high*. Stir in the flour, sugar, and seasonings. Blend in the Half and Half and microwave on high 1 1/2 to 2 1/2 minutes, or until thickened, stirring twice.
3. Pour sauce over the squash and stir lightly to coat.
4. Record total working time: _____ minutes.

Broccoli (Microwave)

Fresh	1 pound	450 g
or		
Frozen	10-ounce package	283-g package

Fresh Broccoli

1. Wash and trim broccoli. If stem ends are tough, remove outer woody portion. Center portion of stems is edible.
2. Cut broccoli pieces so bud portions are approximately 4 inches (10 cm) long. Less-tender stem portions can be cooked for a few minutes before bud ends are added to cooking dish.
3. If stem ends are to be cooked first, place them evenly in a baking dish. Add 1-2 tablespoons (15-30) ml of water. Cover baking dish with waxed paper.
4. Microwave at *high* power for 3 minutes. Turn baking dish 1/4 turn and rearrange broccoli stems so thicker portions remain to the outside of the dish. Cover and microwave for an additional 3 minutes at *high* power.
5. Place bud portion of broccoli in baking dish so buds are toward the center with the heavier stem portions toward the outside of the cooking dish. Cover with waxed paper. Microwave at *high* power for 5 minutes. Turn baking dish 1/4 turn. Microwave 5 minutes. Test stem portion to check degree of doneness. If further cooking is required, microwave at *high* power for 3 minutes. Avoid overcooking.
6. Broccoli may be served with cheese sauce (see separate recipe page 223) or 1 teaspoon of butter or margarine may be melted for each serving of broccoli and spooned over the vegetable.
7. Record total working time: _____ minutes.
8. Refer to page 229 for characteristics of high-quality cooked vegetables.

Frozen Broccoli (Microwave)

1. Remove packaging wrap from broccoli. Place the frozen vegetable in a 1–2 quart (1–2 L) casserole dish. Cover dish with waxed paper.
2. Microwave at *medium* power (50%) for 2 minutes. Separate stalks of broccoli as they become defrosted. Remove defrosted stalks and microwave remaining stalks at *medium* power for 30 seconds.
3. When all stalks have been defrosted, arrange the stalks in the casserole so the bud ends are to the center of the casserole and the stem ends are to the outside of the casserole. Cover the casserole with waxed paper.
4. Microwave at *high* power for 3 minutes. Turn casserole 1/4 turn. Microwave for 3 minutes. Check a stem portion for degree of tenderness. Microwave for 2- or 3-minute intervals at *high* power to reach the desired degree of tenderness. Avoid overcooking.
5. Follow Steps 6, 7, and 8 for fresh broccoli to complete product and assignment.

Fried Parsnips

Parsnips	1 pound	450 g
Margarine or butter	2 tablespoons	30 ml

1. Clean and cook parsnips in salted water (see page 214). Cook parsnips in same frying pan in which the vegetable will be browned. Use only enough water to cook parsnips so most of the water evaporates by the time the parsnips are tender.
2. When parsnips are tender, remove any excess water left in frying pan. Add the butter or margarine to the frying pan. Work melted fat under each piece of vegetable. Fry over low heat until parsnips are golden brown. Parsnips brown more evenly if only a single layer is fried at one time.
3. If glazed parsnips are desired, add up to 2 tablespoons (30 ml) sugar to the frying pan as parsnips are browning. Avoid overcaramelization of the sugar.
4. Record total working time: _____ minutes.

Pan-Fried Eggplant

Eggplant, medium	1	1
Salt	1 1/2 teaspoons	7 ml
Egg	1	1
Water	2 tablespoons	30 ml
Fine crumbs	1 cup	250 ml
Margarine or butter	1/4 cup	60 ml

1. Wash and dry eggplant. Cut into 1/4 inch (0.6 cm) slices. Peel each slice and place on a plate. Sprinkle each slice with some of the salt. Allow to stand for 15 minutes. Rinse salt from eggplant. Dry each slice with paper toweling.
2. Break egg onto a flat plate. Add water. Blend egg and water using a fork.
3. Dip each slice of eggplant in egg mixture so both sides are immersed.
4. Have fine crumbs on either waxed paper or a flat plate.
5. Transfer egg-coated eggplant slices to fine crumbs. Coat each side with crumbs.
6. Melt about half the butter or margarine in a heavy frying pan. Have surface of pan covered with a thin layer of fat. Fat should be hot but *not* smoking as slices of eggplant are added. Carefully brown slices on each side. Add more butter or margarine as necessary. Slices may be tender after they have been browned. Reduce heat for further cooking as necessary.
7. Avoid using too much fat. Eggplant has the ability to absorb fat as a sponge absorbs water.
8. Record total working time: _____ minutes.

Fried Zucchini

Zucchini or summer squash	1/2 pound	225 g
Margarine or butter	2 tablespoons	30 ml
Salt	1/4 teaspoon	1 ml

1. Thoroughly wash zucchini or squash to remove all dirt and sand. Dry with paper toweling.
2. Slice squash into 1/4 inch (0.6 cm) disks. Do not pare.
3. Melt fat in a heavy frying pan, over medium-low heat.
4. Add squash to melted fat; sprinkle salt over squash. Slices of squash may be browned on one or both sides. Cook until tender, 20–25 minutes.*
5. Record total working time: _____ minutes.

*Frying pan may be covered during cooking. Cook over medium-low heat 15–20 minutes or until squash is tender. The vegetables are cooked by steam in this technique.

Sautéed Onions

(See page 177 for recipe and directions.)

Japanese Style Vegetables with Chicken and Shrimp*

**Water	1 cup	250 ml
Soy sauce	4 tablespoons	60 ml
Sugar	3 tablespoons	45 ml
Salt (optional)	1/2 teaspoon	2 ml
†Raw shrimp, peeled and deveined	6	6
Snow peas, fresh	1 cup	250 ml
Sherry, dry (optional)	1/4 cup	60 ml
Chicken	1 1/2 pounds	680 g
Cauliflower, precooked	1 cup	250 ml
Mushrooms, fresh	10	10

1. Skin and bone chicken; cut into bite-size pieces. Peel and devein the shrimp.
2. Clean cauliflower; break into florets. Boil for 4 minutes. Wash and stem the snow peas. Remove the string down the back. Cut into halves or thirds. Hold in ice water until ready to use. The mushrooms are to be cleaned, trimmed, and rinsed under running water.
3. In a bowl mix water, 3 tablespoons (45 ml) soy sauce, sugar, and salt. Drain the snow peas and blot dry.
4. Set all ingredients by the wok in the order listed.
5. Set wok on high (400°F–205°C) heat for 60 seconds; then add the water mixture and bring to a boil.
*6. Add shrimp. Boil until pink and opaque, 2–3 minutes.
7. Remove with slotted spoon to a heated serving plate. Keep warm in an oven set at 200°F (92°C).
8. Add snow peas, sherry, and chicken. Bring to a boil. Stir and cook for 3 minutes. Remove to the heated serving dish with a slotted spoon and sprinkle with the remaining soy sauce. Return to the oven.
9. If water is low, add a little. Add cauliflower and mushrooms and cook 2–3 minutes. Remove to the heated serving dish. Reserve cooking liquid.
10. Arrange all the cooked products separately on the heated platter. Garnish if desired. Pour the cooking liquid into a small pitcher and serve immediately.
11. Record total working time: _____ minutes.

*1. This recipe may be stir-fried in an electric frying pan (Teflon® coated) if a wok is not available.
**2. When water, bouillon, or broth are used in place of oil, "stir-frying" in reality becomes a moist heat method for cooking the meat, poultry, or fish included in the recipe.
3. Rice may be served with this recipe; see page 130.
†4. Shrimp may be cut into halves or thirds.

CHARACTERISTICS OF HIGH-QUALITY COOKED VEGETABLES

Appearance: Pieces intact; cut edge remains distinct. Color is typical of predominant pigment present.

Texture: Cell structure softens without disintegrating.

Tenderness: Tender, yet slightly firm to bite. Vegetables cooked by stir-frying are usually more crisp than vegetables that are sautéed or cooked by other methods.

Flavor: Predominant flavor constituent of the raw vegetable may or may not predominate in the cooked vegetable. Many vegetables may have a slightly sweet note.

CHARACTERISTICS OF HIGH-QUALITY VEGETABLE SAUCES

Cream Sauces (See page 123.)

Cheese Sauce:

Appearance: Color (cheddar cheese in sauce) is a pale apricot (yellow-orange); opaque. Fat remains evenly dispersed throughout the sauce. Cheese is evenly dispersed throughout the sauce.

Consistency: Slightly thicker than heavy whipping cream; flows slowly but is fluid. Starch granules are evenly distributed and gelatinized.

Flavor: Distinct cheese flavor that blends with flavor of vegetable.

Vinegar Sauce on Harvard Beets:

Appearance: Clear; translucent; bright, dark red color.

Consistency: Slightly thinner than whipping cream. Starch granules are evenly distributed and gelatinized.

Flavor: Tart but with a sweet note. Beet flavor will be more distinct when the liquid from the canned beets is used in the sauce.

Note: See page 249 for Review Questions.

Dried Legumes

OBJECTIVES

1. To demonstrate the three stages of preparation essential to transform dried legumes into meal service products:
   a. Rehydration
   b. Cooking in water until tender
   c. Cooking with seasonings to increase palatability
2. To illustrate use of legumes as meat substitutes; therefore, no meat will be used in the recipes that follow.
3. To discuss high nutrient value of dried legumes.
4. To acquaint students with a variety of legumes.

PRODUCTS TO BE PREPARED TO ILLUSTRATE PRINCIPLES

Blackeye beans southern style
Lentils and rice with tomatoes
Curried kidney beans
Western bean stew
Barbecued lima beans

Note: All of the recipes in this section are vegetarian.

PRINCIPLES

1. Dried legumes must be hydrated before cooking. Some legumes are commerically processed to reduce hydration time.
*2. Soda may be added to speed hydration. Before legumes are cooked, soda must be rinsed off to prevent vitamin destruction and cell disintegration by alkali.
3. Legumes must be cooked tender in plain water before ingredients containing acids or calcium are added because
   a. Insoluble calcium pectate can be formed by addition of molasses, brown sugar, or canned tomatoes.
   b. Insoluble pectic substances can be formed by addition of tomatoes, tomato sauce, catsup, or vinegar.
4. Insoluble pectic compounds can be formed if water in which beans have been cooked contains calcium or magnesium ions.

*Use 1/4 teaspoon (1 ml) soda per quart of water for soaking. Rinse legumes carefully to remove soda before cooking.

Blackeye Beans Southern Style

Blackeye beans, dry	1 cup	250 ml
or cooked	3 cups	750 ml
Water to soak dry beans	3 cups	750 ml
*Bacon fat or lard or shortening	1 tablespoon	15 ml
Flour	1 teaspoon	5 ml
Salt	3/4 teaspoon	3 ml
Pepper, black	1/4 teaspoon	1 ml
Cayenne pepper	few grains	few grains
Onion, medium, minced	1	1

1. Sort and wash beans. Cover beans with water and bring to a boil. Boil 2 minutes. Turn off heat. Cover saucepan and allow beans to stand for 1 hour. (*Alternate method:* Soak washed beans overnight before cooking.)
2. Melt bacon fat in a heavy skillet. Stir in flour, seasonings, and onions. Cook until onions are lightly browned.
3. Pour onion mixture into beans. Cover. Simmer until beans are tender, approximately 1 hour.
4. Record total working time: _____ minutes. Yield: 3–4 servings.

*Use bacon fat or lard for authentic Southern style. Use vegetable shortening for vegetarian product.

Lentils and Rice with Tomatoes

Lentils, dry	1 cup	250 ml
or cooked	3 cups	750 ml
Water to soak dry lentils	3 cups	750 ml
Bay leaf	1	1
Parsley	3 sprigs	3 sprigs
Onion, medium, finely chopped	1	1
Margarine or oil	3 tablespoons	45 ml
Rice	1/3 cup	75 ml
Nutmeg, ground	1/4 teaspoon	1 ml
Salt	1 teaspoon	5 ml
Pepper, black	few grains	few grains
Tomatoes, canned	1 cup	250 ml

1. Sort and wash lentils. Soak overnight.
2. Do not rinse. Add bay leaf, parsley, and salt. Cook until lentils are tender, approximately 1 hour.
3. Add the rice to 1 cup (250 ml) boiling salted water (use 1/4 teaspoon [1 ml] salt for each cup water). Cook over low heat until rice is tender. One teaspoon (5 ml) butter or margarine can be added while the rice is cooking.
4. Melt fat in a heavy frying pan or a flame-proof casserole. Add onion. Sauté until onion is lightly browned. Do not burn.
5. Add all other ingredients. Either simmer all ingredients together for 15 minutes or bake for 30 minutes in a 350°F (175°C) oven.
6. Remove bay leaf and cooked parsley before serving.
7. Record total working time: _____ minutes. Yield: 3–4 servings.

Curried Kidney Beans

Kidney beans, dry	1 cup	250 ml
or cooked	3 cups	750 ml
Water to soak dry beans	3 cups	750 ml
Salt	1 teaspoon	5 ml
Onion, medium, sliced	1	1
Pepper	1/8 teaspoon	0.5 ml
Curry powder	1/2–1 teaspoon	2–5 ml
Shortening or oil	2 tablespoons	30 ml

1. Sort and wash kidney beans. Soak overnight in water to cover. (*Alternate method:* Cover beans with water and bring to a boil. Boil 2 minutes. Turn off heat. Cover pan. Let beans stand for 1 hour.)
2. Add salt to soaked beans. Cook beans until tender, about 1 hour. Drain. Reserve liquid.
3. Melt fat in heavy frying pan. Add onion. Sauté until onion is slightly yellow, about 5 minutes.
4. Add cooked beans, pepper, curry powder, and 1/2 cup (125 ml) bean liquid. Simmer together 15–30 minutes for blending of flavors. Add bean liquid as necessary. Beans should be moist but not soupy when served.
5. Record total working time: _____ minutes. Yield: 3–4 servings.

Western Bean Stew

Pinto or cranberry beans, dry	1 cup	250 ml
or cooked	3 cups	750 ml
Water to soak dry beans	3 cups	750 ml
Salt	1/2 teaspoon	2 ml
Tabasco sauce	2–3 drops	2–3 drops
Shortening	2 tablespoons	30 ml
Onion, medium, chopped	1	1
Garlic, small clove, minced	1	1
Tomatoes, canned	1 cup	250 ml
Parsley, minced	2 tablespoons	30 ml
Marjoram, ground	1/4 teaspoon	1 ml
Chili powder	1 teaspoon	5 ml

1. Sort and wash beans. Soak overnight in enough water to cover beans.
2. Add salt and Tabasco sauce to beans. Bring to boil. Reduce heat and simmer until beans are tender, approximately 1 hour. Drain beans and reserve liquid.
3. While beans are cooking, melt fat in a heavy frying pan. Add onions and garlic. Cook until onion is light yellow. Add tomatoes, parsley, 1/2 cup (125 ml) of the reserved bean liquid, and the spices. Simmer together 30 minutes.
4. Add beans to onion mixture. Simmer together for an additional 15 minutes.
5. Record total working time: _____ minutes. Yield: 3–4 servings.

Barbecued Lima Beans

Lima beans, dry	1 cup	250 ml
or cooked	3 cups	750 ml
Water to soak dry beans	3 cups	750 ml
Onion, medium, minced	1	1
Garlic, small clove, minced	1	1
Oil or margarine	2 tablespoons	30 ml
Brown sugar	3 tablespoons	45 ml
Vinegar, cider	2 tablespoons	30 ml
Mustard, prepared	1 teaspoon	5 ml
Tomato sauce—8 ounce (227 g) can	1	1
Tomatoes, canned or juice	1/2 cup	125 ml

1. Sort and wash beans. Soak overnight in enough water to cover beans.
2. Cook beans in salted water (1/4 teaspoon [1 ml] salt per cup of water) until beans are tender. Start with approximately 1 inch of water above beans. Drain cooked beans.
3. Melt fat or heat oil in heavy frying pan or flame-proof casserole. Add onion and garlic. Cook slowly until onion is yellow and transparent but not browned.
4. Add all other ingredients to onion mixture. Simmer over low heat for 30 minutes or bake in a 350°F (175°C) oven approximately 1 hour for a blending of flavors.
5. Record total working time: _____ minutes. Yield: 4–6 servings.

CHARACTERISTICS OF HIGH-QUALITY DRIED LEGUME PRODUCTS

Appearance: Beans or lentils retain shape; liquid well absorbed by legumes (unless a stew or soup product).

Texture: Dried legumes (except soybeans) are mealy.

Tenderness: Little resistance to bite.

*Flavor: Distinctive for variety or type of legume; seasonings well blended.

*Flavor would be improved with longer cooking time than is available in the laboratory period.

REVIEW QUESTIONS

1. What are dried legumes?
2. Discuss briefly the nutritional value of dried legumes.
3. Why are dried legumes soaked in water to which soda has been added?
4. What would happen when the legumes are cooked if the soda was not rinsed off?
5. Why are legumes cooked tender before the addition of flavoring substances (i.e., molasses, tomato)?

Fruits

OBJECTIVES

1. To study the relationship between varietal characteristics of apples and the quality characteristics of selected cooked apple products.
2. To study the factors which affect the cooking of dehydrated fruits.
3. To illustrate the effect of sugar on cell structure.
4. To observe and study conditions which affect enzymatic browning in certain light-colored, fresh, pared, and/or sliced fruit.
5. To study factors affecting formation of pectin gels.

PRODUCTS TO BE PREPARED TO ILLUSTRATE PRINCIPLES

*Raw apples—varietal differences
Raw apples—enzymatic browning
Applesauce
Coddled apples
Baked apples
Prunes
Cranberry sauce
Cranberry jelly
Apple crisp

PRINCIPLES

1. In cooking fruits, softening of cell structure results from
   a. Breakdown of protopectin (cell-cementing substance)
   b. Softening of hemicellulose
2. Agitation during cooking may cause rupturing of cell structure.
3. By osmosis,
   a. Water may pass into cell structure to cause a rupturing of the cell (no sugar present during the cooking period).
   b. Sugar may pass into cell structure to cause a firming of the cell (when fruit is cooked in a dilute sugar syrup).
   c. Sugar in dry form or in concentrated solution may cause dehydration of cell structure, which results in a hard, tough piece of cooked fruit.
4. Sugar and pectin (in the fruit juice) in proper amounts will produce a jelly structure.

*Select apple varieties to include (1) an all-purpose, (2) a cooking, and (3) an eating (raw) variety.

235

5. Light-colored fresh fruits (apples, apricots, avocados, peaches, pears) darken when exposed to air as a result of the presence of oxidative enzymes. Browning is delayed by coating the cut surface.
   a. Hold slices of fruit under cold water until ready to use.
   b. Dip fruit slices in citrus juice.
   c. Combine with commercial ascorbic acid preparations.
   d. Immerse in sugar syrup.
6. Dehydrated fruits (prunes, apricots, apples, pears, raisins) must have water absorbed by plant tissue before the fruit will become soft as a result of cooking. Very dry fruit will require a longer time to absorb water. "Moisturized" fruits may require very short or no special hydration period before they will cook tender in water or steam.
7. Dehydrated and dehydrofrozen fruits will absorb water more rapidly if hot water is added to the fruit for the hydration period.

FRUITS—VARIABLES

Dried Fruits

1. Fruit soaked overnight to rehydrate.
2. Fruit soaked 20 minutes in hot water to rehydrate.

Fresh Fruits

*1. Apples
   a. Sauce prepared from varieties of apples
      (1) Cooking variety—rapid rate of disintegration of cell structure
      (2) Cooking variety—slow rate of disintegration of cell structure
      (3) All-purpose variety—moderate rate of disintegration of cell structure
      (4) Eating raw variety—not suited for cooking
   b. Coddled apples—same varieties as listed above
   c. Baked apples—same varieties as listed above
   d. Evaluate all varieties in raw form.
   e. Use each variety to illustrate the effectiveness of ascorbic acid solution to delay enzymatic browning. Hold cut slices at least 30 minutes before evaluating.
      (1) Raw apple slices not treated
      (2) Raw apple slices dipped in ascorbic acid solution
2. Cranberries
   a. Sauce prepared from whole berries
      (1) Fruit cooked in boiling water, sugar added after cooking
      (2) Fruit cooked in sugar syrup
   b. Jelly prepared by cooking fruit in water, straining fruit to remove seeds and skins, adding sugar and cooking to jelly stage

*Raw apples continue to respire in any type of storage. Apples used shortly after harvest will be of higher quality than apples held in storage. The longer the storage period, the greater the decrease in quality. Respiration is slowest under controlled atmosphere storage.

Browning Reactions in Fresh Fruits

*Apples, for each variety being cooked—2 to 4
Ascorbic acid, commercial mix—1 teaspoon (5 ml)

1. Follow package directions for preparation of the ascorbic acid solution. Prepare 1 or 2 cups (250 or 500 ml) of solution.
2. Wash and dry apples. Cut into quarters. Core.
3. Cut each quarter into 3–5 slices. For half the samples of each variety, dip the slices of apple into the ascorbic acid solution immediately after slicing. Remove slices from solution after each side of slice has been wetted. Arrange on a plate. *Do not cover.* Let stand at least 30 minutes (1 hour preferred) before comparing with products from the second treatment.
4. Arrange the remaining apple slices on a plate as they are cut. *Do not cover.* Allow to remain exposed to air for at least 30 minutes (1 hour preferred).
5. Compare the appearance (surface browning) by the two treatments. Also note whether variety is a factor.

*Avocados, apricots, pears, peaches, or bananas may be substituted for apples.

Applesauce

Apples, medium size	3	3
Water, boiling	3/4 cup	175 ml
Sugar	3 tablespoons	45 ml
No spice for class work		

1. Wash, pare, and cut each apple into 12 to 16 sections.* Core each slice. Cut apples in half from stem end to blossom end. Cut each half into two pieces (quarter of whole apple). Cut each quarter into 3 or 4 equal slices.
2. Add apple slices to boiling water. Cover saucepan. Cook at simmering temperature, 185°–200°F (85°–95°C), until slices are tender and soft, approximately 15 to 20 minutes.
3. Stir cooked apple slices with a fork until slices are broken up. Add sugar and stir until sugar is dissolved.
4. No spice is used for class work so the natural flavor of apples of several varieties can be tested and compared.
5. Record total working time: _____ minutes.

*Some applesauce can be made with apples unpeeled. Wash apples; cut into uniform-sized slices without paring the apples. Apple skins may or may not be removed before sugar is added.

Applesauce (Microwave)

Apples, cooking, medium size	3	3
Water	2 teaspoons	10 ml
Sugar	2–3 tablespoons	30–45 ml
No spice for class		

1. Wash apples. Peel using a vegetable peeler. Quarter each apple. Remove core. Cut each quarter in half lengthwise.
2. Place prepared fruit in a 1-quart (1-L) casserole. Add water. Cover casserole with a piece of waxed paper.
3. Microwave at *high* power for 2 minutes. Stir. Microwave at *high* for 1 more minute.
4. Add sugar. Amount of sugar will vary with the variety of apple used and the degree of ripeness of the apples. Stir in the sugar. If the fruit slices are not yet tender enough to be broken up by stirring, microwave at *high* power for 30-second intervals. Amount of heat will depend on amount of fruit being cooked as well as on the variety and degree of ripeness of the apples.
5. Record total working time: _____ minutes.

CHARACTERISTICS OF HIGH-QUALITY APPLESAUCE

Appearance: Bright yellow color, the shade of yellow depending on the variety of apple used. Pieces of apple pulp should be of uniform size, usually quite small with all the water absorbed by the pulp.

Consistency and Texture: Small even-size pieces of pulp, not easily identifiable. A spoonful mounds up when put on a plate.

Tenderness: Soft, no resistance to bite.

Flavor: Apple flavor identifiable and not masked by sweetness or spice flavor when spices are used.

Coddled Apples

Apples, medium size	2	2
Sugar	2/3 cup	150 ml
Water	1 1/2 cups	375 ml

1. Add sugar to water in a wide-bottomed saucepan. Stir until sugar is dissolved. Bring to a boil.
2. Wash, pare, core, and cut into 1/4 inch (0.6 cm) rings.
3. Add apples to hot syrup and cover saucepan. Reduce heat so apples cook slowly for about 20 minutes or until apple slices are translucent and clear.
4. Record total working time: _____ minutes.

CHARACTERISTICS OF HIGH-QUALITY CODDLED APPLES

Appearance: Slices intact; translucent, bright yellow color, the shade of yellow dependent on the variety of apple used.

Texture: Just firm enough to remain intact.

Tenderness: Slightly firm, little resistance to bite.

Flavor: Apple flavor identifiable and not masked by sweetness.

Apple Crisp

Apples, tart; pared, cored, thinly sliced	4 cups	1000 ml
Sugar, granulated	1/4 cup	60 ml
Oatmeal, quick-cooking	1/2 cup	125 ml
Oatbran or oat flour	1/3 cup	75 ml
Nutmeg	1/2 teaspoon	2 ml
Cinnamon	1/4 teaspoon	1 ml
Brown sugar, packed	1/2 cup	125 ml
Salt	1/4 teaspoon	1 ml
Flour, all-purpose	1/3 cup	75 ml
Margarine or butter, soft	1/3 cup	75 ml
Nuts, coarsely chopped (optional)	1/3 cup	75 ml
Margarine to grease baking pan		

1. Preheat oven to 375°F (190°C).
2. Lightly grease the bottom of an 8" × 8" × 2" (20 cm × 20 cm × 5 cm) baking pan.
3. In a 1 1/2 to 2 quart (1.5–2 L) bowl combine both sugars, salt, all-purpose flour, and both spices. Stir until spices are evenly blended.
4. Add oatmeal, oatbran or oat flour, and softened margarine or butter and, using a pastry blender, cut the fat into the other ingredients until thoroughly blended.
5. Blot the apple slices dry and arrange on the bottom of the greased baking dish.
6. Spread the mixture prepared in Step 4 evenly over the fruit.
7. Sprinkle the chopped nuts, if used, evenly over the top.
8. Bake for 30–40 minutes in the preheated oven.
9. Record the total working time: _____ minutes.

Baked Apples

Apples, medium size	2	2
Sugar	1/4 cup	60 ml
Water	2 teaspoons	10 ml

No spice added for class work

1. Preheat oven to 450°F (230°C).
2. Wash and core apples (use special coring device).
3. Further prepare apples for baking.
   a. On one apple at the blossom end, pare off about 1 1/2 inches (3.8 cm) of skin.
   b. On the second apple, barely cut through the skin around the circumference of the apple, midway between stem and blossom ends.
4. Place the apples in a baking dish.*
5. Fill center cavity of each apple with 2 tablespoons (30 ml) of sugar.
6. Slightly moisten the sugar in each apple with 1 teaspoon (5 ml) of water.
7. Add water to baking dish so bottom of dish is covered with 1/4 inch (0.6 cm) of water.
8. Cover baking dish with aluminum foil for at least the first half of the baking period.
9. Bake at 450°F (230°C) for 10 minutes. Reduce oven setting to 350°F (175°C). Bake 40–50 minutes or until apples are tender. See footnote item 3.*
10. Record total working time: _____ minutes.

*(1) For class discussion, all varieties of apples should be baked in one large baking dish.
 (2) Identify varieties of apples by marking outside of baking pan with marking pencil.
 (3) All varieties of apples do not bake to similar degrees of tenderness within a controlled time limit. This is one way to illustrate varietal differences in apples. Remove the pan of apples from the oven when the all-purpose variety is fork tender.

CHARACTERISTICS OF HIGH-QUALITY BAKED APPLES

Appearance: Apple must remain intact; skin color red to brownish-red depending on variety of apple used.

Tenderness: *Skin*: little resistance to bite. *Pulp*: smooth, soft, no resistance to bite.

Flavor: Apple flavor identifiable and not overpowered by sweetness or spice flavor when spices are used.

Cranberries*—For Each Variable

Cranberries, all edible portion	1 cup	250 ml
Water	1/2 cup	125 ml
Sugar	1/2 cup	125 ml

*Cranberries purchased in season, frozen, and used at a later date will give satisfactory results. Certain varieties of grapes (Concord), crab apples, currants, gooseberries, or loganberries may be substituted for cranberries.

Fruit Sauce (Cooked in Water)*

1. Sort and wash cranberries.
2. Add water and bring to a boil. Boil for 5 minutes or until the skins have popped open.
3. Add sugar and stir until the sugar is dissolved. Simmer, 185°–200°F (85°–95°C), for 5 minutes.
4. Pour into serving dish. Allow to cool before evaluating.
5. Record total working time: _____ minutes.

Fruit Sauce (Cooked in Syrup)*

1. Sort and wash cranberries.
2. Bring water and sugar to a boil. Stir until the sugar is dissolved.
3. Add cranberries to the boiling syrup. Skins will tend to pop open. Cook at 200°–212°F (95°–100°C) for 5 minutes. Do not overstir while the fruit is cooking.
4. Pour into serving dish. Allow to cool before comparing with other products.
5. Record total working time: _____ minutes.

*Compare the tenderness of the cranberry skins for the fruit cooked by each of these methods.

Jelly (Fruit Strained)

1. Sort and wash cranberries.
2. Add water. Bring to a boil. Boil for 5 minutes or until the skins have popped open.
3. Rub the cooked berries through a strainer or put through a food mill, collecting the juice and as much of the pulp as possible in a clean saucepan placed underneath.
4. Add sugar to sieved pulp. Stir until sugar is dissolved.
5. Heat quickly to boiling temperature and boil for about 5 minutes. Mixture may need to be stirred constantly to prevent fruit pulp from sticking to bottom of saucepan and to keep mixture from spattering as it boils.
6. At the end of the cooking period, the mixture should give a jelly "sheeting" test: several drops of juice tend to flow together from the side of the spoon. (Cook until this test is reached.)
7. Pour into a serving dish. *Do not stir* this mixture as it cools.
8. Record total working time: _____ minutes.

CHARACTERISTICS OF HIGH-QUALITY CRANBERRY SAUCE

Appearance: Deep red; translucence is masked by seeds and pulp.
Texture: *Cooked in water*: fluid, no gel structure.
   Cooked in syrup: thicker, may have a tendency to gel.
Tenderness: Skins should be tender with little resistance to bite.
Flavor: Typical of fruit; tart.

CHARACTERISTICS OF HIGH-QUALITY CRANBERRY JELLY

†**Appearance:** Deep red; translucent; seeds may or may not be present.
Consistency and Texture: Firm gel; should hold a cut edge; syneresis at a minimum.
Tenderness: Firm yet soft.
Flavor: Typical of fruit; tart.

†Will depend on size opening of food mill or strainer used after the fruit is cooked.

Prunes—Not Soaked

Prunes, per person	1	1
Water to cover fruit—approximately	1 1/2 cups	375 ml
Sugar—adjust as necessary	1/4 cup	60 ml
Lemon, optional, thin slices	2	2

1. Wash fruit in warm tap water. Lift fruit pieces out of wash water.
2. Add cold water to dried fruit. Quickly heat until water begins to boil. Turn off heat. Cover saucepan with a tight-fitting cover. Allow saucepan to remain on warm burner with the heat off. Soak fruit for 25 minutes.
3. Simmer, 185°–200°F (85°–90°C), fruit for 40 minutes. Keep saucepan covered. Add more hot water as needed. *Do not allow to cook dry.*
4. Remove cover from saucepan. Add sugar, if used.
5. Simmer in an uncovered saucepan for 3 minutes after sugar has been added. (A thin slice of lemon may be added to prunes at the same time as the sugar is added.)
6. If the liquid on the fruit is watery at the end of the 3-minute cooking period, remove fruit from liquid; then continue to heat the water-sugar mixture until it is thicker and somewhat syrupy. Pour the liquid over the fruit for serving.
7. Record total working time: _____ minutes.

Prunes—Soaked Overnight

Prunes, per person	1	1
Water to cover fruit—approximately	1 1/2 cups	375 ml
Sugar—adjust as necessary	1/4 cup	60 ml
Lemon, optional, thin slices	2	2

1. Put soaked fruit and water in a saucepan. Cover saucepan with a tight-fitting lid. Simmer, 185°–200°F (85°–90°C), fruit for 30 minutes. Add more hot water as needed.
2. Remove cover from saucepan. Add sugar, if used.
3. Simmer in an uncovered saucepan for 3 minutes after sugar has been added. (A thin slice of lemon may be added to prunes at the same time as the sugar is added.)
4. If the liquid on the fruit is watery at the end of the 3-minute cooking period, remove fruit from liquid; continue to heat the water-sugar mixture until it is thicker and somewhat syrupy. Pour the liquid over the fruit for serving.
5. Record total working time: _____ minutes.

CHARACTERISTICS OF HIGH-QUALITY PRUNES

Appearance: Intact, plump, not deeply wrinkled.

Tenderness: *Skins:* soft, little resistance to bite.
Pulp: easily removed from pit; smooth, soft, no resistance to bite.

Flavor: Typical. Lemon juice may be used to mask sweetness, but neither sweetness nor lemon flavor should dominate.

OBSERVATIONS ON FRUIT

Fruit	Variety	Color and Appearance	Texture and/or Tenderness	Flavor
Raw apples				

Apple Variety	Treatment	Color and Appearance	Other Comments
	Not treated		
	Ascorbic acid treated		
	Not treated		
	Ascorbic acid treated		
	Not treated		
	Ascorbic acid treated		
	Not treated		
	Ascorbic acid treated		

OBSERVATIONS ON FRUIT (Continued)

Fruit	Variety	Color and Appearance	Texture and/or Tenderness	Flavor
Applesauce				
Coddled apples				
Baked apples				

OBSERVATIONS ON FRUIT (Continued)

Fruit	Treatment	Color and Appearance	Texture and/or Tenderness	Flavor
Prunes	Soaked overnight			
	Soaked in hot water 20 min.			
Cranberry sauce	Cooked in water			
	Cooked in sugar syrup			
Cranberry jelly				

REVIEW QUESTIONS

Questions Applying to Both Fruits and Vegetables

1. Define each of the following terms and discuss its importance in cooking fruits and/or vegetables:
   a. Protopectin
   b. Hemicellulose
   c. Cellulose
   d. Pectin
   e. Calcium pectate
2. a. List four pigments that occur naturally in fruits and vegetables.
   b. Cite examples of a fruit and vegetable containing each of the four pigments.
   c. Describe the action of each of the following agents on each of the four pigments:
      (1) Acid
      (2) Alkali (base)
      (3) Excessive heat
      (4) Iron
   d. Name some specific agents in c(1) and c(2).
3. a. What is the role of pectic substances in raw fruits and vegetables?
   b. What is the effect of acid on pectic substances?
   c. What is the effect of alkali on pectic substances?
4. Explain each of the evaluations on the evaluation sheet on page 251.

Questions Applying to Vegetables Only

1. Define each of the following terms and discuss its importance in cooking vegetables:
   a. Oxalic acid
   b. Solanin
   c. Sinigren
   d. Allyl sulfide
   e. Lignocellulose
   f. Plant acid
2. What determines whether a vegetable is cooked with the lid on or the lid off? Discuss.
3. Discuss the relationship of volume of water used in cooking and nutrient value of a cooked vegetable.
4. The famous French chef, Escoffier, in his recipe for *Choux Rouges à la Flamande* (Flamande Red Cabbage), adds a little vinegar and four peeled and quartered cooking apples. Why are these two items used in preparing this dish?
5. a. Describe the effect of storage temperature on sugar and starch in certain vegetables.
   b. What difficulties might storage temperature cause in cooking potatoes?

Questions Applying to Fruits Only

1. Define each of the following terms and discuss its importance in cooking fruits:
   a. Osmosis
   b. Enzymatic browning
   c. Organic acids
   d. Dehydrated fruits
   e. Gel
2. a. Why must dehydrated fruits be soaked in water before cooking?
   b. What would happen if dehydrated fruits were cooked in a concentrated sugar solution?
3. a. List some fruits which turn brown when cut slices are exposed to the air.
   b. Describe several ways this browning may be delayed.

EVALUATION OF PRODUCTS

Name: _____

Date: _____

Score System

Points	Quality
7	Excellent
6	Very good
5	Good
4	Medium
3	Fair
2	Poor
1	Very poor

Directions:

1. Place the numerical score in the box in the upper left-hand corner.
2. Comments should justify the numerical score. Comments must be brief.
3. Evaluation of the food products must be on an *individual* basis.

Products

Quality Characteristic	Harvard Beets	Baked Potato	Broccoli	Prune	Baked Apple
Appearance	3 — Bluish red	4 — Moist; translucent	3 — Olive green	3 — Shriveled	1 — Fell apart
Consistency or Texture	5	4 — Wet; waxy	5	2 — Firm	1 — Soft and mushy
Tenderness	5	5	4 — Too soft	2 — Tough	1 — Too soft
Flavor	4 — Flat; not tart	6	3 — Bitter	4 — Too sweet	5
Overall Eating Quality	3	4	4	2	1

Soups

OBJECTIVES

1. To acquaint students with the basic types of soups.
2. To illustrate characteristics of a selection of soups.
3. To become acquainted with terminology related to specific types of soups.
4. To review and use methods in preparation of fruits and vegetables.
5. To discuss characteristics of high-quality soups.

PRODUCTS TO BE PREPARED TO ILLUSTRATE PRINCIPLES

Split pea soup
Chicken rice soup
Beef barley soup
Corn chowder
Cream of broccoli soup

Chicken-okra gumbo—Louisiana Cajun
Minestrone soup—Italian
Gazpacho—Spain
Fruit soup—Scandinavian
Cock-O-Leekie soup—Scottish

PRINCIPLES

1. Soups may be classified by
   a. Type of predominant basic liquid
      (1) Broth (stock), i.e., brown stock or white stock
      (2) Milk
   b. Consistency of liquid
      (1) Similar to thin white sauce, i.e., bisque
      (2) Similar to thick white sauce, i.e., chowder
2. Obtain brown stock by browning meat before water is added. Beef is usually the basic meat used for brown stock.
3. Obtain white stock by using veal and/or poultry in its preparation.
4. To prepare a soup low in fat
   a. Remove visible fat from meat or poultry before cooking.
   b. Chill broth to harden fat; then skim fat from surface.
   c. Use a "baster" to suction liquid fat from surface of broth.
5. Prepare broth from less-tender cuts of meat with or without bone and from older poultry. Simmer with water for 1 hour or more until flesh is tender.
6. Broth may be clarified by heating with beaten egg white and crushed egg shell. Coagulated egg traps protein particles of meat. Strain broth to remove egg.
7. Add cold water to meat or poultry to allow better extraction of juices.
8. Dried beans must be rehydrated and may or may not be fully cooked before adding to the broth.

9. Some vegetables may be added to meat at the beginning of the cooking period as a source of additional flavor. These vegetables must be removed before the broth is used in preparation of the soup.
10. Color, flavor, and texture of vegetables can be retained by cooking them the normal time for each vegetable.
11. Pasta or rice may be added in a dry form but a clearer broth results if pasta is pre-cooked.
12. Some fat can be desirable since fat carries some flavor constituents.
13. Fish stock is usually used only in fish soups or stews.
14. Bouillon cubes or granules dissolved in water can substitute for freshly prepared broth and/or intensify flavor of broth.
15. Cut vegetables in assorted sizes to add interest to appearance.
16. Small size pieces of vegetables expose greater surface area to release flavor.
17. Add egg, when used, as the last ingredient to prevent its being overcooked.
18. Fruit soup may be served cold as an appetizer or hot as a dessert.
19. In some soups, meat and vegetables may remain in large pieces. When served, the broth is served as the first course; the meat and vegetables become the entree.
20. Some soups may be served over a slice of bread, as plain bread or toast, or fried (plain bread browned in a small amount of fat).
21. The fat content of creamed soups will depend on
    a. Type and amount of milk or cream used
    b. Addition of added fat as margarine, butter, salt pork, or bacon fat

TERMINOLOGY

1. *Broth* and *stock* are usually used interchangeably. It is the liquid obtained by cooking meat, poultry, fish, shellfish, or vegetables in water with various desired seasonings.
2. *Brown stock* and *white stock*—see Principles.
3. *Fish stock*—see chapter on fish, page 198.
4. *Bouillon* is a lightly seasoned broth or clear soup made from various meats, fish, poultry, or vegetables. Beef is the most common meat used.
5. *Consommé* is a clarified, double strength, brown broth.
6. *Bouillabaisse* is a thick, hearty soup from an assortment of fish and other seafoods.
7. *Chowder* is a thick, hearty soup prepared from meat, poultry, fish, and/or vegetables.
8. *Bisque* is a rich cream soup sometimes containing shellfish.
9. *Minestrone* is a thick vegetable soup.
10. *Gazpacho* is a chilled vegetable soup of finely chopped raw tomatoes, cucumbers, onions, and other vegetables in spiced tomato juice.
11. *Gumbo* is a thick soup/stew characteristic of Creole cooking in Louisiana; also called *okra*.
12. *Okra* is a tall, green plant with edible mucilaginous green pods that impart a characteristic texture and taste; used in soups and gumbos; may also be fried or steamed. *Do not use* filé powder and okra in the same dish.
13. *Filé powder* is made from extracts of the sassafras plant and is used as a thickening agent, but it imparts no flavor to the dish. For this reason many Cajun chefs do not use filé powder.
14. *Blanching* is to briefly heat vegetables or fruits in steam or boiling water to loosen or remove skins; will also set the color. After blanching place the cooking pan in a sink of *cold* water to prevent further cooking.

CHARACTERISTICS OF HIGH-QUALITY SOUPS

Appearance: *Consommé*—broth is clear. *Bouillon*—clear or cloudy depending on the type of soup. The pieces of meat or vegetable have been removed. *Cream soups*—opaque and show no sign of lumpiness.

Tenderness: *Pasta* or *rice* should be cooked *al dente*, i.e., firm but neither soft nor hard. *Vegetables* should be tender without being mushy. *Meat, fish,* and *poultry* should be tender.

Consistency: *Bisque* has the consistency of thin cream. *Chowder* has the consistency of heavy cream or thick white sauce. *Cream soups* should have the consistency of a thin white sauce.

Flavor: Some soups may have a well-blended flavor with no one flavor predominant. Where one vegetable should predominate, as in split pea soup, other ingredients should not mask its flavor.

Recent research indicates the egg yolk should be cooked to the firm stage to avoid the possibility of salmonella food poisoning.

Cock-O-Leekie Soup (Scottish)

Chicken legs or thighs	4 pieces	4 pieces
Leeks	3	3
Onion, small	1	1
Celery, stalk, 10 inches	1	1
Water, cold	6 cups	1500 ml
Salt	2 teaspoons	10 ml
Prunes, optional	—	—
(1 prune per serving)		

1. Trim off stem end and tops of leeks. Useable pieces should be 4–5 inches (10–13 cm) long. Split each piece down through the center to 1 inch (2.5 cm) from the end. Spread out the leaves, and wash carefully to remove any dirt. Drain well.
2. In a 3-quart (3-L) saucepan blanch the leeks in 2 cups of boiling water for 2 minutes. Remove the leeks, draining carefully; retain the cooking water. Squeeze the leaves together to make a tight bundle. Starting at the stem end chop the leeks into a 1/4 inch (0.6 cm) layer (the leaves will fall apart into small pieces).
3. Dice the celery into small pieces.
4. Remove any excess fat from the chicken pieces. Place the chicken pieces in the saucepan containing the cooking liquid from the leeks. Add the remaining 4 cups of water, chopped leeks, celery, and salt. Boil slowly for 7 minutes, then remove from the heat.
5. Remove the chicken pieces from the pan. Remove skin and discard. Remove the chicken meat from the bone, cut into bite-size pieces, and return the meat to the saucepan.
6. If prunes are used, they should be added at this point. Boil slowly for 6–7 minutes. Do not let the prunes start to disintegrate. Remove them from the pan.
7. Serve the soup in a heated bowl, adding one prune to each bowl.
8. Record total working time: _____ minutes.

Beef Barley Soup

Ground beef, extra lean	1/2 pound	225 g
Olive or salad oil	1 tablespoon	15 ml
Water	5 cups	1250 ml
Barley, pearl, quick-cooking	1/4 cup	60 ml
Celery stalk, 10 inches (25 cm)	1	1
Onion, medium–large	1	1
Turnip, medium	1	1
Mixed vegetables, frozen 10-ounce package (283 g)	1 package	1 package
Beef bouillon	2 cubes	2 cubes
Salt	1/2 teaspoon	2 ml
Pepper	1/8 teaspoon	0.5 ml

1. Mixed vegetables—place package in a pan of warm water to thaw.
2. Place oil in a 3-quart (3-L) saucepan. Add ground beef and stir constantly to break the beef into small pieces.
3. Remove dry skin from the onion and chop into small pieces. Add to the browning meat. Heat on medium-high for 3 to 5 minutes, until meat is brown. Add bouillon cubes, salt, and pepper.
4. Add barley and cold water. Bring to a boil and simmer for 20 minutes.
5. Pare the turnip and dice into 3/8 inch (1.0 cm) pieces. Wash celery stalk and cut into 1/8 inch (0.3 cm) slices. Add turnip and celery to the meat mixture. Simmer for 5 minutes.
6. Add the thawed mixed vegetables. Simmer 8–10 minutes or until the vegetables are tender. Add 1 cup (250 ml) of hot water if desired.
7. Serve in heated bowls.
8. Record total working time: _____ minutes.

Split Pea Soup

Split peas, dry, green	1 cup	250 ml
Water, cold	4 cups	1000 ml
Onion, medium–large	1	1
Carrots, medium	2	2
Ham, fully cooked	1 cup	250 ml

1. Directions for preparing ingredients
   a. *Peas*: Sort to remove any foreign particles. Wash and drain by lifting peas out of the wash water.
   b. *Onion*: Chop into small pieces.
   c. *Carrots*: Wash, scrape, and cut into 1/8 inch (0.3 cm) coins.
   d. *Ham*: Dice into small pieces.
2. Place the washed and drained peas in a 3-quart (3-L) saucepan. Add water. Heat to almost simmering temperature. Reduce the heat and hold for 10 minutes.
3. Add onions and carrots. Cook at simmering temperature for 20 minutes or until the peas and vegetables are soft enough to puree.
*4. Place about 1 cup (250 ml) of the cooked vegetables in a blender. Puree until smooth. Repeat the blending procedure until all of the cooked vegetables have been pureed.
5. Return the puree to the saucepan. Stir in the diced ham and heat to serving temperature. *Do not allow to boil.*
6. Serve in heated bowls.
7. Record total working time: _____ minutes.

*Note: If the puree is too thick, additional water can be added until the soup is at the desired consistency.

Chicken Rice Soup

Chicken thighs	4 thighs	4 thighs
Rice, long grain, regular	1/2 cup	125 ml
Onion, medium	1	1
Carrots, medium–large	3	3
Celery stalks, 10 inches (25 cm) long	3	3
Peas, frozen	1 cup	250 ml
Water, cold	4 cups	1000 ml
Salt	1/2 teaspoon	2 ml
Pepper	1/8 teaspoon	0.5 ml
Poultry seasoning	1/8 teaspoon	0.5 ml
Thyme, ground	1/8 teaspoon	0.5 ml
Chicken bouillon cube (optional)	1	1

1. Directions for preparing ingredients
   a. *Chicken thighs*: Remove skin and any visible fat. Wash in cold water.
   b. *Onion*: Cut in half lengthwise; thinly slice crosswise.
   c. *Celery*: Cut into 1/4 inch (0.6 cm) slices.
   d. *Carrots*: Cut into 1/4 inch (0.6 cm) coins.
   e. *Frozen peas*: Place package in a pan of warm water to thaw.
2. Place all of the ingredients except the peas and seasonings in a 3-quart (3-L) saucepan. Simmer over medium heat 25 minutes or until the chicken thighs are tender.
3. Remove the thighs. Cut meat from the bone and cut into small chunks. Add the meat back into the soup.
4. Add the thawed peas and seasonings. Simmer for 10 minutes.
5. Serve in heated bowls.
6. Record total working time: _____ minutes.

Chicken-Okra Gumbo (Louisiana Cajun)

Chicken thigh	4	4
Sausage, Kielbasa	8 ounces	225 g
Water, cold	2 cups	500 ml
Chicken broth, canned, 14 ounce (400 g)	1 can	1 can
Okra, cut, frozen, 10 ounce, (400 g)	1 package	1 package
Onion, medium	1	1
Green pepper, small	1	1
Tomatoes, canned whole, 14 1/2 ounce (411 g)	1 can	1 can
Flour, all-purpose	2 tablespoons	30 ml
Salt	1/2 teaspoon	2 ml
Pepper, black	1/8 teaspoon	0.5 ml
Tabasco, optional	5 drops	5 drops
Rice, quick-cooking (instant)		

1. Directions for preparing ingredients
    a. *Chicken thighs*: Remove the skin and any excess fat. Wash in cold water.
    b. *Okra*: Drain off and discard liquid. Cut into 1/4 inch (0.6 cm) slices.
    c. *Tomatoes*: Reserve the liquid for Step 4. Cut tomatoes into medium-size pieces.
    d. *Rice*: See Step 6.
2. Place chicken thighs and salt in a 3-quart (3-L) saucepan. Add water. Bring to a boil, then reduce heat and simmer for 20 minutes or until chicken is tender. Remove cooked thighs from broth and cool.
3. In a heavy skillet heat dry flour to a medium-brown color, stirring constantly with a wooden spoon. Cool to room temperature.
4. Add onion, green pepper, and okra to broth from the chicken thighs. Bring to a boil, then simmer for 5–10 minutes until the okra is tender.
5. Remove meat from thigh bones and cut into 1/2 inch (1.3 cm) pieces. Add meat and tomatoes to okra mixture. Add salt, pepper, and Tabasco.
6. Cook rice according to package directions, allowing 2 tablespoons of rice per serving. Prepare number of servings for class size.
7. Blend browned flour with half the canned broth, following directions for making a starch paste by Method III, page 121. Also refer to page 118, variable number 7.
8. Add browned flour mixture and remaining canned chicken broth to the okra. Bring to a boil for 2 minutes.
9. To serve, place 2 tablespoons of rice in the center of a heated bowl and add the hot gumbo.
10. Record total working time: _____ minutes.

Fruit Soup (Scandinavian)

Apricots, dried	1 cup	250 ml
Prunes	1 cup	250 ml
Water, cold	4 cups	1000 ml
Cinnamon stick, 3 inches (7.5 cm)	1	1
Lemon	2 slices	2 slices
Tapioca, quick-cooking	2 tablespoons	30 ml
Sugar	1 cup	250 ml
Raisins, golden	3 tablespoons	45 ml
Currants	1 tablespoon	15 ml

1. Directions for preparing ingredients
   a. Wash all of the dried fruit, keeping separate by kind. Lift out of the water to drain.
   b. *Apricots*: Cut the apricots in half with scissors.
   c. *Cinnamon*: Break the stick into small pieces.
   d. *Lemon*: Cut off the ends, discard and cut 2 slices 1/4 inch (0.6 cm) thick.
2. Place the apricots and prunes in a 3-quart (3-L) saucepan and cover with water. Place the pan over medium heat until the water becomes lukewarm. Reduce the heat to low for 10–15 minutes, depending on the moistness of the dried fruits.
3. Add cinnamon pieces, lemon slices, tapioca, and sugar. Bring to a boil. Reduce heat and simmer 10 minutes with saucepan covered. Stir 2–3 times during the heating period to prevent sticking.
4. Add raisins and currants. Simmer 5 minutes or until tender.
5. If soup is to be served hot, serve in heated bowls. If it is to be served cold in class, set the pan in a container of ice water (the ice water in the container should be at least at the same level as the soup in the bowl). Stir the soup frequently to speed cooling. More ice cubes can be added if necessary.
6. Record total working time: _____ minutes.

Minestrone Soup (Italian)

Carrots, medium	2	2
Onion, medium	1	1
Celery, stalk	1	1
Water	4 cups	1000 ml
Olive oil	1 tablespoon	15 ml
Macaroni, elbow, dry	1/2 cup	125 ml
Cabbage, green	1 cup	250 ml
Zucchini	1	1
Beans, canned (great northern or navy)	1 15-ounce can	1 440-g can
Tomatoes, canned	1 16-ounce can	1 454-g can
Peas, frozen, 10 ounce (284 g)	1 package	1 package
Salt	1/2 teaspoon	2 ml
Pepper	1/8 teaspoon	0.5 ml
Basil, dried	1/4 teaspoon	1 ml
Parmesan cheese, shredded, added for garnish (per serving)	1 teaspoon	5 ml

1. Directions for preparing the ingredients
   a. *Peas*: Place frozen peas in a pan of hot water to thaw for use in Step 5.
   b. *Carrots*: Dice into small pieces.
   c. *Onion*: Thinly slice.
   d. *Celery*: Thinly slice.
   e. *Cabbage*: Finely shred.
   f. *Zucchini*: Dice into small pieces.
   g. *Tomato*: Cut into medium-sized pieces; save the juice.
2. Place carrots, onion, and celery in a 3-quart (3-L) saucepan. Add the 4 cups of water and the olive oil.
3. Place the pan over high heat. Bring to a boil. Reduce heat and simmer for 5 minutes.
4. Add cabbage, zucchini, and macaroni. Bring to a boil. Reduce heat and simmer for 5 minutes.
5. Add canned beans with juice, tomatoes with juice, peas with juice, salt, and pepper. Simmer for 10 minutes.
6. Stir in the basil. Serve in heated bowls and garnish with cheese.
7. Record total working time: _____ minutes.

Corn Chowder

Bacon, turkey bacon preferred	4 slices	4 slices
Onion, medium	1	1
Potato, large	1	1
Corn, canned , whole kernel, 12 ounce (340 g)	1 can	1 can
Corn, canned, cream style, 8 ounce (225 g)	1 can	1 can
Celery stalks, 10 inch	2	2
Chicken broth, canned, 14 ounce (400 g)	1 can	1 can
Salt	1/2 teaspoon	2 ml
Pepper, white	1/4 teaspoon	1 ml
Flour, all-purpose	2 tablespoons	30 ml
Milk	2 cups	500 ml

1. Directions for preparing ingredients
   a. *Onion*: Remove dry skin. Trim off both ends and finely dice.
   b. *Potato*: Wash, peel, and cut into small dices.
   c. *Corn, whole kernel*: Drain off and discard liquid.
   d. *Celery*: Cut into 1/4 inch (0.6 cm) slices.
2. In a 3-quart (3-L) saucepan, fry the bacon until crisp. Remove bacon and blot off excess fat on paper towels. Reserve bacon for Step 7.
3. Put the onions into the pan and cook until tender, not brown.
4. Add potato, celery, salt, pepper, and chicken broth. Bring to a boil. Reduce heat and simmer for 15–20 minutes or until potato is tender.
5. Blend flour with 1/2 cup (125 ml) milk until smooth; add to the saucepan. Then add remaining milk. Bring to a boil with constant stirring; boil for 2 minutes.
6. Add the canned corns. Heat to serving temperature. *Do not boil.*
7. Cut the cooked bacon into small pieces with scissors.
8. Serve in heated bowls and garnish each serving with some of the bacon bits.
9. Record total working time: _____ minutes.

Gazpacho (Spain)

Basic Soup

Tomatoes, medium–large, full-ripe	4	4
Cucumber, medium	1/2	1/2
Green pepper, medium–large	1/4	1/4
Garlic clove, small	1/2–1	1/2–1
Bread, crust removed	4 slices	4 slices
Vinegar, cider	2 tablespoons	30 ml
Salt	1/2 teaspoon	2 ml
Olive oil	1 tablespoon	15 ml

Accompaniments (at least two should be served in class) Tomatoes, medium; Cucumber, medium; Scallions, sliced; Green pepper; Croutons; and Hard-cooked eggs, sliced. Ice cubes, one per serving (optional)

1. Directions for preparing the ingredients
   a. *Tomatoes*: Wash, scald with boiling water for about 2 minutes. Peel, remove seeds, and chop coarsely.
   b. *Cucumber*: Pare off skin; trim off both ends. Remove coarse seeds and chop coarsely.
   c. *Green pepper*: Wash. Remove core, seeds, and ribs. Chop coarsely.
   d. *Garlic clove*: Remove dry skin and chop coarsely.
   e. *Scallions*: Cut off the roots. Wash and finely slice white ends only.
2. Remove the outside skin from the garlic clove. Using the back of a tablespoon and a small plate mash the garlic clove and the salt together. Add a little soft, finely crumbled bread, and 1 tablespoon of the juice from the tomatoes to form a well-blended paste.
3. In a 2- or 3-quart (2–3 L) bowl combine remainder of the soft bread crumbs and juice from the tomatoes. Stir vigorously to blend.
4. Reserve portions of tomatoes, cucumber, and green pepper to be served as accompaniments. Add the remaining portions of the vegetables, a few drops of olive oil, and other soup ingredients to the bread-tomato juice mixture. Mix well with a wire whip.
5. Puree about 2 cups (500 ml) at a time in a blender. Pour puree into a 4-quart (4-L) stainless steel or glass bowl. Cover with plastic wrap or aluminum foil. Chill for several hours. For class, place the bowl in a pan of ice water. Stir frequently to chill more rapidly. Add the remaining olive oil and whisk rapidly.
6. To serve, place accompaniments into individual bowls to be passed for addition to soup.
7. If desired, place an ice cube in each chilled bowl. Add cold soup and serve.
8. Record total working time: _____ minutes.

Cream of Broccoli Soup

Broccoli,	1 bunch	1 bunch
chopped stems	3 cups	750 ml
bud clusters	1 1/2 cups	375 ml
Onion, small	1	1
Water	1 1/2 cups	250 ml
Flour, all-purpose	1/2 cup	125 ml
Margarine or butter	2 tablespoons	30 ml
Salt	1/2 teaspoon	2 ml
Milk	3 1/2 cups	875 ml
Pepper	1/8 teaspoon	0.5 ml
Cheese, natural sharp cheddar, shredded	3 1/2 cups	875 ml

1. Cut 1/2 inch (1.3 cm) from stem ends of the broccoli stalks; discard these ends. Cut bud clusters to leave as little of the stem attached as possible but retain buds in small clusters; set the clusters aside. Cut stems into quarters lengthwise; then cut crosswise into 1/4 inch (0.6 cm) pieces.
2. Bring water to a boil in a 3-quart (3-L) saucepan. Add broccoli stem pieces and the onion. Boil for 7–10 minutes or until broccoli is very tender. Saucepan can be partially covered.
3. Puree cooked broccoli in a blender and return the puree to the saucepan. Add the bud pieces and bring to a boil. Simmer 5 minutes or until the buds are crisp tender. Reduce heat and, stirring frequently, hold until the white sauce is ready.
4. Using the fat, flour, salt, pepper, and milk prepare the white sauce. Blend the flour with 1 cup (250 ml) of the milk to form a smooth paste. Add the remaining milk, salt, pepper, and margarine. Bring to a boil with constant stirring and boil for 2 minutes.
5. Add to the cooked broccoli. Heat to serving temperature.
6. Serve in heated bowls. Add 3 tablespoons (45 ml) of the shredded cheese on each serving for garnish.
7. Record total working time: _____ minutes.

REVIEW QUESTIONS

1. Why is cold water recommended to be used in starting the preparation of a soup?
2. How does the size of pieces of vegetables or meat and/or poultry influence the amount of extractives in the broth?
3. In the preparation of a beef broth, what type of cuts would you use? Why?
4. How can an interesting appearance be developed in a predominantly vegetable soup?
5. What is the purpose of blanching a vegetable to be used in a soup? Example: leeks in Cock-O-Leekie soup.
6. The directions say to cook pasta or rice to the *al dente* stage. Describe this stage. Why is it used?
7. Why may it be desirable to clarify a broth?
8. Define the term *consommé*.
9. How may bouillon differ from consommé?
10. Compare the consistencies of a cream soup and a chowder.
11. Why is it desirable to retain a small amount of fat in all soups?
12. The composition of what ingredient in a cream soup may determine the amount of fat in the soup?
13. What is a leek? What flavor does it contribute to the Cock-O-Leekie soup?
14. How does minestrone differ from a gumbo?
15. In what type of soup is okra used? What is the function of the okra?
16. What is the predominant vegetable in gazpacho? At what temperature is gazpacho traditionally served?
17. Where in a meal would you serve a fruit soup?
18. Why should a soup that has flour as an ingredient always be brought to a boil after the flour has been added and is boiled for at least 1 minute?
19. Assume you are preparing a minestrone soup and find you have dry navy beans but no canned beans on hand. What adjustments would be necessary in your procedure for you to use the dry beans?

Salads

OBJECTIVES

1. To study the roles of salads in meals.
2. To discuss and illustrate the preparation and care of selected greens.
3. To discuss and illustrate the arrangement of salad ingredients for serving.
4. To discuss and illustrate marinades and salad dressings.

PRODUCTS TO BE PREPARED TO ILLUSTRATE PRINCIPLES

TYPES OF SALADS

Appetizer	Dinner Accompaniment	Main Course	Dessert
Fruit salad	Cole slaw	Tuna salad	Fresh fruit
Five-bean salad	Tomato (marinated)	Hot potato salad	Frozen fruit
	Caesar-type salad	Chef's salad	Canned fruit
	Sea stix salad	Chicken salad	
		Macaroni salad (page 135)	

PRINCIPLES

1. The type of salad will determine the food combination to be used.
   a. *Appetizer salads* are small servings of salad greens or tart fruit which whet rather than satiate the appetite.
   b. *Dinner accompaniment salads* are relatively small servings of vegetable(s) and/or fruits which complement the entree.
   c. *Main course salads* are generous servings of protein, potato, rice, or pasta usually combined with greens or other succulent vegetables. The salad has high satiety value.
   d. *Dessert salads* are medium to small portions of fruit(s).
2. Quality of ingredients
   a. All ingredients should be edible.
   b. All ingredients should be clean and free from defects (bruises, rotten spots, insects, dirt and sand, and insecticide).
   c. Raw fruits and vegetables should be at their optimum stage of maturity.
   d. All inedible portions should be removed (albedo of citrus fruits, paraffined cucumber skin, for example).
3. Salad greens
   a. Usually all types of salads are served on an underliner of salad greens.
   b. Salad greens may be used alone or in combination with fruits or other vegetables.

    c. Salad greens are palatable only if clean, crisp, and dry. (Exception—wilted lettuce salad.)

    d. When used as underliners for salads, the salad greens should not extend over the edge of the serving plate.

4. Quality characteristics of salads are dependent on

    a. Selecting food combinations for contrast in color, texture, and flavor

    b. Pieces varying in size for contrast and interest

    c. Poultry and fish pieces being large enough to be identified

    d. Pasta remaining in discrete pieces (not gummy masses) by rinsing after cooking

    e. Firm foods (not easily cut with a fork) being in bite-size pieces

5. Marinades

    a. May be used to contribute flavor to pasta or other bland-flavored ingredients; firm fruits and vegetables; or meat, fish, and poultry.

    b. The marinade is drained off before ingredients are combined into a salad.

6. Dressings

    a. Are usually an integral part of the salad.

    b. Flavor of dressing should complement the flavor of the salad.

    c. The type of dressing is determined by how the salad is used in the meal.

Type of Salad	Suggested Dressings*
(1) Appetizer	Tart, usually of French type—an oil and vinegar dressing
(2) Dinner accompaniment	French, mayonnaise, thousand island, Russian, blue cheese, or a special dressing
(3) Main course	Any of those listed for dinner accompaniment salads
(4) Dessert	Mayonnaise or cooked dressings blended with whipped cream. These dressings are usually sweet and rich.

7. A salad must be aesthetically pleasing.

8. All salads must be kept cold prior to serving.

    a. To retain freshness

    b. To prevent bacterial growth in salads containing proteins or carbohydrates

*See pages 277–279 for recipes.

Fruit Salad (Appetizer)

Orange sections or slices	1/2 medium orange
Apple slices, red-skinned apple	1/4 medium apple
Bibb lettuce leaves	3 to 4
French dressing	

1. Pare orange to remove outer white skin with the rind. Either section or cut into slices.
2. Wash and dry the apple. Do not remove red skin. Cut the quarter section into 3 or 4 slices; the skin side should not be more than 1/4 inch (0.6 cm) thick. Dip apple slices in orange juice to delay browning.
3. Lettuce leaves should be washed, drained, and dried.
4. Arrange lettuce leaves on suitable serving plate. Alternate orange sections and apple slices on the bed of lettuce.
5. Serve with French dressing.
6. Record total working time: _____ minutes. Yield: 1 serving.

Five-Bean Salad (Appetizer)

*Green beans, whole	1 can	1 can
*Yellow wax beans, cut	1 can	1 can
*Kidney beans	1 can	1 can
*Garbanzo beans	1 can	1 can
*Butter beans	1 can	1 can
Green pepper, large	1	1
Sweet onion, 3 inch (7 cm) diameter	1/2	1/2
Celery, 1/4 inch (0.6 cm) slices	2 cups	500 ml
**Cider vinegar	3 cups	750 ml
Sugar	3 cups	750 ml
Vegetable oil (optional)	1/4 cup	60 ml
Lettuce cups or leaves for each serving		

1. Empty cans of green and yellow wax beans into a collander or strainer. Allow to drain thoroughly. Transfer to a 4-quart (4-L) bowl.
2. Empty kidney beans into a collander or strainer. Carefully rinse under cold, running tap water. Drain thoroughly. Transfer to bowl containing green and wax beans. Follow same procedure for garbanzo and butter beans.
3. Wash green pepper, dry, and slice into lengthwise strips. Add to beans.
4. Remove dry skin from onion. Wash and dry. Slice into rings approximately 1/8 inch (0.3 cm) thick. Separate rings. Add to beans.
5. Wash celery, dry, and slice. Add to beans.
6. If oil is used, add to beans.
7. In a 2-quart (2-L) saucepan combine vinegar and sugar. Bring to a boil. Pour over vegetables.
8. Lightly toss vegetables with two forks. Do this several times as the mixture cools.
9. Cover the bowl. Refrigerate at least 4 hours before serving. The salad will be more flavorful if it can marinate 24 hours before serving.
10. To serve: Wash, drain, and dry lettuce. Place on serving plate. Drain bean mixture and arrange on lettuce, 1/2 cup (125 ml) approximate serving portion. No salad dressing is needed.
11. Record total working time: _____ minutes. Yield: 16–20 servings.

*Approximate can size = 1 pound (454 grams).
**If vinegar has a very tart flavor, 1/2 cup (125 ml) water can be added.

Tomato Salad—Marinated (Dinner Accompaniment)

Tomatoes, medium large	2	2
French dressing (temporary emulsion)	1/2 cup	125 ml
Parsley, finely minced	1 tablespoon	15 ml
Chives, finely minced	1/2 teaspoon	2 ml
Lettuce cups or leaves	4	4

1. Wash tomatoes and skin by impaling on fork through the core and dipping tomato into boiling water for 5–10 seconds. Plunge into cold water. Slice tomatoes 3/8 inch (1 cm) thick. Arrange in single layer so dressing can be spooned over each slice.
2. Wash parsley and dry. Finely mince using scissors. Wash chives and dry; finely mince. Combine parsley and chives with French dressing. Allow to stand 5 minutes. Spoon over tomatoes. Refrigerate 1 hour before serving.
3. Wash lettuce. Remove excess moisture. Place on serving plate.
4. Drain excess dressing from tomato slices before serving on lettuce.
5. Record total working time: _____ minutes. Yield: 4 servings.

Cole Slaw (Dinner Accompaniment)

*Cabbage, green	2 cups	500 ml
Dairy sour cream	1/2 cup	125 ml
Cider vinegar	2 tablespoons	30 ml
Sugar	2 teaspoons	10 ml
Salt	few grains	few grains

1. Wash, dry cabbage; shred into thin, long shreds. Width of shred should not be more than 1/16 inch (0.2 cm). Shreds should be approximately 2 inches (5 cm) in length.
2. Combine the sour cream, vinegar, and sugar.
3. Toss the dressing lightly with the shredded cabbage.
4. Serve on a lettuce leaf, if desired.
5. Record total working time: _____ minutes. Yield: 2 servings.

*When green cabbage is not available, 1–2 tablespoons (15–30 ml) shredded carrot or thin slivers of green pepper can be added to provide color to the salad. A mixture of 3 parts green cabbage and 1 part red cabbage may also be used for color contrast.

Sea Stix Salad (Dinner Accompaniment)

Sea stix (6)	1/2 pound	225 g
Celery, 1 stalk	10 inch	25.4 cm
Pepper, red sweet	2 tablespoons	30 ml
Onions, green (4)	1/4 cup	60 ml
Mayonnaise	2 tablespoons	30 ml
Lettuce cups or leaves		

1. Remove wrappers from sea stix. Wash in cold water and blot dry.
2. Cut stix in 1/4 inch (0.6 cm) pieces.
3. Chop celery, pepper, and onions into medium pieces.
4. Combine stix, vegetables, and mayonnaise in 1-quart (1-L) bowl.
5. Serve in lettuce cups or on leaves.
6. Record total working time: _____ minutes. Yield: 4 servings.

Caesar-Type Salad* (Dinner Accompaniment)

**Salad greens	1 quart	1 L
Seasoned croutons	1 cup	250 ml
Salad oil	1/4 cup	60 ml
Worcestershire sauce	1/2 teaspoon	2 ml
Lemon juice	2 tablespoons	30 ml
Black pepper, freshly ground	few grains	few grains
Blue cheese or Roquefort, crumbled	1 ounce	30 g

1. Wash and dry salad greens. Break into bite-size pieces. Place in an appropriate size bowl.
2. Add the lemon juice, pepper, and Worcestershire sauce to the 1/4 cup (60 ml) salad oil.
3. Pour oil mixture over salad greens. Add about half of the croutons and toss lightly.
4. Crumble the blue cheese over the top. Add the last portion of croutons.
5. Serve cold.
6. Record total working time: _____ minutes. Yield: 4–6 servings.

*A true Caesar salad requires a raw egg.

**Romaine used by itself is traditional. If romaine is unavailable, use a combination of head lettuce, Bibb lettuce, and endive.

Seasoned Croutons*

Bread cubes	1 cup	250 ml
Salad oil (olive oil will give distinctive flavor)	1 tablespoon	15 ml
Garlic clove, small	1	1

1. Cut bread into 3/8 inch (1 cm) cubes. Arrange cubes in single layer on baking pan. Brown in a 375°F (190°C) oven.
2. Pour garlic flavored oil over croutons. Toss well.
3. Garlic-flavored oil is prepared by allowing a clove of garlic to soak overnight in the oil. Remove garlic clove before using the oil.

*Commercial seasoned croutons may be used as purchased.

Chef's Salad (Main Course)

*Salad greens	1 1/2 cups	375 ml
Swiss cheese	2 ounces	60 g
Brick cheese	1 ounce	30 g
Boiled ham	2 ounces	60 g
Egg, hard-cooked	1	1
French dressing	2 tablespoons	30 ml
Lettuce cups or leaves		

1. Start egg to hard cook. (See page 155.)
2. Wash and remove excess water from salad greens. Tear endive, spinach, and romaine into bite-size pieces.
3. Use the lettuce cups or larger leaves as underliners in the salad bowl.
4. In a small bowl, lightly toss together the greens with the French dressing.
5. Place greens in salad bowl, slightly mounding them toward center of bowl.
6. Cut cheese into lengthwise strips, 3/8 inch × 1/8 inch (1 cm × 0.3 cm). Cut ham into lengthwise strips, 1/4 inch × 1/4 inch (0.6 cm × 0.6 cm). Cut egg lengthwise into quarters. Arrange cheeses, ham, and hard-cooked egg on top of greens.
7. Serve with additional French dressing as desired.
8. Record total working time: _____ minutes. Yield: 1 serving.

*Use a combination of head lettuce chunks, endive, spinach, and romaine.

Hot Potato Salad (Main Course)

Potatoes, waxy variety, medium size	4	4
Salt	1/2 teaspoon	2 ml
Pepper, white	few grains	few grains
Bacon slices	8	8
Eggs, hard-cooked	4	4
Green onions	4	4
Bacon fat	2 tablespoons	30 ml
Vinegar, cider	1/2 cup	125 ml

1. Wash potatoes. Pare and cut into 1-inch (2.5-cm) cubes. Cook until tender.
2. Start egg to hard cook. (See page 155.)
3. Cut bacon into 1-inch (2.5-cm) pieces. Place in cold frying pan. Cook at low heat, 300°F (150°C) in an electric frying pan, until bacon is crisp. Remove bacon pieces. Measure drippings. Return 2 tablespoons (30 ml) to frying pan.
4. When potatoes are cool enough to handle (but not cold), cut into pieces approximately 1/4 inch × 1 inch (0.6 cm × 2.5 cm).
5. Remove roots from green onions. Wash, dry, and finely chop.
6. Add the vinegar to the drippings. Heat quickly to boiling. Add potatoes, green onions, seasonings, and sliced hard-cooked eggs. (Reserve several slices of eggs for garnish, if desired.) Lightly toss ingredients together using forks. Add the pieces of bacon. Garnish and serve. (This can be served from electric frying pan to keep the salad hot.)
7. Record total working time: _____ minutes. Yield: 4 servings.

Tuna Salad (Main Course)

Tuna, "whole meat" style	1 cup	250 ml
Cucumber	1/2 cup	125 ml
Celery	1/2 cup	125 ml
Egg, hard-cooked	1	1
*Mayonnaise	1/2 cup	125 ml
Lettuce cups or leaves	2	2

1. Start egg to hard cook. (See page 155.)
2. Leave tuna fish in large chunks. Drain off excess oil. Place tuna in a small bowl.
3. Wash and dry celery and cucumber. Dice celery into 1/4 inch (0.6 cm) dice. Slice cucumber into 1/8 inch (0.3 cm) slices. Add mayonnaise, celery, and cucumber to tuna. Toss lightly together using two forks. *Do not overwork.*
4. Place lettuce on an appropriate-size plate. Place tuna mixture into lettuce cup.
5. Cut hard-cooked egg into quarters lengthwise. Use for garnish.
6. Serve with additional mayonnaise as desired.
7. Record total working time: _____ minutes. Yield: 2 servings.

*Use a commercial mayonnaise containing pasteurized eggs.

Chicken Salad (Main Course)

Chicken, cooked	1 cup	250 ml
Salt	1/16 teaspoon	0.2 ml
Celery	1/2 cup	125 ml
Pineapple chunks, well drained	1/2 cup	125 ml
Ripe olives, pitted	6	6
Slivered almonds, toasted	2 tablespoons	30 ml
*Mayonnaise	1/4 cup	60 ml
Lettuce cups or leaves	2	2

1. Place almonds in a heavy frying pan. Place pan over low heat. Stir nuts occasionally for even browning. Cool nuts before adding to other ingredients. Use to garnish salad.
2. Cut chicken into 3/4 inch (2 cm) cubes. Place chicken in a small bowl. Add salt. Use two forks to lightly toss chicken to distribute salt. *Do not overwork.*
3. Cut each pineapple chunk into 2 or 3 pieces. Add to chicken.
4. Wash and drain celery. Cut into 1/4 inch (0.6 cm) dice. Add to chicken.
5. Halve or quarter olives. Add olives and mayonnaise to chicken. Use two forks to lightly toss ingredients together. *Do not overwork.*
6. Wash lettuce and drain thoroughly. Arrange on appropriate-size plates.
7. Serve half of chicken mixture in each lettuce cup. Garnish with toasted almonds.
8. Serve with additional mayonnaise as desired.
9. Record total working time: _____ minutes. Yield: 2 servings.

*Use a commercial mayonnaise containing pasteurized eggs.

Fresh Fruit Salad (Dessert)

Orange sections or slices	1/3 medium orange
Pineapple, fresh	3 or 4 chunks or pieces
Banana	4 to 5 slices
Grapes, dark skinned preferred	3 to 5 seeded
Boston or Bibb lettuce leaves	1 to 4
Honey-lemon-oil dressing	

1. Pare orange to remove outer white skin with the rind. Either section or cut into slices.
2. Remove heavy skin from a 1/2 inch (1.3 cm) slice of fresh pineapple. Cut slice in half. Remove core. Cut a half-slice into several pieces.
3. Cut bananas into 1/4–3/8 inch (0.6–1 cm) slices. The banana could first be scored with a fork, if desired. Dip banana slices in orange juice to delay browning.
4. Wash and dry grapes. Cut in half if large. Remove any seeds that may be present.
5. Lettuce leaves should be washed, drained, and dried. Put lettuce leaves on serving plate.
6. Arrange fruit casually on lettuce. Avoid a "worked-over" appearance. Serve with honey-lemon-oil dressing (page 278.)
7. Record total working time: _____ minutes. Yield: 1 serving.

Canned Fruit Salad (Dessert)

Pineapple chunks	2 cups	500 ml
Apricot halves	8–10	8–10
Maraschino cherries	8	8
Marshmallows, large	8	8
Whipping cream	1/2 cup	125 ml
Fruit salad dressing	1/2 cup	125 ml
Slivered almonds, toasted	2 tablespoons	30 ml
Boston or Bibb lettuce leaves for 4 servings		

1. Thoroughly drain the canned fruits. Cut the apricot halves into two or three slices. Cut the maraschino cherries into halves. Cut the marshmallows into quarters.
2. Whip the cream. Blend with the fruit salad dressing. Use approximately 1/2 cup (125 ml) of the blended dressing to mix lightly with the fruit. Do not overblend so fruit becomes mushy. This mixture should stand at least 1 hour before serving for better blending of flavors.
3. Lettuce leaves should be washed, drained, and, if necessary, dried.
4. Put lettuce leaves on serving plate. Add fruit mixture. Sprinkle with toasted, slivered almonds. Serve with remaining portion of whipped cream dressing.
5. Record total working time: _____ minutes. Yield: 4 servings.

Frozen Fruit Salad (Dessert)

Apricot halves or peach slices, canned	1 1/2 cups	375 ml
Pineapple chunks, canned	1 cup	250 ml
*White grapes, canned	3/4 cup	175 ml
Cream cheese, 3 ounce (approx. 90 g) package	1	1
Lemon juice	1 tablespoon	15 ml
Sugar	1 tablespoon	15 ml
Whipping cream	1/2 cup	125 ml
**Mayonnaise	1/2 cup	125 ml
Mint sprigs (fresh), if desired		

1. Thoroughly drain all canned fruits. Apricot halves may be cut into thirds. Peach slices may be cut in half. Pineapple chunks may be cut into thirds.
2. In a 2-quart (2-L) bowl, blend the cream cheese with the lemon juice and sugar. Blend until smooth.
3. Add the mayonnaise dressing gradually to the cheese mixture, blending after each addition to keep the mixture smooth.
4. Whip the cream; add to the cream cheese–mayonnaise mixture. *Do not overblend.*
5. Add the drained fruits. Blend. Pour mixture into refrigerator trays for freezing. Freeze until firm (approximately 2–3 hours).
6. For serving, slice into serving portions. Place a portion on washed, drained, and dried lettuce leaves. Garnish with a sprig of mint, if desired.
7. Record total working time: _____ minutes. Yield: 9 servings.

*Minted pears or green maraschino cherries could be substituted for the grapes.
**Use a commercial mayonnaise containing pasteurized eggs.

CHARACTERISTICS OF HIGH-QUALITY SALADS

Appearance: *Greens*—crisp, moist (not wet). *Fruits, vegetables,* and *meat*—pieces large enough to be identified. Aesthetically pleasing, simple, and casual.

Color: Pleasing selection of contrasting colors *or* a blend of monochromatic colors.

Texture: *Greens*—firm and crisp. *Fruits, vegetables,* and *meat*—firm. All pieces in a combination salad must be of compatible texture. *Pasta*—soft and free of any gumminess.

Tenderness: *Greens*—firm, crisp. *Fruits, vegetables, meat,* and *pasta*—little resistance to bite. Skins of fruits and vegetables (apple, tomato, cucumber) must be tender.

*Ease of eating: Pieces of firm, raw vegetables (carrots, cauliflower, and so on) of a size to be easily managed with a fork; connective membranes of citrus fruit removed or cut for ease in eating.

Flavor: Appropriate for use of salad; balanced, well blended.

*This characteristic is important enough in salads to be evaluated along with the other characteristics.

REVIEW QUESTIONS

1. List the four types of salads as identified with their place in the meal. Briefly describe each type.
2. a. List the four requirements for quality of ingredients.
   b. List factors to consider in care and use of salad greens.
   c. Why should salad greens be torn rather than cut?
   d. Why must salad greens be dry when used?
   e. Why should cleaned salad greens be refrigerated in a tightly closed container?
3. a. List several factors to be considered in arranging an attractive salad.
   b. Discuss several ways in which contrast (variety) might be obtained in a salad.
4. What are marinades and how are they used?
5. Discuss factors to consider when deciding what type of salad dressing to use.
6. Why is it necessary to keep all salads cold prior to serving?

Salad Dressings

OBJECTIVES

1. To discuss and review the principles of emulsion formation.
2. To illustrate the preparation of a food emulsion.
3. To introduce students to the principles of reforming "broken" emulsions.
4. To discuss composition of types of dressings used in salad preparation.
5. To emphasize the bacteriological implications in using mayonnaise dressing or salad dressings.
6. To review principles of starch-egg cookery.

PRODUCTS TO BE PREPARED TO ILLUSTRATE PRINCIPLES

Mayonnaise dressing
French dressing (optional)

Honey-lemon-oil dressing
Fruit salad dressing

PRINCIPLES

1. Emulsions may be either *temporary* or *permanent* depending on stability.
2. Stability of an emulsion system depends on particle size and the presence of an emulsifier.
3. Temperature of ingredients determines the ease of forming an emulsion.
4. Temperature of storage in part determines the stability of the emulsion.
5. A "broken" emulsion can be re-emulsified because
   a. Adding the broken emulsion to an egg yolk is similar to adding oil to the egg yolk as in the original production.
   b. By adding the broken emulsion to water or vinegar, the liquid dilutes the emulsifier present in the broken emulsion so the emulsifier can again function.
6. The term *salad dressing* is extremely broad; it can apply to any type of dressing used on a salad. Specific Standards of Identity which define the composition and ingredients used are found in the Code of Federal Regulations: Title 21–, Part 169, dated April 1, 1993.

Mayonnaise Dressing (Permanent Emulsion)

*Egg yolk	1	1
Salt	1/4 teaspoon	1 ml
Cayenne	few grains	few grains
Mustard, dry	1/2 teaspoon	2 ml
Sugar	1/2 teaspoon	2 ml
Vinegar	2 tablespoons	30 ml
Vegetable oil	1 cup	250 ml

1. Put the egg yolk in a small, deep bowl. Add salt, cayenne, mustard, and sugar; mix.
2. Mix in 1 tablespoon (15 ml) vinegar.
**3. Add 1–2 drops of oil and beat vigorously, using rotary beater or electric mixer. Continue adding the oil a few drops at a time, beating vigorously after each addition until about 1/4 cup (60 ml) of oil has been used.
4. Beat in the remaining oil. Add 1–2 tablespoons (15–30 ml) at a time. Beat in remaining vinegar when the mixture becomes quite thick (about half the oil has been added).
5. Record total working time: _____ minutes.

*In order to take out the raw egg yolk, two options are available. Replace the egg yolk with (1) one tablespoon (15 ml) of cold water, or (2) an egg substitute equivalent to one (1) egg yolk. See directions on the package.

**Amount of oil added as one addition should never be more than half the volume of the emulsion already formed.

Re-Emulsification of Mayonnaise

The emulsion in mayonnaise may break, permitting the oil and water to separate into layers. Freezing or storage at too low a temperature will cause this breakdown. Mayonnaise which is too thick may separate on standing. The emulsion may be restored by the following procedure:

1. Place one egg yolk* in a small, deep bowl. Beat lightly with rotary beater.
2. Add the broken mayonnaise 1–2 teaspoons (5–10 ml) at a time. Use a rotary beater or electric mixer to beat thoroughly after each addition until the emulsion re-forms. Larger amounts of broken emulsion can be added as the emulsion is re-formed. (See the second footnote for mayonnaise dressing.)

*One tablespoon (15 ml) of water or vinegar may be used in place of the egg yolk.

CHARACTERISTICS OF HIGH-QUALITY MAYONNAISE DRESSING

Appearance: Shiny; emulsion stable.

Color: Yellow; shade dependent on color of egg yolk and source of acid.

Consistency: Mounds firmly on spoon even when diluted with other ingredients such as whipped cream, chili sauce, catsup, or pickle relish.

Mouth Feel: Somewhat oily.

Flavor: Spices well blended; slightly tart.

French Dressing (Temporary Emulsion)

Vegetable oil	2/3 cup	150 ml
*Vinegar	1/3 cup	75 ml
Sugar	1 teaspoon	5 ml
Salt	1/4 teaspoon	1 ml
Paprika	1/4 teaspoon	1 ml
Mustard, dry	1/4 teaspoon	1 ml
Cayenne	few grains	few grains

1. Blend together all dry ingredients. Place in a 2-cup (500-ml) container with a tight closure.
2. Add the vinegar and the vegetable oil. Shake the mixture vigorously before using.
3. Record total working time: _____ minutes. Yield: 1 cup (250 ml).

*Either white or cider vinegar can be used. Cider vinegar contributes a slightly fruity flavor but does give a darker color to the dressing. For a fruity flavor, use lemon juice in place of the vinegar.

Honey-Lemon-Oil Dressing (Temporary Emulsion)

Lemon juice	1/4 cup	60 ml
Honey	1/4 cup	60 ml
Salad oil	1/4 cup	60 ml
Celery seed (optional)	1/8 teaspoon	0.5 ml

1. Place all ingredients in a 1-cup (250-ml) container with a tightly fitting closure.
2. Shake ingredients together vigorously just before serving.
3. Record total working time: _____ minutes. Yield: 3/4 cup (175 ml).

Fruit Salad Dressing (Cooked-Starch Based)

Pineapple juice	1/4 cup	60 ml
Orange juice	1/2 cup	125 ml
Lemon juice	2 tablespoons	30 ml
Water	1/4 cup	60 ml
Salt	1/8 teaspoon	0.5 ml
Sugar	1/3 cup	75 ml
Flour	2 tablespoons	30 ml
Egg	1	1
Whipping cream	1/2 cup	125 ml

1. Blend together in a 1 or 1 1/2 quart (1–1.5 L) saucepan the salt, sugar, and flour.
2. Gradually add the fruit juices and water. Stir until all ingredients are evenly blended.
3. Place over heat. Stir constantly. Bring to a boil and boil 1 minute. Remove from heat.
4. Blend egg in a 2–3 cup (500–750 ml) bowl.
5. Gradually add hot starch mixture, about 1 tablespoon (15 ml) at a time, to egg. Stir after each addition to thoroughly blend. When approximately half the starch has been added to the egg, pour all of egg-starch mixture into remaining starch paste. Blend thoroughly.
6. Return egg-starch mixture to medium heat. Stir constantly until egg is coagulated, about 4–5 minutes. Mixture should be near boiling point but should not boil. Remove from heat.
7. Cool dressing before using on fruit salad.
8. Whip cream just before using dressing. Fold into dressing.
9. Record total working time: _____ minutes. Yield: 2–2 1/2 cups (500–625 ml).

REVIEW QUESTIONS

1. a. What is the difference between a temporary and a permanent emulsion?
   b. Which ingredients function as emulsifying agents in mayonnaise?
   c. List some other ingredients which function as emulsifying agents in salad dressings. (*Note:* Read the ingredient lists on samples of commercial products.)
2. According to Standards of Identity how do mayonnaise and salad dressing differ?
   a. In composition
   b. In permitted ingredients
3. What problems might arise in making mayonnaise with fresh whole eggs?

Gelatin

OBJECTIVES

1. To illustrate principles involved in the preparation of gelatin products.
2. To compare quality characteristics of a gelatin prepared from plain, dry gelatin and a commercial gelatin mix.
3. To illustrate and discuss factors that affect the strength of a gelatin gel.
4. To illustrate and discuss factors that affect a gelatin foam.
5. To illustrate and discuss basic ingredients of typical gelatin food products.

PRODUCTS TO BE PREPARED TO ILLUSTRATE PRINCIPLES

Plain jellies   Spanish cream
Gelatin foam   Bavarian creams
Gelatin sponges   Chiffons

PRINCIPLES

1. Dry gelatin particles must be separated before heating by
   a. Mixing gelatin granules with cold water
   b. Diluting with other dry ingredients (sugar, acids, and salts, as in the commercial mix)
2. All gelatin granules are dissolved in the water by the application of heat to form gelatin sols.
3. Factors that affect transformation of gelatin sols to gels
   a. Concentration of gelatin
   b. Temperature
   c. Acidity
   d. Sugar
   e. Buffer salts
4. The effect of the five factors listed in Principle 3 are observed as
   a. Rate of gel formation
   b. Strength of the gel
5. Pieces of added food materials that are too large will rupture a gel structure.
6. In formation of gelatin foam, air incorporation increases the volume and decreases intensity of color and flavor.
7. Dissolved gelatin will not retain air for foam formation until it has attained the consistency of raw egg white.
8. A gelatin solution that sets prematurely (before whipping or before adding fruit or vegetable pieces) can be reliquified (by heating) and rechilled to desired consistency.

PLAIN JELLIES AND GELATIN FOAM

Orange Jelly

Gelatin	1 tablespoon	15 ml
Water	1/3 cup	75 ml
Sugar	1/2 cup	125 ml
Lemon juice, fresh	2 tablespoons	30 ml
Frozen, concentrated orange juice, unsweetened	1/3 cup	75 ml
Water	1 cup	250 ml

1. Allow orange juice to thaw.
2. Place 1/3 cup (75 ml) cold water in the upper part of a double boiler. Sprinkle the gelatin over the top of the water. Allow to stand for 5 minutes.
3. Place the hydrated gelatin over boiling water. Stir until gelatin has dissolved. No particles of gelatin should be seen.
4. Add sugar and stir until dissolved. Add all other ingredients.
*5. Stir until thoroughly blended. Pour half into mold. Chill mold in a pan of chipped ice. When firm, unmold for evaluation.
6. Use the remaining half portion as directed next for Orange Gelatin Foam.
7. Record total working time: _____ minutes.

Orange Gelatin Foam

1. Place the remaining half portion of orange jelly in a 1-quart (1-L) glass measuring cup. Measure quantity. Place the glass cup in a pan of chipped ice. Chill until the gelatin has the consistency of raw egg white.
2. Leave the mixture in the glass cup. Beat with an electric mixer at high speed until the mixture is light and holds up in soft peaks. Measure quantity of foam. Foam can be left to become firm in glass cup or may be transferred to a mold for gelatin.*
3. Compare color and flavor of the jelly product with color and flavor of the foam product. Compare volume of jelly product with volume of foam product.
4. Record total working time: _____ minutes.

Orange Jelly—Commercial Mix Product

Gelatin mix, orange flavor, 3 ounces (approx. 90 g)	1 package	1 package
Water	2 cups	500 ml

1. Prepare by directions on package.
*2. Dissolved gelatin can be molded as just plain jelly, or a comparison of jelly and foam as outlined above may be followed.
3. Record total working time: _____ minutes.

*Small ring molds are preferred for most of the gelatin products since the products can be chilled rapidly. Individual molds can be used, but are time consuming to fill and to wash and dry.
A small ring mold holds approximately 2 cups (500 ml).
An individual mold contains approximately 1/3 cup (75 ml).

Orange Jelly—Artificially Sweetened, Commercial Mix Product

Gelatin mix, orange flavor, artificially sweetened	1 package	1 package
Water	2 cups	500 ml

1. Prepare by the directions on the package.
2. Dissolved gelatin can be molded as just plain jelly, or a comparison of jelly and foam as outlined above may be followed.
3. Record total working time: _____ minutes.

Note: A package of this type of product weighs 0.3 ounces (approx. 8.5 g).

Perfection Salad

Gelatin	1 tablespoon	15 ml
*Sugar	1/4 cup	60 ml
Salt	1/2 teaspoon	2 ml
Water	1 1/4 cup	300 ml
Vinegar	2 tablespoons	30 ml
Lemon juice	1 tablespoon	15 ml
Cabbage	1/2 cup	125 ml
Celery	1 cup	250 ml
Green pepper	1 tablespoon	15 ml
Sweet red pepper or canned pimiento	1 tablespoon	15 ml

1. Mix gelatin, sugar, and salt together in a saucepan. Add 1/2 cup (125 ml) of the water. Place over low heat. Stir constantly until the gelatin is dissolved.
2. Remove from heat. Stir in remaining water, vinegar, and lemon juice.
3. Chill until the consistency of raw egg white.
4. Wash cabbage. Use french knife to shred into fine shreds, 1/8 inch wide × 2 inches long (0.3 cm × 5 cm). Wash celery and drain off excess water. Cut into 1/4 inch (0.6 cm) dice. Wash green pepper, dry, and cut into 1/4 inch (0.6 cm) dice. If fresh, sweet red pepper is used, follow directions for green pepper, or cut pimiento into thin strips. Fold prepared vegetables into the gelatin when it has the consistency of raw egg white.
**5. Spoon into a 2-cup (500-ml) mold. Chill until firm.
6. Record total working time: _____ minutes.

*May substitute a synthetic sweetner for sugar; see package for equivalents.
**See footnote on page 281.

Reception Salad

Lime gelatin dessert mix, 3 ounces (approx. 90 g)	1 package	1 package
Plain gelatin	1 teaspoon	5 ml
Water	3/4 cup	175 ml
Canned pear liquid	3/4 cup	175 ml
Salt	1/2 teaspoon	2 ml
Canned pear halves	4–5	4–5
Cottage cheese	3/4 cup	175 ml
Ginger	1/2 teaspoon	2 ml
Lemon juice	1 tablespoon	15 ml
Red-skinned apple, unpeeled	1	1

1. Bring to a boil 3/4 cup (175 ml) water. Add to the lime gelatin mixed with the plain gelatin. Stir until all gelatin is dissolved.
2. Add the pear syrup, salt, and lemon juice, and mix.
3. Pour one-third gelatin mixture into the bottom of a 1-quart (1-L) ring mold. Allow to chill until the gelatin is the consistency of raw egg white. Arrange alternate slices of apples and pears so the fruit is perpendicular to the bottom of the mold (see Steps 4 and 5). Fruit slices must not extend above the rim of the mold.
4. Wash and dry the apple. *Do not peel.* Cut the apple into quarters, lengthwise. Core. Cut each quarter into lengthwise wedges so each wedge is approximately 1/4 inch (0.6 cm) wide on the skin side. Red skin of apples will be at the outside of the mold.
5. Cut each pear half into lengthwise slices approximately 1/2 inch (1.3 cm) wide on the outside.
6. Chill remaining gelatin mixture until it is the consistency of raw egg white. Whip until the mixture holds in soft peaks.
7. Cream the cottage cheese, using an electric mixer. Add ginger and blend thoroughly.
8. Fold cheese mixture into whipped gelatin. Pour cheese-gelatin foam over the fruit. Chill until gelatin is firm.
9. Record total working time: _____ minutes.

Tomato Aspic

Gelatin	1 tablespoon	15 ml
Tomato juice	1 3/4 cups	425 ml
Salt	1/4 teaspoon	1 ml
Sugar	1/2 teaspoon	2 ml
Worcestershire sauce	1/2 teaspoon	2 ml
Tabasco sauce	1–2 drops	1–2 drops
Lemon juice, fresh	2 tablespoons	30 ml

1. Place 1/2 cup (125 ml) of the tomato juice in the upper part of the double boiler. Add the gelatin. Allow to stand 5 minutes.
2. Dissolve the hydrated gelatin over boiling water. Be sure all gelatin is dissolved.
*3. Add remaining ingredients. Stir until all are blended and sugar and salt are dissolved. Pour into mold; chill until firm.
4. Record total working time: _____ minutes.

*See footnote on page 281.

BLENDED FOAMS: GELATIN SPONGES, BAVARIANS, CHIFFONS

Note: In any of these products, a synthetic sweetner can replace the sugar. See equivalents on the package.

Lemon Sponge or Snow Pudding

Gelatin	2 teaspoons	10 ml
Water, cold	1/4 cup	60 ml
Sugar	1/4 cup	60 ml
Water	1/4 cup	60 ml
Lemon juice	3 tablespoons	45 ml
Whipped topping	1 cup	250 ml

1. Place 1/4 cup (60 ml) of cold water in the upper part of the double boiler. Add 2 teaspoons (10 ml) of gelatin and allow to stand 5 minutes.
2. Place hydrated gelatin over boiling water. Heat until the gelatin is dissolved. All gelatin must be dissolved.
3. Remove from heat. Add the sugar and stir until the sugar is dissolved.
4. Add the second portion of water and the lemon juice. Chill until the mixture has the consistency of raw egg white.
5. Beat mixture until light and foamy using electric mixer. The foam should hold soft peaks.
*6. Fold the whipped topping into the beaten gelatin. *Do not overfold.* Spoon into a mold and chill until firm.
7. Serve with a stirred custard prepared from
    1 cup milk (250 ml)
    1 egg yolk
    1 whole egg (2 egg yolks may be substituted)
    2 tablespoons sugar (30 ml)
    1/4 teaspoon vanilla (1 ml)
    (See page 152 for the method.)
8. Record total working time: _____ minutes.

*See footnote on page 281.

Apricot Sponge

Gelatin	2 teaspoons	10 ml
Apricot nectar	1/4 cup	60 ml
Lemon juice	1 tablespoon	15 ml
Sugar	2 tablespoons	30 ml
Apricot pulp from dried apricots	1/2 cup	125 ml
Whipped topping	1 cup	250 ml

1. Place the apricot nectar in the upper part of a double boiler. Add the gelatin. Allow to stand 5 minutes.
2. Dissolve the hydrated gelatin over boiling water. Be sure all gelatin is dissolved. Add the sugar and stir until sugar is dissolved. Remove from heat.
*3. Add lemon juice and apricot pulp. Chill until the consistency of raw egg white. Beat mixture until light and foamy using electric mixer. The foam should stand in soft peaks.
**4. Fold the whipped topping into the beaten gelatin. *Do not overfold.* Spoon into a mold and chill until firm.
5. Serve with whipped cream. This may be further garnished with apricot halves.
6. Record total working time: _____ minutes.

*Prepare apricot pulp: Wash 4 ounces (120 g) dried apricots. Place in small saucepan and cover with water. Hold over low heat for 20 minutes. Bring to a boil. Cook until tender. Remove apricots from liquid. Puree in a blender or put through a food mill.
**See footnote on page 281.

Spanish Cream—Modified Sponge

Gelatin	1 tablespoon	15 ml
Cold milk	1/4 cup	60 ml
Scalded milk	1 1/3 cups	325 ml
Eggs	2	2
Sugar	1/3 cup	75 ml
Salt	1/8 teaspoon	0.5 ml
Vanilla	1 teaspoon	5 ml

1. Place 1/4 cup (60 ml) cold milk in a custard cup. Add the gelatin. Allow to stand while making a stirred custard from the remaining milk, salt, 2 tablespoons (30 ml) of the sugar, and the eggs. Cook this custard mixture over warm, not boiling, water until the mixture coats the spoon.
2. Add the hydrated gelatin to the warm custard. Stir until the gelatin is dissolved. Add the vanilla. Chill until the consistency of raw egg white.
3. Beat the eggs until they form soft peaks. Gradually add remaining sugar with some beating. Peaks should remain slightly soft.
*4. Add the gelatin mixture and fold until just blended. Place in a 4-cup (1-L) ring mold. Chill until firm.
5. Serve with whipped cream and/or frozen raspberries.
6. Record total working time: _____ minutes.

*See footnote on page 281.

Pineapple Bavarian Cream

Gelatin	2 teaspoons	10 ml
Cold water	1/4 cup	60 ml
Sugar	1/4 cup	60 ml
*Crushed pineapple with syrup	1 cup	250 ml
Lemon juice	1 tablespoon	15 ml
Whipped topping	1 cup	250 ml

1. Add the gelatin to 1/4 cup (60 ml) cold water. Let stand while preparing the liquid in Step 2. Put the gelatin in the 2-quart (2-L) bowl to hydrate.
2. Drain syrup from crushed pineapple. Add enough water to give 1/2 cup (125 ml) of the blended liquids. Bring to a boil.
3. Add the boiling liquid to the hydrated gelatin. Stir until the gelatin is dissolved. Place over low heat if necessary until gelatin is dissolved.
4. Add the sugar and stir until sugar is dissolved. Add the lemon juice.
5. Chill the mixture in an ice bath until it has the consistency of raw egg white. Beat with electric mixer until light and foamy. The mixture should hold in soft peaks.
**6. Fold the whipped topping into the beaten gelatin. Fold in the pineapple fruit along with the whipped topping. *Do not overfold.* Spoon into mold. Chill until firm.
7. Record total working time: _____ minutes.

*Fresh or frozen pineapple cannot be used in gelatin products.
**See footnote on page 281.

Lime Bavarian—Modified Bavarian Cream

Evaporated milk	2/3 cup	150 ml
Lime gelatin mix	1 1/2 ounces	45 ml
Plain gelatin	1 teaspoon	5 ml
Boiling water	3/4 cup	175 ml
Sugar	1/2 cup	125 ml
Lime juice	2 tablespoons	30 ml
Lemon juice	1 tablespoon	15 ml
Lime rind, grated	1 teaspoon	5 ml
Chocolate wafer crumbs	1 1/2 cups	375 ml
Butter or margarine	1/3 cup	75 ml
Semisweet chocolate, grated	1 ounce	30 g

1. Chill evaporated milk in an ice tray in the freezing compartment of the refrigerator until ice crystals are formed on the insides of the tray (approximately 2 hours).
2. Place chocolate wafer cookies on breadboard. Crush to fine crumbs with rolling pin. Melt butter or margarine. Add wafer crumbs and blend thoroughly. Pack into two trays, 10 x 4 x 2 inches (25 x 10 x 5 cm). Chill.
*3. In a 2-quart (2-L) bowl, blend plain gelatin, lime gelatin mix, and sugar. Add boiling water. Stir until gelatin and sugar are dissolved. Add lime juice and lemon juice.
4. Chill mixture in a pan of chipped ice until gelatin is the consistency of raw egg white.
5. Remove bowl from chipped ice. Use an electric mixer to beat the gelatin until it is light and begins to hold soft peaks. Blend in the lime rind with the electric mixer.
6. Quickly beat the icy cold evaporated milk until it forms soft peaks. (Use electric mixer.)
7. Add the beaten milk to the beaten gelatin, folding or whipping as necessary.
8. Pour and/or spoon the blended mixture over the chocolate crumbs in the trays.
9. Sprinkle grated chocolate over the top. Chill until firm.
10. Record total working time: _____ minutes.

*Grate lime before extracting juice.

Strawberry Chiffon[†]

Gelatin	1 tablespoon	15 ml
Cold water	1/4 cup	60 ml
*Sugar	1/4 cup	60 ml
Lemon juice	1 tablespoon	15 ml
Frozen strawberries, 1 package	1 pound	450 g
or Fresh, crushed strawberries	1 1/2 cups	375 ml
Whipped topping	1 cup	250 ml

1. Put water in upper part of double boiler. Add gelatin. Allow to stand 5 minutes.
2. Dissolve the hydrated gelatin over boiling water. Be sure all gelatin is dissolved. Add sugar and stir until sugar is dissolved. Remove from heat.
3. Add lemon juice and berries. Chill until the consistency of raw egg white. Beat mixture until light and foamy using electric mixer. The foam should stand in soft peaks.
4. Fold the whipped topping into the gelatin mixture. Spoon into a 1-quart (1-L) ring mold. Chill until firm.
5. Record total working time: _____ minutes.

[†]This recipe can be used as a pie filling.
*Increase sugar to 1/2 cup (125 ml) if fresh berries or unsweetened frozen berries are used.

REMOVING GELATIN PRODUCTS FROM MOLDS

1. Run warm water into a pan large enough and deep enough so that the gelatin mold can be placed in water the depth of the gelatin in the mold. (*Remember:* Heat melts gelatin.)
2. Hold the mold in the warm water for approximately 5 seconds, then remove.
3. It may be desirable to quickly run the tip of a knife blade around the edge of the gelatin—not more than 1/16 inch into gelatin. (Do this to both the inner and outer edges of a ring mold.) Jar the mold to see that the gelatin is loosened.
4. Hold the mold close to the serving dish; invert mold *quickly.* (At times it may be desirable to place the inverted serving dish over the gelatin mold and then invert both serving dish and mold.)

CHARACTERISTICS OF HIGH-QUALITY GELATIN JELLIES

Appearance: Gelatin is usually clear; tomato aspic or orange jelly (from juice) may be cloudy or even opaque; fruit pieces small enough to remain evenly distributed; vegetable pieces slightly smaller than fruit pieces; cabbage, finely shredded. Gelatin retains shape of mold.

Texture: Gelatin firm yet resilient.

Tenderness: Easily masticated. Pieces of fruit and/or vegetable may have contrasting tenderness yet blend together well.

Flavor: Plain unflavored gelatin, very bland. In some products (tomato aspic, orange jelly, and so on) one flavor will predominate. Flavor of fruits and/or vegetables should be well blended. Jellies made from commercial gelatin mixes should have the characteristic fruit (or vegetable) flavor indicated on the label. Tartness should not be dominant.

CHARACTERISTICS OF HIGH-QUALITY WHIPS (GELATIN FOAMS)

Appearance: Very small air cells, uniform in size, evenly distributed; opaque, pale pastel color.

Texture: Firm, slightly resilient.

Tenderness: Delicate, tender, no resistance to bite.

Flavor: Typical of fruit used; weaker and more delicate than comparable plain jelly.

CHARACTERISTICS OF HIGH-QUALITY BLENDED FOAM PRODUCTS (GELATIN FOAM COMBINED WITH WHIPPED TOPPING AND/OR WHIPPED CREAM)

Appearance: Foam structures blended into a homogeneous, smooth foam; fruit, when used, in identifiable pieces.

Tenderness: Soft, delicate; fruit, little resistance to bite.

Flavor: Typical of fruit or flavoring material used (canned pineapple, coffee, strawberry, apricot).

REVIEW QUESTIONS

1. What steps are necessary to dissolve gelatin? (How is the gelatin sol formed?)
2. Explain why plain gelatin must be soaked in cold water while a commercial gelatin mix can be added directly to boiling water.
3. a. Define gelatin.
   b. In the preparation of gelatin desserts, what causes gelation to take place?
   c. In the case of gelatin the sol-gel transformation is said to be reversible. What is meant by this? What is the practical importance of this?
4. What is the effect of each of the following ingredients on the rate of gel formation and the strength of the resulting gel?
   a. Sugar
   b. Acid
   c. Buffer salts
5. In making Perfection Salad, what would happen if the pieces of vegetable were cut too coarsely?
6. a. Discuss the essential requirement for the formation of a stable gelatin foam.
   b. Compare the color and flavor of a plain jelly and a gelatin foam, both made from the same mix.
7. a. What is the common ingredient in the following products?
      (1) Gelatin jelly
      (2) Gelatin foam
      (3) Lemon sponge
      (4) Spanish cream
      (5) Bavarian cream
      (6) Chiffons
   b. What ingredient(s) or treatment identifies each product in part (a)?

Beverages

OBJECTIVES

To illustrate selected factors that may affect the quality characteristics of beverages
  a. Method of commercial processing
  b. Method of preparation of beverage

PRODUCTS TO BE PREPARED TO ILLUSTRATE PRINCIPLES

Percolated coffee   Green tea   Chocolate
Dripped coffee   Black tea   Cocoa
Vacuum coffee   Iced tea (black)
Decaffeinated coffee   Instant tea
Instant coffee   Instant iced tea
Freeze-dried coffee

PRINCIPLES

1. Some beverages such as tea and coffee are composed of water-soluble constituents extracted from certain leaves, berries, or roots.
    a. Solubility of the beverage components depend on
        (1) Temperature of water
        (2) Length of steeping period
        (3) Effect of acid on the solubility of tannin
    b. Quality characteristics of tea and coffee depend on
        (1) Volatile flavoring constituents
        (2) Polyphenols (tannins)
        (3) Caffeine
        (4) Type of water used for extraction of soluble constituents
        (5) Individual consumer standards of acceptability
    c. Commercial processing of the base ingredient (tea leaves or coffee berries) influences the following:
        (1) Color of beverage
        (2) Volatile flavoring constituents developed
        (3) Solubility of polyphenols (tannins)
        (4) Presence of caffeine (decaffeinated coffee)
    d. Nutrient content of steeped infusion is negligible.

2. For some beverages the base ingredient becomes an integral part of the beverage, as in chocolate and cocoa. For Standards of Identity see Code of Federal Regulations: Title 21–, part 163, dated April 1, 1993.
   a. Chocolate contains not less than 50% cacao fat.
   b. Cocoa may contain variable amounts of cacao fat. Breakfast cocoa may contain not less than 22% cacao fat.
   c. Special alkalizing treatment (Dutch process) produces a redder-colored product with slightly milder flavor.
   d. Chocolate and cocoa contain starch, which must be gelatinized to contribute to the stability of the beverage.
   e. Fluid milk or dried milk solids and water are the usual liquids used in preparing the beverage; milk becomes an integral component of these beverages (chocolate, cocoa).
   f. Coagulation of heat-coagulable proteins (lactalbumin, lactoglobulin) may result in an undesirable film on the surface of the beverage.
   g. Nutrient content is relatively high and depends on
      (1) Use of chocolate or cocoa
      (2) Type and amount of milk used
3. Effect of acids on solubility of polyphenols in preparation of iced tea.

STANDARD CAFFEINE CONTENT VALUES

Coffee (5 ounces)	mg
Brewed from ground roasted	80
Instant	60
Decaffeinated	3

Tea (5 ounces)	
Brewed from leaf or bag	40
Instant	30

Cocoa and Chocolate	
Cocoa, hot chocolate (5 ounces)	4
Chocolate milk (8 ounces)	5

Food Technology 37: (No. 9), 32–39 (1983).

COFFEE BEVERAGES

	U.S.A.			Metric	
	Amount of Ground Coffee			**Amount of Ground Coffee**	
Water (8 oz cup)	**Recommended***	**Laboratory**	**Water**	**Recommended***	**Laboratory**
3 cups	1/2 cup	1/4 cup plus 2 tablespoons	0.75 L	125 ml	80 ml
4 1/2 cups	3/4 cup	1/2 cup plus 1 tablespoon	1.12 L	175 ml	140 ml
6 cups	1 cup	3/4 cup	1.50 L	250 ml	175 ml

*Ratio of ground coffee to water recommended by The Coffee Brewing Institute, Inc.

Method of Preparation	**Type of Grind**
Steeping	Regular
Percolate	Regular
Drip or ADC	Drip or ADC
Vacuum	Drip or fine

Recommendation: Do not brew less than two-thirds of the capacity of the coffee maker for best results from the coffee maker.

Percolated Coffee

1. Put water into percolator pot.
2. Place ground coffee in the basket section of the percolator.
3. Heat. Keep the water percolating moderately for 5 minutes if heating over a gas or electric burner. *Or* when using an electric percolator, allow to heat until the signal light is lighted or until the percolating process stops.*
4. Record total working time: _____ minutes.

*Most electric percolators must not be placed in water as they are washed. Their electric units must be kept out of the water. Some new models, however, do have immersible electric units. Always check to see which type of electric unit is in the coffee maker you have used.

*Filtered Coffee—Drip Process**

1. Put ground coffee in basket part of dripolator. Fit basket into lower section. Put upper section (for water) in position.
2. Bring water to an active boil, 212°F (100°C). Use saucepan.
3. Pour boiling water into upper section of dripolator. Have the dripolator sitting near a warm burner.
4. After water has filtered through the coffee grounds, heat the beverage to 200°F (94°C) for serving.
5. Record total working time: _____ minutes.

   *Principles of beverage extraction also apply in automatic coffee makers.

Filtered Coffee—Vacuum Process

1. Put the water in the lower section of the coffee maker.
2. Adjust closure for the upper part of the coffee maker. Add the ground coffee. Firmly fit the upper section onto the lower section of the coffee maker.
3. Heat until water is forced up into the ground coffee.
4. Remove coffee maker from heat. As the coffee maker cools, the coffee beverage should filter into the lower section of the coffee maker.
5. When the beverage has filtered into the lower section, remove the upper section.
6. Reheat beverage to 200°F (94°C), if necessary, for serving.
7. Record total working time: _____ minutes.

Instant Coffee

Coffee, instant—3–4 tablespoons (45–60 ml)
Water—4 cups (1 L)

1. Put instant coffee into an enamel or heat resistant glass coffeepot.
2. Add water.
3. Heat to 200°F (94°C). Hold at this temperature for 5 minutes.
4. Serve.
5. Record total working time: _____ minutes.

Freeze-Dried Coffee

Coffee, freeze dried—2–3 tablespoons (30–45 ml)
Water—4 cups (1 L)

1. Put the freeze-dried coffee into a preheated coffeepot.
2. Bring the water to a boil in a saucepan and add to the coffee.
3. Allow to set over a warm burner (200°F or 94°C) for 5 minutes before serving.
4. Record total working time: _____ minutes.

CHARACTERISTICS OF HIGH-QUALITY COFFEE BEVERAGES

Appearance: Clear, bright.

Aroma: Pleasingly fragrant.

Flavor: Fresh coffee flavor with no bitterness.

TEA BEVERAGES

Green or Black Tea

Tea bag—1 (2.2 grams or 0.08 ounce) or 3/4–1 teaspoon (3–5 ml)
Water—1 cup (250 ml)

1. Preheat teapot by filling with boiling water. Allow to stand while bringing fresh water to a boil.
2. Discard water from teapot. Place tea bag in the preheated pot.
3. Add the freshly boiled water. Keep the teapot on a warm burner (but not over direct heat). Allow tea to steep for 3 minutes.
4. Serve in white-lined cups when comparing beverages prepared from several types of tea.
5. Record total working time: _____ minutes.

Iced Tea

Tea	3 teaspoons	6.6 g
or	3 bags	3 bags
Water, boiling	2 cups	500 ml
Chipped ice	2 cups	500 ml
Lemon juice	2 teaspoons	10 ml

1. Preheat pint- or quart-size (500 ml–1 L) glass measuring cup with boiling water.
2. Discard water from cup. Put the tea bags in the preheated cup.
3. Add freshly boiled water. Keep cup warm. Allow to steep for 8 minutes.
4. Place 1/2 cup (125 ml) chipped ice into each of 4 glasses.
5. Pour an equal amount of the hot tea beverage into each of the glasses.
6. Add 1 teaspoon (5 ml) lemon juice into each of 2 glasses.*
7. Record total working time: _____ minutes.

*If beverage is cloudy, more lemon juice may be added.

Instant Tea and Instant Iced Tea

Follow the directions on each of the containers.

CHARACTERISTICS OF HIGH-QUALITY TEA BEVERAGES

Appearance: Clear, bright.

Color: Depth of color somewhat dependent on time of steeping. *Green tea*: yellow to green. *Black tea*: amber.

Flavor: Distinctive of type; green tea will be somewhat more bitter than black tea.

CHOCOLATE AND COCOA BEVERAGES

Chocolate

Chocolate	1/4 square (1/4 ounce)	1/4 square (7 g)
Sugar	1 tablespoon	15 ml
Water	1/4 cup	60 ml
Milk	1 cup	250 ml
Vanilla	1/8 teaspoon	0.5 ml

1. Combine water, chocolate, and sugar in small saucepan. Heat to boiling with constant stirring. Continue boiling (with stirring) until a smooth paste forms. *Caution:* Do not scorch mixture as it reaches consistency of paste.
2. Add milk. Heat to 200°F (94°C). Add vanilla and serve.
3. Record total working time: _____ minutes.

Cocoa

Cocoa	1 tablespoon	15 ml
Sugar	1 tablespoon	15 ml
Water	1/4 cup	60 ml
Milk	1 cup	250 ml
Vanilla	1/8 teaspoon	0.5 ml

1. Mix together cocoa and sugar in small saucepan. Add water and blend.
2. Heat to boiling with constant stirring. Continue boiling (with stirring) until smooth paste forms. Do not allow mixture to scorch as it reaches consistency of paste.
3. Add milk. Heat to 200°F (94°C). Add vanilla and serve.
4. Record total working time: _____ minutes.

CHARACTERISTICS OF HIGH-QUALITY CHOCOLATE OR COCOA BEVERAGES

Appearance: Surface is free from milk scum or a layer of fat.

Consistency: Smooth, even consistency of thin cream.

Flavor: Definite, well-blended chocolate flavor. Vanilla should be well blended with the chocolate to enhance the chocolate flavor.

REVIEW QUESTIONS

General

1. Discuss the effect of brewing time and temperature of water on extraction of soluble constituents in making coffee and tea.
2. Discuss the use of hard water in making coffee and tea.
3. List the factors which will determine the color, aroma, and flavor of coffee and tea.
4. Discuss the nutrient content of
   a. Coffee
   b. Tea
   c. Hot chocolate

Coffee

1. Discuss the principles which apply to brewing coffee by each of the three basic methods.
2. Why are coffee beans roasted before grinding?
3. Discuss the importance of using the correct grind of coffee for each method.
4. a. Discuss the staling of coffee.
   b. What is the relationship of packaging of coffee to staling?

Tea

1. What factors determine the grade of tea?
2. a. List the principal types of tea.
   b. Discuss the differences in manufacture of the different types.
   c. How do these differences in methods of manufacture affect the beverage as served?
3. Why does too long a brewing period produce a bitter flavor in the beverage?
4. a. What is the effect of adding lemon to tea?
   b. Explain why this happens.

Chocolate and Cocoa

1. Discuss the Standards of Identity as applied to cocoa and chocolate.
2. a. What are the two processes for making cocoa from cacao nibs?
   b. What are the characteristics of cocoa produced by each process?
3. What is accomplished by forming chocolate or cocoa pastes before adding the milk?

Crystallization: Sugar (Candies)

OBJECTIVES

1. To acquaint students with selected factors that affect crystallization of sugar syrup mixtures.
   a. Concentration of sugar
   b. Temperature
      (1) To which sugar syrups are cooked
      (2) To which sugar syrups may be cooled before beating
   c. Extent of beating
   d. Addition of interfering agents
      (1) Those that cause hydrolysis
      (2) Those that have "coating" action
2. To give students the opportunity to compare textures of selected crystalline and amorphous candies.

PRODUCTS TO BE PREPARED TO ILLUSTRATE PRINCIPLES

Crystalline Products

Chocolate fudge
Penuche fudge
Divinity fudge

Amorphous Products

Caramels
Peanut brittle
Lollipops

PRINCIPLES

1. Factors that affect the concentration of sugar in a syrup
   a. At any given temperature, a certain amount of sugar (sucrose) can be dissolved to make a syrup.
   b. The concentration of sugar in solution becomes greater as the temperature increases.
   c. A solution is said to be supersaturated when the amount of sugar in solution exceeds that theoretically possible at any temperature.
   d. Supersaturation results from cooling a sugar syrup which has been heated to increase the concentration of sugar in the syrup.

2. Factors that affect the crystallization of sugar in a sugar syrup
   a. When supersaturation occurs, the sugar may crystallize.
   b. Nuclei must be present for crystallization. The following substances can act as nuclei:
      (1) A minute crystal of sugar
      (2) A particle of colloidal dimension
      (3) A scratch or rough spot on the pan
   c. Nuclei formation may also be spontaneous within the sugar syrup.
   d. The greater the degree of supersaturation, the larger the number of crystals formed and the smaller the size of the crystals formed when the cooked, cooled sugar syrup is beaten.
   e. The viscosity of a cooked sugar syrup increases with cooling; increased viscosity fosters formation of many small crystals.
   f. Beating a cooked, cooled sugar syrup fosters the formation of many small crystals.
   g. A cooked sugar syrup beaten at high temperature crystallizes with formation of fewer and larger crystals.
   h. Crystals continue to grow in size in an underbeaten crystalline candy.
3. Effect of other ingredients on sucrose crystallization
   a. Substances which alter rate of crystallization or size of crystals are called *interfering agents* or *doctoring agents*.
   b. Each sugar has its own rate of crystallization; therefore, the presence of any other sugar(s) will delay or inhibit crystallization of sucrose.
   c. Fat and/or protein in a cooked, cooled sugar syrup may
      (1) Foster formation of many small crystals
      (2) Delay or prevent crystallization of sucrose
4. Syrups for amorphous candies are cooked to higher temperatures than syrups for crystalline candies.
5. Factors that prevent crystallization
   a. An increased concentration of interfering agents inhibits and prevents crystallization.
   b. The higher the end temperature, the greater the viscosity of the syrup.
   c. Stirring during cooking may be essential to prevent scorching of milk, chocolate or cocoa, or butter.
   d. Stirring must be kept at a minimum to prevent formation of nuclei.
   e. Cooked syrups must be cooked without agitation.

Note of caution: Temperatures used in sugar cookery, 238–310°F (114–154°C), are much above the boiling point of water. *Handle hot syrups with extreme caution!*

Comment: Traditionally "fondant" and "fudge" are crystalline candies. Sucrose is dissolved in water; the sugar solution is heated to a high temperature, 234–240°F (112–116°C), to produce a supersaturated sugar solution when the syrup is cooled. See Principles 1, 2, and 3, pages 297–298, for factors which affect the size of the sugar crystals during recrystallization. The smaller the crystals formed, the smoother and creamier the fondant or fudge.

Uncooked candies prepared from powdered sugar cannot be classified as true fondants or fudges because there is *no* control of the size of the sugar crystals.

Chocolate Fudge

Sugar, granulated	1 1/2 cups	375 ml
Milk	1/2 cup	125 ml
Corn syrup, light	2 tablespoons	30 ml
Chocolate	1 1/2 squares	1 1/2 squares
Margarine or butter	2 tablespoons	30 ml
Vanilla	1/2 teaspoon	2 ml
Nuts, coarsely broken (optional)	1/2 cup	125 ml
Margarine or butter to grease pie plate		

1. Check boiling point of water on candy thermometer.
2. Lightly butter a 6 inch (15 cm) diameter glass pie plate.
3. Use a 5-cup (1.25-L) saucepan with a diameter of 6 inches (15 cm). Blend together the sugar, corn syrup, and milk. Stir with a wooden spoon. Place the candy thermometer in the saucepan.
4. Bring the mixture to 238°F (115°C) with as constant stirring as necessary to keep from scorching. Remember to adjust final temperature. If water boiled at 210°F (99°C), cook mixture to 236°F (114°C). During the cooking period it may be desirable to wipe undissolved sugar crystals from the side of the pan with a damp cheesecloth wrapped around a fork.
5. Remove pan from heat. Add the butter and the chocolate. Do not cut up the chocolate before adding it to the cooked mixture. *Do not stir* the mixture, but allow the cooked syrup to cool to 110°F (43°C). If time is limited, it may be necessary to set the pan containing the cooked syrup into a pan of cold water to which 2 or 3 ice cubes have been added so the temperature can be reduced more quickly. It is preferable to reduce the heat without using the cold water.
6. Remove candy thermometer and add the vanilla. Use a wooden spoon to beat mixture until the mass begins to hold its shape as the spoon is pulled through it. This beating may take as long as 20 minutes. Quickly add nuts (when used) and press the mixture into a buttered pie plate. Do not use nuts for class evaluation of crystalline candy.
7. Record total working time: _____ minutes.

Penuche Fudge

Light brown sugar	1 1/2 cups	375 ml
Half and Half (light cream)	1/2 cup	125 ml
Margarine or butter	2 tablespoons	30 ml
Vanilla	1/2 teaspoon	2 ml
Nuts, coarsely broken (optional)	1/2 cup	125 ml
Margarine or butter to grease pie plate		

1. Check boiling point of water on candy thermometer.
2. Lightly butter a 6-inch (15-cm) glass pie plate.
3. Use a 5-cup (1.25-L) saucepan 6 inches (15 cm) in diameter. Blend together the brown sugar and the Half and Half (light cream). Stir with a wooden spoon. Place the candy thermometer in the saucepan.
4. Bring the mixture to 238°F (115°C) with as constant stirring as necessary to keep mixture from scorching. Remember to adjust final temperature. If water boiled at 210°F (99°C), cook mixture to 236°F (114°C). During the cooking period it may be desirable to wipe undissolved sugar crystals from the side of the pan with a damp cheesecloth wrapped around a fork.
5. Remove pan from heat and add the butter. *Do not stir* the mixture, but allow the cooked syrup to cool to 110°F (43°C). If time is limited, it may be necessary to set the pan containing the cooked syrup into a pan of cold water to which 2 or 3 ice cubes have been added so the temperature can be reduced more quickly. It is preferable to reduce the heat without using the cold water bath.
6. Remove candy thermometer and add vanilla. Use a wooden spoon to beat mixture until the mass begins to hold its shape as the spoon is pulled through it. This beating may take as long as 20 minutes. Quickly add nuts (when used) and press mixture into buttered pie plate. Do not use nuts for class evaluation of crystalline candy.
7. Record total working time: _____ minutes.

CHARACTERISTICS OF HIGH-QUALITY CRYSTALLINE CANDIES

Appearance: Surface should have a high sheen; satiny.

Consistency: Firm enough to hold shape or cut edge when spooned into individual portions or when cut in pieces.

Texture: Smooth feel on tongue without stickiness (pastiness) or graininess. Very fine crystals can be identified as portion of fudge is pressed against the roof of the mouth by the tongue.

Flavor: Sweetness well blended with other ingredients that may contribute to flavor, like chocolate, vanilla, brown sugar. Nuts, when used, must be fresh.

Divinity Fudge

Sugar, granulated	1 cup	250 ml
Corn syrup, light	1/4 cup	60 ml
Water	1/4 cup	60 ml
Egg white	1	1
Vanilla	1/2 teaspoon	2 ml
Nut meats, broken	1/3 cup (optional)	75 ml

1. Check the temperature at which water boils vigorously on the candy thermometer.
2. Cover a baking sheet 12 × 14 inches (30 × 35 cm) with heavy waxed paper.
3. Use the upper section of the double boiler, 3-cup (750-ml) capacity, for a saucepan. (The narrow, deep pan holds the cooking syrup over the mercury bulb of the thermometer.)
4. Place the sugar, corn syrup, and water in the saucepan (see Step 3). Stir to blend ingredients; sugar will not be dissolved. Place candy thermometer in pan.
5. Place the pan over high heat to cook as rapidly as possible without having the syrup "boil over" the top of the pan. Cook to an end temperature of 264°F (130°C). If thermometer has shown water boils at 210°F (99°C), cook syrup to 262°F (128°C).
6. Do not beat egg white until syrup reaches 260°F (127°C). Place the egg white in a 1 1/2–2 quart (1.5–2 L) bowl. The bowl should be deep with a narrow bottom so the egg white will be easily caught into the egg beater. Use a hand electric mixer at highest speed to beat egg white until soft peaks form. The tips of the egg white fall over as the beater is removed. (Check page 160 for stages of beating egg white.)
7. Remove cooked syrup from the heat.
8. Pour the hot syrup in a thin stream (as thin as a thread) onto the beaten egg white with continuous beating. Have the mixer at highest speed. *Be sure the syrup goes onto the egg white and not into the beater blades nor into the sides of the bowl.** Take 5 or more minutes to add the syrup to the egg white. Do not scrape the last portion of syrup from the pan.
9. Keep beating the mixture at highest speed until the mixture cools and begins to stiffen. Reduce mixer speed to medium and to low depending on the stiffness of the divinity mixture.
10. Stop the mixer and add the vanilla. Beat the divinity mixture at lowest mixer speed until the candy appears to hold its shape as the beater is pulled out of the candy. *This is a critical step.* The candy mixture must be beaten until crystallization begins; beating must be stopped before crystallization is completed.
11. If nuts are used, quickly add at this step. Do not have nuts cut too finely; this would detract from appearance. Do not use nuts for class evaluation.
12. Quickly drop candy onto waxed paper by teaspoons. Use one spoon to cut a portion of candy; use a second spoon to push the candy onto the waxed paper.
13. Record total working time: _____ minutes.

*Syrup hardens quickly and will gum up the beaters or form a heavy coating on the sides of the bowl.

CHARACTERISTICS OF HIGH-QUALITY DIVINITY FUDGE (CRYSTALLINE CANDY)

Appearance: Slight sheen, white, opaque.

Texture: Very fine crystals, smooth.

Consistency: Firm enough to hold shape, yet soft to the bite.

Flavor: Sweet, mild vanilla when no nuts have been added.

Caramels

Sugar, granulated	1 cup	250 ml
Corn syrup, light	2/3 cup	150 ml
Sweetened condensed milk	2/3 cup	150 ml
Margarine or butter	1/2 cup	125 ml
Vanilla	1 teaspoon	5 ml
Brazil nuts, whole, unblanched	1 cup	250 ml

Margarine or butter to grease pie pan and knife to cut caramels

1. Check boiling point of water on candy thermometer.
2. Lightly butter the bottom and sides of a pan 7 × 7 inches (18 × 18 cm). When used, spread nuts evenly over the bottom of the pan.
3. Use a 5-cup (1.25-L) saucepan with a 6-inch (15-cm) diameter. Blend together the sugar, corn syrup, and butter. Bring to a boil with constant stirring.
4. Very gradually, with constant stirring, add the sweetened condensed milk. The milk should be added without reducing the boiling of the sugar syrup. Continue stirring the boiling mixture for 15 minutes. (Be sure to keep the bottom of the saucepan scraped clean. The sweetened condensed milk scorches very quickly. The scorched portions give lumpy caramels.)
5. Remove the saucepan from the heat and quickly and carefully put the candy thermometer in position. Return the caramel mixture to the heat. Cook with constant stirring to 246°F (119°C). Be sure to adjust final temperature; if water has boiled at 210°F (99°C) on the candy thermometer, remove cooked caramels at 244°F (118°C).
6. Remove from heat. Remove candy thermometer. Quickly stir in the vanilla. Quickly pour caramels into buttered pan. *Caution:* Scrapings must be put into a second buttered pan.
7. When scraping the pan, remember the scrapings will be very hot; *avoid burns.*
8. Allow caramels to set until cool. Then loosen caramels from sides of pan with case knife. Place heavy waxed paper on breadboard. Invert caramels onto the waxed paper. If caramels have become cold, lightly warm the bottom of the pan to melt the fat so the caramels will fall free from the pan.
9. Cut individual caramels using a lightly buttered french knife and/or scissors. Wrap individual caramels in heavy waxed paper. Save for class evaluation.
10. Do not use nuts for class evaluation.
11. Record total working time: _____ minutes.

CHARACTERISTICS OF HIGH-QUALITY CARAMEL CANDY

Appearance: Tan to brown color, medium brown being most desirable;* smooth with a sheen.

Texture and Tenderness: Firm, smooth feel in the mouth. Acceptable texture may vary from being somewhat short (friable, easily broken) to being chewy without being gummy and sticky.

Flavor: Rich, sweet, a distinct flavor; well rounded.

*Color will be deep reddish brown if chocolate or cocoa is added.

Peanut Brittle

Sugar, granulated	1 1/2 cups	375 ml
Corn syrup, light	1/2 cup	125 ml
Water	1/2 cup	125 ml
Margarine or butter	3 tablespoons	45 ml
*Soda	1/2 teaspoon	2 ml
Peanuts, raw or roasted	1 1/2 cups	375 ml
Vanilla	1/2 teaspoon	2 ml

1. Check boiling point of water on candy thermometer.
2. Use 1 tablespoon (15 ml) of butter or margarine to lightly grease the surface of three inverted baking sheets, 10 1/2 × 15 1/2 inches (26 × 38 cm). (There should be no sides surrounding the surface used, because the sides interfere in the stretching or pulling of the cooked brittle.)
3. Use a 2-quart (2-L) saucepan with a diameter of 6 inches (15 cm). Combine the water, corn syrup, and sugar in the saucepan. Place the thermometer in position in the saucepan.
4. Heat the sugar mixture rapidly to 280°F (138°C). Stir as little as possible to keep mixture from scorching. It may be desirable to wipe undissolved sugar crystals from the side of the pan with damp cheesecloth wrapped around a fork.
5. When the syrup reaches 280°F (138°C), add the peanuts and the butter or margarine. Stir the mixture continuously and heat to 306°F (152°C). Remove pan from heat immediately. Remember to make temperature adjustments for original thermometer reading for boiling water; if water boiled at 210°F (99°C), cook to 304°F (151°C).
6. Add the soda and the vanilla. Stir these ingredients in as quickly as possible. *Do not overstir or the foam structure will be lost.*
7. Pour approximately one-third of the final mixture on each of the three baking sheets. Pour into as thin a layer as possible, but do not try to spread the mixture with a spatula.
8. After the edges of the candy have cooled slightly—about 2 minutes—start to gently pull and stretch the candy into a relatively thin sheet. Try to keep the nuts fairly evenly distributed during stretching. Continue to stretch the candy until the center of the mass has also been stretched.
9. Record total working time: _____ minutes.

*If soda is omitted, a very hard, glassy type peanut brittle will result.

CHARACTERISTICS OF HIGH-QUALITY PEANUT BRITTLE

Appearance: Candy mass should appear somewhat aerated or foamy. The candy mass should be pale golden with the peanuts slightly darker.

Texture: Foam structure may not be apparent; candy mass is brittle and easily breaks up.

Flavor: Mild caramel flavor for the candy mass.

Lollipops or Hard Candy

Sugar, granulated	1 cup	250 ml
Corn syrup, light	1/3 cup	75 ml
Water	1/2 cup	125 ml

*Flavoring
**Coloring
Round toothpicks or wood skewers
Margarine or butter to grease baking sheets

1. Check boiling point of water on candy thermometer.
2. Lightly grease the bottoms of two cookie sheets, 10 1/2 × 15 1/2 inches (26 × 38 cm). Use butter or margarine.
3. Cook sugar, corn syrup, and water to 310°F (154°C) with as little stirring as possible. It may be desirable to wipe undissolved sugar crystals from the side of the pan with a damp cheesecloth wrapped around a fork.
4. Remove the cooked syrup from the heat. Quickly add the desired coloring and flavor ingredients with as little stirring as possible.
5. Use a metal tablespoon to quickly spoon the syrup onto the buttered baking pans. Try to keep the spooned mixture in rounds or "lollipop" shape. Round toothpicks or skewers can be quickly pressed onto the hot candies.
6. Carefully loosen the candies from the buttered baking sheet.
7. Record total working time: _____ minutes.

*If oils are used for flavoring—for example, oil of cloves—the quantity used for flavoring can easily be less than one drop. The amount of oil that can be held on the end of a toothpick may give an adequate amount of flavoring to the candy. Flavor extracts are less potent than oils as a source of flavor, but care should also be taken with extracts not to get too much extract in the candies.

**Coloring materials are also very concentrated so a small amount of coloring is added—again about as much as will remain on the end of a toothpick.

CHARACTERISTICS OF HIGH-QUALITY HARD CANDIES

Appearance: Candies are generally translucent and solid without air bubbles.

Texture: Smooth with no graininess as the candy dissolves in the mouth.

Flavor: Distinct for type of flavoring used.

REVIEW QUESTIONS

1. Define or explain each of the following terms:
   a. Crystalline (candy)
   b. Amorphous (candy)
   c. Saturated solution
   d. Supersaturation
   e. Nuclei
   f. Interfering (doctoring) agents
   g. Hydrolysis
   h. Sucrose
   i. Invert sugar
   j. Viscosity
2. a. List the three essential steps in preparing any crystalline candy.
   b. Briefly describe each of the three steps listed in (a).
   c. Indicate what is being accomplished at each step with regard to the crystalline structure of the candy.
3. a. Compare the ratio of sugar to corn syrup in the chocolate fudge recipe and the caramel recipe.
   b. Explain why the ratio differs for the two types of candy.
4. A recipe for chocolate fudge contains brown sugar, heavy cream, butter, and chocolate. What expectations might be held with regard to
   a. Preparation
   b. Finished product
5. Discuss the importance of the degree of beating in making divinity (foam) fudge.
6. In making amorphous candies, what is the importance of each of the following steps?
   a. Stirring constantly to add milk
   b. Not scraping the cooking pan after pouring candy
   c. Cooking lollipops with minimal stirring
7. Why is the baking soda used in making peanut brittle?

Crystallization: Water (Frozen Desserts)

OBJECTIVES

1. To acquaint students with selected factors that affect crystallization of water to ice in frozen dessert mixtures.
    a. Chemical factors
        (1) In the frozen dessert mixture
            (a) Type and concentration of sugars
            (b) Role of fat
            (c) Nonfat milk solids
            (d) Other solids
            (e) Stabilizers and emulsifiers
        (2) In the freezing mixture
            (a) Ratio of ice to salt
            (b) Role of water
    b. Physical factors
        (1) In the frozen dessert mixture
            (a) Interfering substances
            (b) Role of agitation
            (c) Overrun
            (d) Hardening
        (2) In the frozen dessert mixture
            (a) Role of agitation
            (b) Rate of agitation
2. To give students the opportunity to compare the texture and flavor of selected frozen desserts.

PRODUCTS TO BE PREPARED TO ILLUSTRATE PRINCIPLES

Ice Creams*	Sherbets*	Still Frozen
Vanilla	Orange	Chocolate mousse
Chocolate		
Strawberry		

*Note: These products require not less than 3 hours preparation time. The ice cream mix can be prepared through Step 7 and held in the refrigerator. The freezing process (page 308) can then be started at the beginning of the laboratory period. The sherbet mix can be prepared through Step 4 and held in the freezer. At the start of the laboratory period, remove the frozen mix from the tray in chunks; hold at room temperature for about 5 minutes. Then proceed with Step 5.

PRINCIPLES

1. Frozen desserts consist of ice crystals suspended in a sugar syrup into which air bubbles have been beaten.
2. Sugars in solution
    a. Lower the freezing point of the solution. One gram-molecular-weight of sugar lowers the freezing point by 1.86 degrees Celsius.
    b. In frozen dessert mixes, act to control size of ice crystals
    c. Sugar will affect the freezing point of the mix
3. Fats
    a. Are interfering substances which cause more ice crystals to be formed
    b. Affect the texture of the frozen desserts
4. Milk solids affect the viscosity of the mix and aid in the incorporation of air into the mix.
5. Gelatin and egg white may be added to a frozen dessert mix to increase viscosity and aid in the incorporation of air (overrun).
6. Emulsifiers are added to commercial ice cream mixes to aid in emulsification, viscosity, and foam stability.
7. Agitation (rapid mixing) when the mix is close to the freezing point favors the formation of many small crystals.
8. Frozen desserts need to be hardened after the freezing process has been terminated. The hardness of the frozen dessert will depend upon
    a. The lowest temperature reached
    b. Quantity of sugar in the mix

Freezing Desserts in an Ice Cream Freezer

1. The freezer is designed so the mix will be well agitated during the freezing process.
2. The freezing mixture consists of ice, salt, and brine.
3. Salt is more effective than sugar in lowering the freezing point.
4. The brine absorbs the heat from the frozen dessert mix.

Vanilla Ice Cream—Custard Base

Note: This is a variation of the method presented in the starch-egg chapter (page 169).

Milk	2 cups	500 ml
Sugar	3/4 cup	175 ml
Half and Half	1 cup	250 ml
Heavy cream	1 cup	250 ml
Eggs (beaten)	2	2
Flour	1 tablespoon	15 ml
Salt	1/4 teaspoon	1 ml
Vanilla	2 teaspoons	10 ml

1. Combine milk, flour, and salt in a 2-quart (2-L) saucepan. Heat on medium, with constant stirring, to boiling; boil for 1 minute.
2. Cool pan until you can hold your hand on the bottom of the pan.
3. Add sugar and beaten egg by adding 2 tablespoons of the warm mixture to the mixed sugar and egg. Then add this mixture back to the pan containing the milk and flour.
4. Return the pan to the heat and stir constantly until slightly thickened.
5. Cool by placing pan in sink in cold water.
6. Add Half and Half, cream, and vanilla; mix well.
7. Chill the mixture well, then freeze according to directions.

Variations

Chocolate Ice Cream

Add 2 ounces of unsweetened chocolate to cold mild and allow to melt as milk mixture is heated. Beat with a rotary beater until smooth.

Strawberry or Raspberry Ice Cream

When ready to freeze, stir in one pint of crushed sweetened berries; omit the vanilla.

FREEZING

1. Use finely crushed ice and rock salt.
2. Mix ice (5 parts) and salt (1 part) in a plastic dish pan.
3. Place beaters in the can and put can in the tub. Be sure that the socket hole in the bottom of the can rests on the center point of the casting in the bottom of the tub.
4. Pour in mixture—never over 3/4 full.
5. Adjust cover and gear frame—fasten down latch(es).
6. Pack ice/salt mixture around the can, covering it completely.
7. Turn occasionally while packing. Allow to stand 1 minute after packing.
8. Turn on motor and beat until hard to turn.
9. Remove the beaters and scrape the ice cream into the can. Be careful not to let any salt/ice/brine mixture get into the can. Replace cover and plug hole tightly.
10. Allow the ice cream to ripen (harden) for 30–60 minutes.
11. Record total working time: _____ minutes.

CHARACTERISTICS OF HIGH-QUALITY ICE CREAM

Appearance: Color according to flavor; *vanilla*: creamy white to light yellow; *chocolate*: medium chocolate brown (slight red cast if "Dutched" cocoa is used); *strawberry*: creamy pink; strawberry seeds may show; *raspberry*: bluish pink; pieces of fruit may show.

Consistency: Firm enough to hold shape.

Texture: Should feel smooth (fine crystals) on the tongue.

Body: Thick and smooth as it begins to melt.

Flavor: Slightly sweet characteristic of flavor.

Chocolate Mousse

Chocolate chips, semisweet	1 cup	250 ml
Water, boiling	1/2 cup	125 ml
Eggs, separated	4	4
Vanilla	2 teaspoons	10 ml
Sugar	1 tablespoon	15 ml
Cream, heavy	1 cup	250 ml
Almonds, toasted and slivered	2 tablespoons	30 ml

1. Put the chocolate chips and boiling water into a blender. Mix at "Blend" (3/4 maximum speed) for 1 minute. Cool.
2. Add egg yolks and vanilla. Mix at "Blend" for 1 minute.
3. Beat egg whites in a large mixing bowl, adding sugar gradually, to the stiff peak stage.
4. Fold chocolate mixture into beaten egg whites.
5. Whip the heavy cream to stiff peak stage and fold into the chocolate–egg white mixture.
6. Pour into serving dishes and freeze to soft stage.
7. Record total working time: _____ minutes.

CHARACTERISTICS OF HIGH-QUALITY CHOCOLATE MOUSSE

Appearance: Medium chocolate brown; may have slight red cast.

Consistency: Firm enough to hold shape.

Texture: Should feel smooth (fine crystals) on the tongue.

Body: Medium thick and smooth as it begins to melt.

Flavor: Sweet; distinct chocolate flavor.

Orange Sherbet

Milk, whole	2 cups	500 ml
Gelatin, plain	1 envelope (1/4 oz)	7 g
Sugar	1 cup	250 ml
Orange juice	1 cup	250 ml
Lemon juice, fresh	2 tablespoons	30 ml
Salt	1/2 teaspoon	2 ml
Yellow food color	6 drops	6 drops
Red food color	3 drops	3 drops

1. Place only 1 cup of milk in a 2-quart (2-L) saucepan. Sprinkle gelatin over the surface and allow to stand for 5 minutes.
2. Heat slowly with constant stirring until gelatin dissolves.
3. Remove from heat and add all of the other ingredients. Stir until the sugar is dissolved.
4. Pour into a 9″ × 9″ (23 cm × 23 cm) aluminum pan. Cover pan with plastic wrap or foil and place in the freezer. Freeze until firm and hard (1 1/2–2 hours).
5. Remove from freezer. Cut into chunks and put into a large bowl (3–4 quarts). Allow to stand for 10 minutes to soften.
6. Beat until it increases in volume and becomes smooth (do not allow to melt). Pour back into the pan. Re-cover and return to the freezer.
7. Allow to freeze until just firm (about 1 hour). Remove and serve.
8. Record total working time: _____ minutes.

Alternate Freezing Method
Mix: Follow Steps 1, 2, and 3 for orange sherbet.
Freeze in ice cream freezer. See directions for vanilla ice cream on page 308.

CHARACTERISTICS OF HIGH-QUALITY SHERBET

Appearance: Color according to flavor; should be a muted shade.

Consistency: Firm enough to hold shape.

Texture: Should feel smooth (fine crystals) on the tongue.

Body: Thin to medium thick and smooth as it begins to melt.

Flavor: Sweet note but also a tart note; characteristic orange flavor.

EVALUATION OF PRODUCTS
(FROZEN DESSERT)

Name: _____

Date: _____

Score System

Points	Quality
7	Excellent
6	Very good
5	Good
4	Medium
3	Fair
2	Poor
1	Very poor

Directions:

1. Place the numerical score in the box in the upper left-hand corner.
2. Comments should justify the numerical score. Comments must be brief.
3. Evaluation of the food products must be on an *individual* basis.

Products

Quality Characteristic					
Appearance					
Consistency					
Texture					
Body					
Flavor					

REVIEW QUESTIONS

1. Define or explain each of the following terms:
   a. Heat of fusion
   b. Molal lowering of freezing point
   c. Viscosity
   d. Crystallization
   e. Brine
2. Explain the role of each of the following ingredients or procedures in ice crystal formation:
   a. Sugar (2 ways)
   b. Fat
   c. Nonfat milk solids
   d. Other solids (eggs, gelatin)
   e. Emulsifiers
   f. Agitation
3. Discuss the ratio of salt to ice in the freezing mixtures for ice cream as contrasted with sherbet.
4. Why is it necessary to be careful to keep the salt/ice/brine mixture from getting into the frozen dessert?
5. a. When ice cream is held in storage, how can the growth of ice crystals be inhibited?
   b. How would growth of ice crystals affect the quality of any frozen dessert?

Meal Planning

This is a planning exercise only and will not involve preparation of food in the laboratory. Students should reread the chapter entitled Nutritional Labeling and Education Act of 1990. The Food Pyramid will be used in this lesson.

This lesson will also take up the section of the 1990 Act directed to the nutrition information found on packages or on charts in stores (for meat, fish, poultry, and produce, i.e., fruits and vegetables).

OBJECTIVES

1. To use the information in the Dietary Guidelines to plan a menu for three meals (breakfast, lunch, and dinner) for one day.
2. To use the Food Guide Pyramid to select individual food items that are nutritionally accurate.
3. To use other information, i.e., nutrition facts, in planning the menu.
4. To become familiar with and use the new nutritional information which is available only in grocery stores.
5. To study and use the other nonnutritional factors which affect the choice of foods.
6. To see the relationship between nutritional requirements and the preparation of high-quality food products.

The First Steps in Menu Planning

1. Before you can decide how many servings you will need from each food group on the pyramid, you must know your caloric requirements for the day. Following are some values for adults and teens:

1,600	*2,200*	*2,800*
Number of calories is about right for many sedentary women and some older adults.	Number of calories is about right for most children, teenage girls, active women, and many sedentary men.	Number of calories is about right for teenage boys, many active men, and some very, very active women.

2. Sample diets for a day at 3 calorie levels:

	1,600	**2,200**	**2,800**
Bread group servings	6	9	11
Vegetable group servings	3	4	5
Fruit group servings	2	3	4
Milk group servings	2–3	2–3	2–3
Meat group (ounces)	5	6	7
Total fat (grams)	53	73	93
Total added sugars (teaspoons)	6	13	18

The steps to meet the nutritional requirements have been provided; the other nonnutritional factors will be presented.

Nonnutritional Factors in Meal Planning

1. Base the selection on foods you know and like, but be open-minded enough to try new foods.
2. Include foods of different colors, shapes, and sizes.
3. Introduce several food textures for different mouth feel.
4. Introduce a variety of flavors, saving sweet for the end of the meal.
5. Use variations of foods and methods of preparation.
6. Plan foods which can be prepared in the time available.
7. Select foods with prices which will fit in your budget.

Meal Patterns

The first step in planning a menu is to prepare a meal pattern. The pattern will be generated from the Food Pyramid and from the desired caloric intake. If snacks are to be included in the food intake, they need to be provided for in the meal pattern. The "three square meals a day" may not be appropriate for many in today's society, but it will facilitate the planning of meals. The actual time and place of meals may vary.

Of all the meals of the day, breakfast is the most important and should never be skipped. Good breakfasts may be prepared without cooking and can be laid out the night before. An example of a breakfast pattern based on the Food Pyramid and three caloric levels follows. Note that a specific food is not mentioned but rather the Food Groups (some slightly modified) are listed here.

1,600 calories	*2,200 calories*	*2,800 calories*
Fruit/fruit juice	Fruit/fruit juice	Fruit/fruit juice
Cereal and/or bread	Cereal and/or bread	Cereal
Milk	Protein food	Bread
Beverage	Milk	Protein food
	Beverage	Milk
		Beverage

When the meal pattern and the menu are finished, the job is half done. The second half of the job, meal preparation, is just as important as the nutritional planning. This manual has stressed the Characteristics of High-Quality foods. Without high-quality foods, there cannot be good nutrition.

Nutrition Facts and Meal Planning

The Nutrition Act of 1990 and The American Technology Preeminence Act of 1991, which took effect February 14, 1994, mandate that certain information be printed on each food package. Nutrition facts that appear on the side panel of most packages is helpful in the planning of meals. A reproduction and explanation of the information on the panel is shown in Appendix E.

Nutrition Facts contains a section on percentage (%) of Daily Value, which indicates how much of each of the listed nutrients are included in the product. The figures are shown both in weight (grams) and as a percentage (%) of daily value. Refer to page 341 for a detailed description of each of the sections.

Answer the following questions:

1. Are you satisfied and pleased with your menu selections. If not, why not?

   _____

   Go back and make another selection.

2. Will your meal be attractive, a good mixture of colors and textures? _____

3. Will the flavors go well together?_____

   If not, why not?_____

4. Are there any other changes you want to make? _____

REFERENCES

Anon. (1993). The New Nutrition Panel. Dairy Council Digest *64:* No. 3, 15.

Anon. (1994) Pamphlet. The New Food Labels. American Institute for Cancer Research.

Kurtzweil, Paula (1993). Daily Values Encourage Healthy Diet. FDA Consumer *27*: No. 4, May, 28–32.

Kurtzweil, Paula (1993). Good Reading for Good Eating. FDA Consumer *27*: No. 4, May, 7–13.

Kurtzweil, Paula (1993). "Nutrition Facts" to Help Consumers Eat Smart. FDA Consumer *27*: No. 4, May, 22–27.

Kurtzweil, Paula (1994). Food Label Close-Up. FDA Consumer *28*: No. 3, April, 15–19.

Marmelstein, N.H. (1993). A New Era in Food Labeling. Food Technology *47*: No. 2, 15.

MEAL PLAN—ASSIGNMENT AND WORKSHEET

Assignment

1. You are to make a Meal Plan for one day, including breakfast, lunch, dinner, and all snacks.
2. Select the number of calories for the day: _____ calories.
3. In the space provided indicate the food group and the number (N) of servings for each group. Do this for each of the three meals.
4. After you have completed the worksheet, total the number of servings for each food group and record in the box below.
5. If you do not have the desired number of servings in any food group, adjust your worksheet to get the correct number.

WORKSHEET

Breakfast Group	N	Lunch Group	N	Dinner Group	N	Snacks Group	N

NUMBER OF SERVINGS

Food Group	Desired	Worksheet
Bread, cereal, rice, and pasta		
Vegetable		
Fruit		
Meat, poultry, fish, dry beans, eggs, and nuts		
Milk, yogurt, and cheese		

When this assignment is completed satisfactorily, prepare your menu from the items in your Food Plan above. Refer to the nonnutritional factors to help you make your decisions.

PREPARATION OF THE MENU

Item from the Food Group	Food Selected

BREAKFAST

LUNCH

DINNER

SNACKS

APPENDIX A

Carbohydrate Content (Total, Complex, Dietary Fiber, Other—Sucrose, etc.) of Selected Cereals

SOURCE OF INFORMATION

The data for the four tables in Appendixes A, B, C, and D was collected from August through October 1993 at a large supermarket in northeastern Ohio. The mention of brand names and manufacturers does not imply endorsement of these products by the authors, the publisher, or the two universities with which the authors were previously connected.

The data presented here will aid students in making the connection between good nutrition and the purchase of food items to ensure that the foods selected are the best nutritionally. In selecting food items for purchase, you must consider other factors. Most important is palatability, which includes appearance, flavor, texture, and mouth feel. Other important factors are the customers' preferences, price, shelf life, and how the product maintains its quality during use.

The best cereals will be low in fat, cholesterol, and sugar; dietary fiber and complex carbohydrates should be high. For the fats and oils, the best products will be low in saturated fats and cholesterol; the polyunsaturated and, to a certain extent, the monounsaturated fats will be high.

CARBOHYDRATE CONTENT (Total, Complex, Dietary Fiber, Other [Sucrose, etc.]) OF SELECTED CEREALS

Cereal	Manufacturer	Total	Complex	Dietary Fiber	Other
			As grams per 1 ounce serving		
Group 1, no fiber					
Cocoa Pebbles	Post	25	12	0	13
Honey Comb	Post	25	14	0	11
Nut & Honey Crunch	Kellogg	24	15	0	9
Fruit Rings	Food Club	26	13	0	13
Rice Krispy Treat	Kellogg	24	15	0	9
Golden Grahams	General Mills	24	14	0	10
Triples	General Mills	24	18	0	6
Kix	General Mills	24	21	0	3
Count Dracula	General Mills	25	12	0	13
Puffed Wheat (in bag)	Topco	11	10	0	1
Puffed Rice	Quaker	13	13	0	0
Group 2, 1–4 grams of fiber					
Life	Quaker Oats	20	12	2	6
Toasted Oatmeal	Quaker Oats	22	14	2	6
Puffed Kashi	Kashi	21	19	2	0
Natural Cereal	Food Club	19	9	2	8
Fruit/Oat Bran Crunch	Koln	21	17	4	0
Familia	Muesli	31	18	4	9
Shredded Wheat, Spoon	Nabisco	23	20	3	0
Frosted Wheat Squares	Nabisco	24	15	3	6
Shredded Wheat N'Bran	Nabisco	23	19	4	0
Honey Bunches of Oats	Post	23	15	2	6
Sweetened Wheat Puffs	Food Club	25	10	1	14
Raisin Brand	Food Club	30	16	4	10
Bran'nola	Post	23	12	3	8
Common Sense Oat Bran	Kellogg	23	13	4	8
Product 19	Kellogg	25	21	1	3
Low Fat Granola	Kellogg	23	13	2	8
Special K	Kellogg	22	18	1	3
Cracklin' Oat Bran	Kellogg	21	10	4	7
Corn Flakes	Food Club	25	22	1	2
Bran Flakes	Food Club	23	14	4	5
Mueslix, Crispy	Kellogg	33	17	3	13
Just Right	Kellogg	24	17	1	6
Just Right, Fruit & Nut	Kellogg	46	31	3	12
Toasted Oats	Food Club	20	17	2	1
Ripple Crisp	General Mills	24	18	1	5
Total Raisin Bran	General Mills	33	14	4	15
Total	General Mills	23	15.5	2.5	5
Wheaties	General Mills	23	17	3	3

continued

CARBOHYDRATE CONTENT OF SELECTED CEREALS (Continued)

Cereal	Manufacturer	Total	Complex	Dietary Fiber	Other
			As grams per 1 ounce serving		
Group 3, 5–9 grams of fiber					
Natural Bran Flakes	Post	23	13	5	5
Raisin Bran	Post	31	11	5	7
Raisin Bran	Kellogg	48	21	8	19
Original All Bran	Kellogg	21	7	9	5
Complete Bran Flakes	Kellogg	23	13	5	5
100% Bran	Nabisco	21	6	9	6
Group 4, 10–15 grams of fiber					
All Bran, Extra Fiber	Kellogg	22	7	15	0
Fiber N Bran	General Mills	23	10	13	0
Cooked Cereals					
Instant Grits	Quaker Oats	22	22	0	0
Oats	Quaker Oats	27	22	4	1
Wheat Germ	Kretchmer	12	6	3	3
Oat Bran	Quaker Oats	17	13	4	0
Cream of Rice	Nabisco	23	23	0	0
Cream of Wheat	Nabisco	23	21	1	0
Malt-O-Meal	Malt-O-Meal	21	20	1	0
100% Wheat Hot Cereal	Ralston	27	21	6	0
Wheatena	American Home	32	27	5	0
Maypo Oatmeal	American Home	19	16	0	3
Inst. Oatmeal–Kid's Choice	Quaker	30	27.4	2.6	0
CO-CO Wheat	Little Crow Foods	28	27	1	0

APPENDIX B

Composition of Dietary Fats and Oils

COMPOSITION OF DIETARY FATS AND OILS

Dietary Fat	Cholesterol Mg./Tbsp.	Saturated Fat %	Monoun-saturated %	Polyun-saturated %	Alpha Lin-oleic Acid %
Canola oil	0	6	58	26	10
Safflower oil	0	9	13	78	0
Sunflower oil	0	11	20	69	0
Corn oil	0	13	25	61	1
Olive oil	0	14	77	8	1
Soybean oil	0	15	24	54	7
Peanut oil	0	18	48	34	0
Cottonseed oil	0	27	19	54	0
Lard	12	41	47	11	1
Palm oil	0	51	39	10	0
Beef tallow	14	52	44	3	1
Butterfat	33	66	30	2	2
Coconut oil	0	92	6	2	0

Agricultural Handbook 8–4
Home and Garden, Bulletin Number 72

APPENDIX C

Fatty Acid Content of Selected Fats and Oils

FATTY ACID CONTENT OF SELECTED FATS AND OILS (Expressed as grams per tablespoon [14 g] oil)

Type Oil	Brand Name	Class Oil	Monounsaturated	Polyunsaturated	Saturated
Olive	Berio	Mild	75 %	na*	na
Olive	Berio	X-Mild	77 %	na	na
Olive	Devino	xtravir	10.0	1.0	2.0
Olive	Rubino	X-light	11.0	1.0	2.0
Olive	Bertolli	Classico	11.0	1.0	2.0
Olive	Food Club	100% Pure	9.0	1.0	2.0
Canola	Wesson	—	9.0	4.0	1.0
Canola	Food Club	—	9.0	4.0	1.0
Canola	Crisco	Puritan	9.0	4.0	1.0
Corn	Mazola	100% Pure	4.0	8.0	2.0
Corn	Food Club	100% Pure	4.0	8.0	2.0
Sesame	Hain	—	6.0	6.0	2.0
Safflower	Holywood	—	2.0	11.0	1.0
Sunflower	Food Club	—	2.0	10.0	2.0
Peanut	Planters	—	6.0	4.0	2.0
Vegetable	Crisco	**	7.0	7.0	1.0
Vegetable	Food Club	100% Soya	3.0	9.0	2.0
Vegetable	Wesson	Soy and Cotton-seed Oils	na	na	na
Solid Fats (Hydrogenated)					
	Crisco		6.0	3.0	3.0
	Food Club		6.0	3.0	3.0
	Wesson		na	na	na

*na = not available

**Canola, sunflower, soya

APPENDIX D

Composition of Selected Margarines and Margarine Spreads

COMPOSITION OF SELECTED MARGARINES AND MARGARINE SPREADS (Expressed as grams of fat per tablespoon [14] of margarine)

Brand	Total Fat	Polyunsaturated	Monounsaturated	Saturated	P/S Ratio
Corn Oil Margarines					
Fleischmann's Orig.	11	4	5	2	2.0
Food Club	11	4	5	2	2.0
Soy Bean Oil Margarines					
Chiffon, soft	10	4	4	2	2.0
Blue Bonnet, soft	11	4	5	2	2.0
Parkay, soft	10	4	4	2	2.0
Spreads, Margarine-Type (See Note 1 below)					
Promise, 70% Oil Extra light	6	2	3	>1	2.0
Promise, 68% Oil	10	5	4	1	5.0
Promise, 26% Oil	4	1	3	0	0.0
Promise, Fat Free	0	0	0	0	0.0
Fleischmann, 68% Oil	10	3	5	2	0.6
Fleischmann, 67% Oil	9	2	5	1	2.0
Fleischmann, 60% Oil	8	3	4	1	3.0
Fleischmann, 56% Oil	8	3	4	1	3.0
Fleischmann, 40% Oil	6	2	3	1	2.0
Blue Bonnet, 75% Oil	11	3	6	2	0.6
Blue Bonnet, 68% Oil	10	3	5	2	0.6
Blue Bonnet, 60% Oil	8	2	5	1	2.0
Blue Bonnet, 48% Oil	7	2	4	1	2.0
Parkay, 70% Oil	10	1	7	2	0.5
Parkay, 53% Oil	7	1	5	1	1.0
Parkay, 50% Oil	7	2	4	1	2.0
Country Crock, 64% Oil	9	2	5	2	1.0
Country Crock, 48% Oil	7	3	3	1	3.0
Shedds Spread, 48% Oil	7	3	3	1	3.0
Kraft, 47% Oil	7	2	4	1	2.0
Weight Watchers, 30% Oil	4	2	1	1	2.0
Squeeze Bottles					
Fleischmann, 70% Oil	10	5	4	1	5.0
*Not Butter, 70% Oil	10	4	4	2	2.0
Parkay, 64% Oil	9	5	3	1	5.0
Shedds, 64% Oil	9	4	4	1	4.0

*I Can't Believe It's Not Butter

Note 1. The Food and Drug Administration has not issued any Standards of Identity for the Margarine-type Spreads. Therefore, the manufacturer is free to formulate the spread as desired as long as all ingredients are listed on the package. Read carefully the Ingredient List and any notes on the package. For example, some brands of spreads cannot be used for baking or frying.

APPENDIX E

Key Aspects of the New Nutrition Label

Key Aspects of the New Nutrition Label

A number of consumer studies conducted by FDA, as well as outside groups, enabled FDA and the Food Safety and Inspection Service of the U.S. Department of Agriculture to agree on a new nutrition label. The new label is seen as offering the best opportunity to help consumers make informed food choices and to understand how a particular food fits into the total daily diet.

New heading signals a new label. ⟶

More consistent serving sizes, in both household and metric measures, replace those that used to be set by manufacturers.

Nutrients required on nutrition panel are those most important to the health of today's consumers, most of whom need to worry about getting too much of certain items (fat, for example), rather than too few vitamins or minerals, as in the past. ⟶

Conversion guide helps consumers learn caloric value of the energy-producing nutrients. ⟶

New mandatory component helps consumers meet dietary guidelines recommending no more than 30 percent of calories from fat.

% Daily Value shows how a food fits into the overall daily diet.

Reference values help consumers learn good diet basics. They can be adjusted, depending on a person's calorie needs.

Nutrition Facts

Serving Size 1 cup (228g)
Servings per Container 2

Amount per Serving

Calories 260   Calories from Fat 120

% Daily Value*

Total Fat 13g	**20%**
Saturated Fat 5g	**25%**
Cholesterol 30mg	**10%**
Sodium 660mg	**28%**
Total Carbohydrate 31g	**10%**
Dietary Fiber 0g	**0%**
Sugars 5g	
Protein 5g	

Vitamin A 4%	•	Vitamin C 2%
Calcium 15%	•	Iron 4%

*Percent Daily Values are based on a 2,000 calorie diet. Your daily values may be higher or lower depending on your calorie needs:

	Calories:	2,000	2,500
Total Fat	Less than	65g	80g
Sat Fat	Less than	20g	25g
Cholesterol	Less than	300mg	300mg
Sodium	Less than	2,400mg	2,400mg
Total Carbohydrate		300g	375g
Dietary Fiber		25g	30g

Calories per gram:
Fat 9 • Carbohydrate 4 • Protein 4

Recipe Index

Subject Index